ASEAN Post-50

Aida Idris · Nurliana Kamaruddin
Editors

ASEAN Post-50

Emerging Issues and Challenges

Editors
Aida Idris
Faculty of Business and Accountancy
University of Malaya
Kuala Lumpur, Malaysia

Nurliana Kamaruddin
Asia-Europe Institute
University of Malaya
Kuala Lumpur, Malaysia

ISBN 978-981-13-8042-6   ISBN 978-981-13-8043-3   (eBook)
https://doi.org/10.1007/978-981-13-8043-3

© The Editor(s) (if applicable) and The Author(s), under exclusive license to Springer Nature Singapore Pte Ltd. 2019
This work is subject to copyright. All rights are solely and exclusively licensed by the Publisher, whether the whole or part of the material is concerned, specifically the rights of translation, reprinting, reuse of illustrations, recitation, broadcasting, reproduction on microfilms or in any other physical way, and transmission or information storage and retrieval, electronic adaptation, computer software, or by similar or dissimilar methodology now known or hereafter developed.
The use of general descriptive names, registered names, trademarks, service marks, etc. in this publication does not imply, even in the absence of a specific statement, that such names are exempt from the relevant protective laws and regulations and therefore free for general use.
The publisher, the authors and the editors are safe to assume that the advice and information in this book are believed to be true and accurate at the date of publication. Neither the publisher nor the authors or the editors give a warranty, expressed or implied, with respect to the material contained herein or for any errors or omissions that may have been made. The publisher remains neutral with regard to jurisdictional claims in published maps and institutional affiliations.

This Palgrave Macmillan imprint is published by the registered company Springer Nature Singapore Pte Ltd.
The registered company address is: 152 Beach Road, #21-01/04 Gateway East, Singapore 189721, Singapore

Foreword

Although there is a large scholarly literature on the Association of Southeast Asian Nations (ASEAN), much of it has been written by outsiders rather than Southeast Asians. This means that we often learn more about the expectations and judgements of foreigners than we do about the priorities and concerns of people living in the region.

This volume includes work from people based in Singapore and the Philippines—as well as South Korea—but it is most of all a Malaysian collection. The essays—which are the product of research rather than mere opinion—give a sense of the type of issue that is attracting concern in Malaysia and other parts of Southeast Asia today. The authors are not merely specialists in international relations and economics—who often dominate the analysis of regionalism—but also include scholars in such areas as law, economics, town planning, rural politics and youth development.

ASEAN is a genuinely interesting topic for discussion. After the European Union, it is probably the most significant experiment in regionalism in the modern world. It is also gradually becoming a player in global relations. How ASEAN relates to major powers is at present a matter for urgent attention, and this volume gives particular and sensitive attention to ASEAN's engagement with China.

Internal developments in ASEAN are also vital—and it is important that the essays below focus not only on economic issues (such as the development gap between member countries of the ASEAN organization), but also on such under-studied areas as youth development and the harmonization of nutrition labeling in food packaging. Problems of urbanization and environmental concerns, and also intra-regional migration, are also given special treatment—and so is the role of ethnicity and religion in serious social tension (such as the Rohingya crisis).

What needs to be stressed is that these and other issues are dealt with in a regional and not merely national context. This shift from nation to region as the key unit of analysis is an important development in academic investigation. The specific concerns of Malaysia and other ASEAN countries are not ignored in this volume—but the centrality of a specifically regional perspective deserves to be highlighted.

Such books as this—grounded in the region and not merely nation—make their own input to the growth of regionalism. They are an academic contribution to the demanding task of building an ASEAN "community". Promoting such a sense of community is vital, as the editors explain. Having past its 30th anniversary, ASEAN's principal task is "generating and maintaining the political will to commit to the various initiatives established under the ASEAN aegis".

Canberra, Australia

Anthony Milner
Visiting Professor
Centre for ASEAN Regionalism
University of Malaya

Professorial Fellow, Asia Institute
University of Melbourne

Co-Chair, Australian Committee
of the Council for Security
Cooperation in the Asia Pacific
(CSCAP)

Contents

1 Overview of ASEAN   1
Aida Idris and Nurliana Kamaruddin

2 ASEAN at 50: The Rise of China and the Emerging Regional Integration Architecture   13
Kee Cheok Cheong, Ran Li and Qianyi Wang

3 The ASEAN-ROK Economic Relations: Challenges and Opportunities   35
Nurliana Kamaruddin and Jan Vincent Galas

4 Determinants of Chinese Overseas FDI in ASEAN Countries   53
Jie Zheng and Mohd Nazari Ismail

5 Empowerment for Economic and Human Capital Development Through Education   81
Wendy Mei Tien Yee and Serina Rahman

viii   Contents

6   ASEAN Qualification Reference Framework:
     Harmonization of ASEAN Higher Education Area   101
     Zita Mohd Fahmi, Usharani Balasingam
     and Jake M. Laguador

7   Representing Migration in ASEAN: Challenges
     to Regional Integration   135
     Charity Lee

8   Environmental Challenges Within ASEAN:
     Contemporary Legal Issues and Future Considerations   155
     Sarah Yen Ling Tan and Hanim Kamaruddin

9   Environmental Threats to the Performance of Urban
     Areas in ASEAN Integration   177
     Zakaria Alcheikh Mahmoud, Yahaya Ahmad,
     Melasutra Md. Dali and Nikmatul Adha Nordin

10   Regulatory Incoherence in Nutrition Labelling
     of Pre-packaged Food in ASEAN: What Next?   203
     Evelyn S. Devadason and VGR Chandran Govindaraju

11   Real-Life Moral Dilemma Discussion (Re-LiMDD)
     Among Young Adolescents: A Comparison Between
     Malaysia and Indonesia   231
     Vishalache Balakrishnan

12   Challenges and Opportunities; Lessons for ASEAN
     Post 50   239
     Nurliana Kamaruddin and Aida Idris

Index   249

Notes on Contributors

Nikmatul Adha Nordin obtained her first and Master's Degree from Universiti Sains Malaysia in the field of Urban and Regional Planning. She was awarded a doctoral degree from USM in 2011 in the field of social and physical planning. She is a Graduate Member of the Malaysian Institute of Planners (MIP). She started her career as Research Officer in USM, served a stint as Research Executive at a private consultant firm before settling for an academic career in Universiti Malaya starting 2004. Her research interest is on participatory urban planning, tourism planning and community development planning.

Yahaya Ahmad started his academic career at the University of Malaya in 1995, as one of the pioneering staff to establish the Department of Architecture and the Faculty of Built Environment. Now is the Dean of the Faculty and Director of ASEAN University Network-Disability and Public Policy. He specializes on conservation of heritage buildings and sites. His main contribution besides restoration of many heritage buildings includes as head and member of expert teams to prepare UNESCO nomination dossiers for Melaka and George Town Malaysia, Ahmadabad City India and Coral Stone Mosques of Maldives to the UNESCO World Heritage List.

x   Notes on Contributors

Vishalache Balakrishnan served as a teacher of Moral Education before becoming a lecturer at the University of Malaya in 2002. She has a basic and specialist teaching certificate. She pursued her studies at the University of Malaya for Bachelor of Education (1999) and Master of Education (2002). She completed her Doctoral Studies in Moral Education (2009) at Victoria University of Wellington, New Zealand and a postgraduate studies in critical psychology education at Waikato University, New Zealand (2016). Dr. Vishalache Balakrishnan is Director of Research Center for International and Comparative Education (CRICE) at University of Malaya, Malaysia.

Usharani Balasingam is a senior lecturer at the Faculty of Law University of Malaya. She was an active legal practitioner of law as an Advocate and Solicitor and in legal corporate advisory before entering academia. She has a doctorate in education. She has published in local and international journals and in book chapters in the areas of education, law, elder and ethics. She is the co-editor of the book Protecting the Elderly Against Abuse and Neglect (UM Press 2017) and co-author of Navigating the Companies Act 2016 for SMEs (2018, Sweet & Maxwell).

Kee Cheok Cheong is Senior Advisor, Asia-Europe Institute and Senior Research Fellow, Institute of China Studies, University of Malaya. A graduate of the University of Malaya (UM), he obtained his Ph.D. at the London School of Economics. Upon his return, he joined the Faculty of Economics and Administration, UM, where he held the positions of Deputy Dean and Dean of Faculty. After a decade at UM, he spent 16 years at the World Bank as Economist and subsequently Senior Economist. Back with UM since 2010, he has co-authored books, book chapters, and published in international academic journals.

Evelyn S. Devadason is a professor at the Faculty of Economics and Administration, University of Malaya. She obtained her Ph.D. (Economics) from the University of Malaya and M.Soc. Sci. (Economics) from the National University of Singapore. Her research focuses on international trade and regional integration. Her research work has seen print in international journals such as

World Development, Journal of International Development, Pacific Review, Journal of Contemporary Asia, Journal of Contemporary China, among others. She has also been engaged in several international research projects, including the ICFTU-APRO, ADBI, ADB, World Bank, ERIA-UNCTAD, FIA, UNEP-DTU and more recently in the European Union's Horizon 2020—Research and Innovation Framework Programme on CRISEA.

Zita Mohd Fahmi J.M.N. began her career as a law lecturer, served as Dean of the Law Faculty and retired as a Professor of Law with UiTM. Her work and experience in the development and practice of field of quality assurance in higher education and training begun in 1997 with Lembaga Akreditasi Negara and continued with the Malaysian Qualifications Agency till 2017. She had major responsibility in the development, implementation and the review of Malaysian Qualifications Framework. She chaired comparability projects which supported mutual recognition of qualifications with New Zealand (NZQA), Taiwan (HEEACT) and Japan (NIAD QE).

Jan Vincent Galas is currently an associate professor at College of Business and Economics at Chung-Ang University. Jan completed his M.A. and Ph.D. in International Studies at Sogang University in South Korea. His research interests focus on ASEAN and East Asian studies, particularly in the intersections of constructivism, strategic culture and theories of development, communication and cooperation. Jan is also an international debating consultant and has worked as a debate coach or trainer in East Asian countries.

VGR Chandran Govindaraju is an associate professor at the Faculty of Economics and Administration, University of Malaya. He obtained his Ph.D. (Economics) from the University of Malaya and M.Sc. (Environmental Management) from the National University of Malaysia. His research interests include innovation, technology and industrial development. He has published several articles in international journals, such as *Economics of New Technology and Innovation, Policy Modelling*, among others. He has worked as consultants to international organizations such as UNCTAD, UNIDO, UNESCO, UNEP,

xii   **Notes on Contributors**

ERIA and OECD. He was also engaged as a local expert to the Ministry of Science, Technology and Innovation, Economic Planning Unit, Academic of Sciences, Ministry of International Trade and Industry, MIGHT, Prime Minister's Department and the Malaysian Productivity Corporation.

Aida Idris is an associate professor at the Faculty of Business and Accountancy, University of Malaya (UM). She obtained her Ph.D. from the same university and now specializes in Entrepreneurship, SME Development and Cross-cultural Management. Before entering academia, she had worked as an engineer and a management consultant in several multinational corporations. Throughout her service in UM, she has held several administrative positions, including as Director of Academic Development Centre and Deputy Executive Director of Asia-Europe Institute. Dr. Idris is an active researcher and has produced more than 50 publications in books, journals and conference proceedings. In 2015, she was awarded a two-year scholarship by the Ministry of Education, Malaysia, to pursue a postdoctoral program at Trinity College Dublin, Ireland, where she collaborated with a number of European scholars on the subject of international education.

Mohd Nazari Ismail is a professor at the Faculty of Business and Accounting, University of Malaya, and former dean of the faculty. An author of six books, he was also the 1999 Fulbright Foundation Malaysian Scholar at the University of Michigan at Ann Arbor, the Fulbright Visiting Specialist at Pfeiffer University, North Carolina and a visiting fellow at Oxford Center for Islamic Studies, Oxford, UK. He obtained his B.Sc. Economics (Hon.) from the University of Wales, UK, M.B.A. from the State University of New York and Ph.D. from the University of Manchester, UK.

Hanim Kamaruddin is a senior lecturer at the Faculty of Law, Universiti Kebangsaan Malaysia. Her research focuses on environmental law particularly on various aspects of transboundary haze pollution in Malaysia and ASEAN. She has published law articles, chapters in books and conference proceedings on issues related to environmental law. Dr. Hanim is a member in the Disciplinary Board of Bar Council Malaysia, a certified mediator, Malaysia, and Country Focal Person (CFP) for Malaysia's Train the Trainers Asian Development Bank (ADB). She has co-authored a book entitled *The Environmental Quality Act (EQA) 1974 Statutory Instruments and Amendments* in 2016.

Nurliana Kamaruddin is a senior lecturer at the Asia-Europe Institute, University of Malaya. She earned her Ph.D. in International Studies majoring in Development Cooperation at Ewha Womans University, Seoul, and M.A. in International Cooperation at Yonsei University, Seoul, South Korea. Nurliana was a recipient of the Korea Foundation ASEAN Fellowship (2013–2015) and the POSCO TJ Park Foundation Asia Fellowship (2009–2011). Her research interest includes international development, non-traditional security, governance and international cooperation with an area focus of East Asia.

Jake M. Laguador is currently the Research Director and former Dean of the Graduate School in Lyceum of the Philippines University—Batangas. He finished Bachelor's Degree in Computer Engineering, Master's Degrees in Educational Administration and Public Administration, and Doctorate Degree in Educational Management while currently taking up Doctor of Philosophy in Management. He has published more than 80 research articles in different journals of social sciences, education, business, information technology, engineering, educational psychology and management. He landed Top 80 in ranking of scientists in Philippine Institutions according to Google Scholar Citations Public Profiles in 2016.

Charity Lee is currently a senior lecturer at the Department of Asian and European Languages, Faculty of Languages and Linguistics, University of Malaya. Her main areas of research include narrative analysis and critical discourse analysis, particularly involving social practices surrounding migrant and vulnerable groups and mainly employing narrative and participatory action research methodologies. She also studies communication practices found in media and political discourses. She teaches German linguistics at the undergraduate level and discourse analysis at the postgraduate levels.

Ran Li is Research Fellow at Institute of China Studies, University of Malaya. She obtained her doctoral degree in Economics from the University of Malaya in 2014. Her specialization is in the transformation of China's state enterprises, state enterprise system and China's political-economic system, and her current areas of research include China's global strategy and China–Malaysia economic relations. Her previous writings have appeared in a number of international journals such as *China: An International Journal, Engineering Economics, Cities, International Journal of China Studies* and *Journal of Contemporary Asia.*

Sarah Yen Ling Tan is a senior lecturer at the Faculty of Law, University Malaya. Her research is focused on international and national environmental law and legal issues, in particular, constitutional environmental rights, environmental justice and energy. She has published articles in legal journals, online, chapters in books and conference proceedings and co-authored a book. She is a member of the World Commission on Environmental Law, Advisor to the Steering Committee Rules and Procedures of the Environmental Court, the Managing Editor of the *Journal of Malaysian and Comparative Law* and the Editorial Advisor to the University of Malaya Law Review.

Zakaria Alcheikh Mahmoud is a senior lecturer in the Faculty of Built Environment, University of Malaya. He has been in the academic as well as professional field for more than 20 years in various parts of the world. He carried out his undergraduate study at Al-Baath University, in Syria while his Master's Degree as well as Ph.D. in Urban Planning was received from the School of Planning and Architecture, India. Built environment has been his major concern throughout his career as he carried out and produced several researches and publications as well as presented papers in conferences. At present, Zakaria is living in Kuala Lumpur, Malaysia.

Melasutra Md. Dali is a Registered Town Planner and also a member of Malaysian Association of Social Impact Assessment. She has been as a lecturer at Faculty of Arts and Social Sciences and Faculty of Built Environment. While serving UM, she also involved in several researches and consultancy services on Social Impact Assessment, Urban Redevelopment, Development Plan studies. She has been appointed as

Council Member for Petaling Jaya City Council in 2008–2012 and be part of the One Stop Center committee. She is now carrying out collaboration research with Nippon Foundation under the preview of ASEAN University Network—Disability and Public Policy on research Towards Inclusive Learning Environment.

Serina Rahman is a visiting fellow in the Malaysia Programme at the ISEAS-Yusof Ishak Institute, Singapore, conducting research in the fields of rural politics, sustainable development, environmental anthropology and the socio-economics of the environment. Serina co-founded Kelab Alami, an organization formed to empower a Johor fishing community through environmental education for habitat conservation and economic participation in coastal development. She has trained local youth in this area as habitat guides, scientific fieldworkers and community researchers as they work to combine scientific data with local ecological and cultural knowledge. She received her Ph.D. in Science from Universiti Teknologi Mara in 2014.

Wendy Mei Tien Yee is a senior lecturer of Ethnic Relations and Peace Studies at the University of Malaya. She received her Ph.D. (2008) in Youth Studies from University Putra Malaysia. She also obtained a Certificate in International Relations and Human Rights Studies from the United Nations University, Tokyo (2006). In 2014, she obtained a certificate in Peacebuilding and Intercultural Dialogue from the Institute for Peace and Dialogue in Switzerland. She conducts her research in the fields of youth development, ethnic relations and national unity. She's involved in the development of University Course Module with the Ministry of Higher Education.

Qianyi Wang received her Ph.D. from the Faculty of Economics and Administration, University of Malaya, and is now in the Economic School of Shandong Technology and Business University, China. Her research interests include development studies, urban studies with particular reference to China and China–Malaysian relations. She has published in international journals in all these areas and is participating in various research projects related to urbanization in China, the Malaysian Chinese, including a Malaysian Chinese Biographical Dictionary, Malaysia–China Relations and China's role in ASEAN.

Jie Zheng was a part-time student of Faculty of Business and Accounting, University of Malaya concentrating in International Business. During her pursuant of M.B.A. from September 2015 to March 2018, she worked diligently, fulfilling all the university graduation requirement and was awarded the Master of Business Administration (with Distinction). Her research project under the supervision of Prof. Mohd Nazari Ismail was evaluated with an A grade. Zheng Jie also works with Sinohydro Bureau 8 Co., Ltd. as the Manager of Malaysia Office, her scope of work is business development in the field of construction, specializing in the energy sector.

List of Figures

Fig. 1.1	ASEAN's trade and inflow FDI growth (2007–2016)	9
Fig. 4.1	Conceptual model	64
Fig. 9.1	Contribution of healthy performance of urban areas to regional integration of ASEAN 2025 vision	180
Fig. 10.1	ASEAN—TBTs and labelling requirements for TBT reasons in pre-packaged food (%). TBTs—share of total public (mandatory) NTMs in the PPF sector. B31—share of total TBTs in the PPF sector	206
Fig. 10.2	ASEAN7*—regulatory distance of labelling requirements for TBT reasons in pre-packaged food. *ASEAN7 excludes Cambodia, Lao and Myanmar. MY—Malaysia; SGP—Singapore; THA—Thailand; PHL—Philippines; IDN—Indonesia; BRN—Brunei; CAM—Cambodia; MYA—Myanmar; LAO—Lao; VNM—Vietnam	207
Fig. 11.1	Four components of Re-LIMDD	235

xvii

List of Tables

Table 1.1	Human development index of ASEAN member countries	4
Table 1.2	Diversity in language, culture and political system	5
Table 2.1	China's importance in the trade of ASEAN countries, 2013	20
Table 2.2	China's outward FDI in ASEAN countries, 2004–2012, US$ Million	21
Table 3.1	South Korea trade value with ASEAN (1989–2017)	41
Table 3.2	South Korea's Foreign Direct Investment in ASEAN (2010–2016) (US$ million)	42
Table 3.3	South Korea's top ten ODA partners of 2015 disbursement value received (2011–2015) (US$ millions)	43
Table 3.4	South Korea's disbursement of ODA to ASEAN countries 2011–2016 (current price US$ millions)	44
Table 3.5	Projects approved by South Korea's EDCF in ASEAN countries for 2016	44
Table 4.1	Foreign direct investment: inward and outward flows and stock USD in millions	55
Table 4.2	Comparison of ASEAN inward FDI from world and China	56
Table 4.3	Source of secondary data	65
Table 4.4	Descriptive statistics	67

xix

xx   List of Tables

Table 4.5	Reliability analysis	68
Table 4.6	Regression analysis	70
Table 4.7	Overview of the study	73
Table 6.1	AQRF level descriptors	112
Table 6.2	National qualification framework (NQF) summary	114
Table 6.3	Summary of ASEAN national qualification framework	115
Table 6.4	Types of qualification framework functions	117
Table 6.5	Key characteristic of regional qualifications framework	118
Table 7.1	Bilateral migration matrix World Bank estimates, ASEAN member states, 2013	137
Table 7.2	Employed migrants by economic domain, ASEAN member states, latest year	138
Table 7.3	Employed migrants by level of education, ASEAN member states, 2013 Member States, latest year (%)	139
Table 8.1	Relevant framework on renewable and sustainable energy development in ASEAN	163
Table 8.2	Per cent increase in FAO total oil palm planted area from 1989 to 2013 in selected ASEAN countries and estimated per cent of oil palm planted areas from deforestation since 1989	164
Table 8.3	Ranking climate risk of ASEAN countries	166
Table 8.4	ASEAN's reaction to the United States withdrawal from Paris Agreement	168
Table 9.1	Rate of Urban population share in ASEAN Countries—1975–2050	178
Table 9.2	PM2.5 level in some ASEAN cities	182
Table 10.1	ASEAN7—regulatory distance of labelling requirements for TBT reasons for pre-packaged food, by subsectors	208
Table 10.2	Distribution of responses based on level of complexity of nutrition labelling	211
Table 10.3	Reasons for complexity in nutrition labelling	212
Table 10.4	Compliance costs and problems related to nutrition labelling	215
Table 10.5	Suggested changes for consistency in nutrition labelling	217
Table 10.6	Product description for subcategories of pre-packaged food	224
Table 10.7	Core elements of nutrition labelling	225
Table 11.1	Comparison of moral dilemmas	237

1

Overview of ASEAN

Aida Idris and Nurliana Kamaruddin

Background

The Association of Southeast Asian Nations (ASEAN) was formed on 8 August 1967 through the signing of the Bangkok Declaration by five founding member countries, namely Indonesia, Malaysia, Philippines, Singapore and Thailand. The primary motivation for the establishment of this regional pact was to promote regional peace and resilience amidst the volatilities of the Cold War (Hoang et al. 2016). With the successive inclusion of Brunei, Vietnam, Lao PDR, Myanmar (Burma) and Cambodia over the next few decades, ASEAN's membership has grown to the present ten states.

A. Idris (✉)
Faculty of Business and Accountancy, University of Malaya,
Kuala Lumpur, Malaysia
e-mail: aida_idris@um.edu.my

N. Kamaruddin
Asia-Europe Institute, University of Malaya, Kuala Lumpur, Malaysia
e-mail: nurliana.k@um.edu.my

© The Author(s) 2019
A. Idris and N. Kamaruddin (eds.), *ASEAN Post-50*,
https://doi.org/10.1007/978-981-13-8043-3_1

The benefits of economic and sociocultural cooperation have underlined the importance of solidarity among these neighbouring countries. By the end of the 1990s, ASEAN had emerged as one of the world's most successful models of regional integration, spurred by its Vision 2020 (ASEAN Secretariat 2017a) of "a concert of Southeast Asian nations, outward looking, living in peace, stability and prosperity, bonded together in partnership in dynamic development and in a community of caring societies".

Due to its track record in regional economic development and political cooperation, ASEAN has often been compared to the European Union (EU). However, unlike the EU, ASEAN was never intended to be a supranational organization; rather, it prides itself as a collection of diverse neighbouring nations which are committed to maintaining regional peace and stability through a process of peaceful talks and negotiations, known as the ASEAN Way (Yukawa 2018). Another important philosophy which revolves around the region is ASEAN "centrality".

According to Acharya (2017), the notion of ASEAN centrality means that ASEAN lies at the core of Asia or Asia Pacific regional institutions, providing the institutional platform within which the wider Asia Pacific and East Asian regional institutions are anchored. In other words, without ASEAN, it would not have been possible to construct these wider regional bodies. ASEAN centrality also implies that Southeast Asia is at the hub of Asian regionalist debates over norms and mechanisms for regional cooperation in Asia, such as the discourse on non-interference and legalization.

Regional peace in ASEAN has led to stable economic growth, resulting in substantial reduction in extreme poverty across the region, where the percentage of population living below USD1.25 per day has decreased from 47% in 1990 to 14% in 2015 (ASEAN Secretariat 2017a). Significant improvements have also been recorded in health and education, as evidenced by rising tertiary enrolment rates and life expectancy, especially in the lower income CLMV states (comprising Cambodia, Lao PDR, Myanmar and Vietnam).

Having celebrated its 50th anniversary recently, ASEAN now stands as the third largest economy in Asia and seventh globally

(ASEAN Secretariat 2017b). With the formal establishment of the ASEAN Community in November 2015, leaders of member states adopted the *ASEAN 2025* document which sets out the direction for a "politically cohesive, economically integrated, socially responsible and a truly rules-based, people-oriented, people-centred ASEAN". Three pillars define the ASEAN Community—the ASEAN Political-Security Community, the ASEAN Economic Community and the ASEAN Socio-Cultural Community. The formation of this Community, supported by a collective population of about 635 million people and a consumer market of USD2.6 trillion, has obviously introduced enormous opportunities for ASEAN and its partners.

Nevertheless, ASEAN is currently at a turning point as it moves forward in a turbulent and uncertain twenty-first century. Although the first fifty years of integration has brought about peace and prosperity to the region, the next fifty undoubtedly will be fraught with unprecedented challenges. Today ASEAN not only has to contend with its own internal challenges arising from highly diverse political, economic and sociocultural systems of its member countries, it also has to deal with external factors amidst shifts in geostrategic balance, fraying global consensus on free trade, populism and xenophobia, ideological extremism, climate change, digital revolutions and cybercrimes. These issues are summarized in the following sections.

Diversity Among Member Countries

The entry of the CLMV countries into ASEAN in the late 1990s raised concerns over the possible emergence of a two-tier region, resulting from a development gap between them and the six older member states, popularly known as the ASEAN6. The Human Development Index (HDI) reported by the United Nations Development Programme (UNDP 2018) suggests clear discrepancies in average income, health and education between CLMV and ASEAN6 populations. As indicated in Table 1.1, Singapore, Brunei and Malaysia are categorized as very high HDI, while Thailand is high. The remaining six members are considered medium scorers, with the Philippines and Indonesia

Table 1.1 Human development index of ASEAN member countries

Country	HDI (2017)	
Singapore	0.932	very high
Brunei	0.853	very high
Malaysia	0.802	very high
Thailand	0.755	high
Philippines	0.699	medium
Indonesia	0.694	medium
Vietnam	0.694	medium
Laos	0.601	medium
Cambodia	0.582	medium
Myanmar	0.578	medium

Source UNDP (2018)

leading the CLMV countries. These gaps appear to be mainly related to differences in population distribution between urban and rural areas (ASEAN Secretariat 2017a). Whereas more than half of the population in ASEAN6 live in cities, only a third of CLMV population do so. In other words, a huge majority of CLMV population live in rural areas, with less access to education, health and business infrastructure than that of ASEAN6.

Furthermore, even though recent reports (ASEAN Secretariat 2017a) show that CLMV represent around 27% of the total ASEAN population, their share of the region's gross domestic product (GDP) is only about 12%. Also worth noting is their heavier dependence on trade in goods (approximately 18% of the total ASEAN value in 2016), while the services trade sector is significantly less productive, fluctuating around 9–12% of the total for ASEAN since 1999 and even recording a decline in recent years (from 13.4% in 2015 to 12.0% in 2016). In contrast, the positive trend in services trade for ASEAN6 has been consistent at more than 10% growth annually during the same period. Since the service sectors typically reflect a connection to knowledge-based economic activities, the above figures underline a lag in the development of a knowledge economy among the CLMV countries, relative to the ASEAN6.

Diversity among ASEAN member states also exists in their official language or native tongue, cultural and religious values, and political

1 Overview of ASEAN **5**

Table 1.2 Diversity in language, culture and political system

Country	Primary language/Mother tongue	Ethnic majority/Official religion
Brunei	Malay	Malay/Islam
Cambodia	Khmer	Khmer/Buddhism
Indonesia	Indonesian	Javanese/Islam
Laos	Lao	Lao/Buddhism
Malaysia	Malay	Malay/Islam
Myanmar	Burmese	Bamar/Buddhism
Philippines	Filipino	Visayan and Tagalog/Christianity
Singapore	English	Chinese/Buddhism
Thailand	Thai	Thai/Buddhism
Vietnam	Vietnamese	Vietnamese/Folk

Source Compiled from various government websites 2019

ideology, as listed in Table 1.2. These differences can hamper regional integration through a lack of trust, communication barriers and contradicting priorities between the various ASEAN communities. An example of this complex situation is the plight of the Rohingyas in Myanmar, a conflict which has often been linked to ethnic, religious and ideological gaps between the majority Buddhist population and the minority Muslim Rohinghya (IRIN News 2013; Mohajan 2018; Ware 2015). As a result of religious persecution and ethnic cleansing, hundreds of thousands of Rohingya have fled their homes and become refugees in other ASEAN member states, especially Muslim majority countries such as Malaysia and Indonesia. This has prompted some government leaders in these countries to issue statements protesting against the lack of action by the Myanmar government to resolve the situation, despite the principle of non-interference among member states. Clearly with such a sensitive mix of ethnicity and religion in the background, the issue of the Rohingya refugees will continue to be a serious impediment to ASEAN's integration, unless the ASEAN Way of peaceful negotiations can effectively guarantee minority rights across the region.

Changing Relationships with United States, China and Other Dialogue Partners

While still celebrating its 50th anniversary, ASEAN is now contending with shifting geopolitical and geo-economic landscape. When the newly elected US President Donald Trump visited Asia in November 2017 for the APEC Economic Leaders' Meeting, his "America First" agenda was seen to be undoing much of what the Obama administration had tried to accomplish with ASEAN previously. The ambiguity of the Trump administration in the United States and his aggressive foreign policy has increased growing global political uncertainty. The Trump administration is concerned of China and Russia challenging the US dominance and declared that the administration aims to "advance American influence" through trade and engagement with multilateral organizations (The White House 2017, 2–4).

The current policy adopted by the United States towards China and North Korea appears to be provocative and inconsistent. This is highlighted by their earlier close cooperation with China in the case of North Korea's nuclear threat (ISEAS 2017) but which has since then reversed into a trade war, with far-reaching implications on the ASEAN economy (Moeller 2018; Pereira 2018). The tougher trade policies have not only resulted in the trade war with China in 2018 but also tension with long-term allies: Canada and members of the EU such as France and Germany.

In the meantime, ASEAN importance that was highlighted under the Obama administration mentioned earlier has been subsumed in the larger security concerns of the South China Sea and an "Indo-Pacific" approach (The White House 2017, 45). In the National Security Strategy document published by the White House in 2017, ASEAN is mentioned as a centrepiece "of the Indo-Pacific's regional architecture and platforms for promoting an order based on freedom" (The White House 2017, 46). However, there has been little engagement from the current administration.

The present sentiment in ASEAN is not so much looking forward to better ties with the United States, as finding ways to manage future risks and uncertainties due to the latter's unclear direction concerning major issues such as the South China Sea disputes, Comprehensive and Progressive Agreement for Trans-Pacific Partnership, climate and environment protection, etc. In view of a receding US influence in Southeast Asia, ASEAN has attempted to improve existing ties with key Asian economies, namely China, Japan and South Korea, using the ASEAN + 3 platform. Within ASEAN + 3, China especially has dominated ASEAN's landscape in recent years.

This is demonstrated by its increased level of investment across Southeast Asia involving megaprojects such as the "Belt and Road Initiative" and the mobility of Chinese nationals in the region, either as students or tourists. With the inclusion of Australia, New Zealand and India, there is also the ASEAN + 6, which stands as the linchpin of Asia Pacific's economic, political, security, sociocultural architecture. The relationship among these countries has seen progress through the development of the Regional Comprehensive Economic Partnership (RCEP), a proposed free-trade agreement involving the 16 countries of ASEAN + 6. Regional experts argue that, relative to the Trans-Pacific Partnership, RCEP will allow its members better protection against global competition (Fukunaga 2014; Wilson 2015).

Another major dialogue partner for ASEAN is the EU. Prior to Brexit, the EU was ASEAN's main reference for best practices in regionalization, serving as the benchmark for human capital mobility, shared open market, sustainable development, as well as a collective response towards ideological extremism and forced migration. Although challenges pertaining to Brexit have now raised fresh questions about these traditional perceptions of the EU, ASEAN still believes that it has a lot to learn from the EU experience. Because of this, post-Brexit EU and the UK will continue to be influential partners of ASEAN as it moves into the next fifty years of regional cooperation.

Unlike its relationship with the United States, China and Japan, ASEAN's ties with the EU have thus far been driven almost completely by economic factors with little geopolitical undertones (Yeo 2016). Various forms of support extended by the EU towards ASEAN, which include improving the latter's regulatory framework and harmonization of quality standards, also benefit the EU in its attempts to revive its sluggish economy. The EU is ASEAN's second largest trading partner, with a 7% average growth in annual trade over the past two decades (Pardo 2016). It has also become the largest provider of foreign direct investment (FDI) in ASEAN, responsible for 22% of the total FDI flow into the region. Hence, emerging conflicts such as the palm oil ban imposed by the EU on ASEAN producers will have to be negotiated skilfully to maintain the goodwill between the two regional blocs.

Promoting Sustainable Growth and Development

Socio-economic growth across ASEAN has thus far been driven mainly by contract manufacturing. Because of its regional peace and stability, ASEAN has been a major FDI destination for multinational corporations (MNCs) looking to establish plants to produce goods which are then exported to other parts of the world. This provides jobs and raises the income of the local population, while improving the regional GDP. However, the choice of FDI destination for contract manufacturing is primarily determined by the cost of operation in a particular setting.

As a country modernizes and improves its standard of living, the costs of operation in that country (such as wages and raw materials) will also rise; thus with modernization, a country will often lose its attractiveness as a contract manufacturer for large MNCs and will be replaced by others that can operate at lower costs. An example of this phenomenon is the electronics industry where traditional leaders such as Singapore and Malaysia are fast being replaced by Vietnam and Thailand. The cycle is continuous, so that even the lower-cost ASEAN countries are also increasingly facing cost-related threats, particularly from China. Such trends have had negative implications on ASEAN's trade and inflow FDI growth, as indicated in Fig. 1.1, where the figures have been gradually stagnating since 2012.

The above situation clearly describes the importance of achieving and maintaining sustainable growth. In this regard, some of the more pertinent issues facing ASEAN are quality of education, lifelong learning, knowledge economy and innovation, as well as modernization

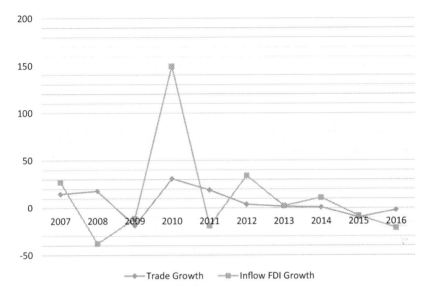

Fig. 1.1 ASEAN's trade and inflow FDI growth (2007–2016) (*Source* ASEAN Secretariat 2017c)

and management of urban poverty. In addition, since the concept of sustainable growth is closely related to the implementation of sustainable development practices, challenges associated with environment protection, biodiversity and indigenous economic activities have also begun to capture the attention of academics, practitioners and policymakers in recent years.

Organization of the Book

Set against the above background, this book delves into a number of related issues and challenges faced by ASEAN in its journey towards a more cohesive and dynamic regional integration. It serves as a compilation of works involving authors from several Asian countries and is intended as supplementary reading for students, researchers and scholars of ASEAN studies. The book chapters discuss some essential topics in ASEAN's post-50 environment according to the three pillars of the ASEAN Community: politics and security, economy and socio-culture.

Following this introductory note, the following three chapters revolve around a very significant topic in the post-50 ASEAN environment, namely its changing relationships with key dialogue partners, particularly the United States, China and South Korea. In these chapters, the authors describe how the diminishing presence of the United States in Southeast Asia has opened up huge opportunities for China and South Korea to pursue their interests in the region, especially in economic and trade activities.

Chapters 5 and 6 deal with education management issues. While the former discusses the role of knowledge as an empowerment tool for ASEAN societies moving towards sustainable socio-economic development, the latter argues for a systematic infrastructure for higher education which can improve and standardize quality between the ASEAN6 and CLMV countries.

The next two chapters investigate another critical emerging issue in the region, namely green management and environment protection. Chapter 7 discusses legal and policy consideration regarding biodiversity, deforestation and climate change, whereas Chapter 8 explores energy consumption and pollution in urban areas as ASEAN progressively becomes more modernized.

Chapters 9, 10 and 11 are independent topics focusing, respectively, on immigration and political-security, food labelling regulations for cross-border consumption, and the question of moral or ethics in a multicultural environment. The book concludes with Chapter 12, which summarizes the various perspectives of regional integration challenges proposed in the preceding chapters, with a special emphasis on policy recommendations and future directions.

References

Acharya, Amitav. 2017. "The Myth of ASEAN Centrality?" *Contemporary Southeast Asia: A Journal of International and Strategic Affairs* 39 (2): 273–279.

ASEAN Secretariat. 2017a. *Celebrating ASEAN: 50 Years of Evolution and Progress*. Jakarta: ASEAN.

ASEAN Secretariat. 2017b. *ASEAN Community Progress Monitoring System.* Jakarta: ASEAN.

ASEAN Secretariat. 2017c. *ASEAN Economic Integration Brief.* Jakarta: ASEAN.

Fukunaga, Yoshifumi. 2014. "ASEAN's Leadership in the Regional Comprehensive Economic Partnership." *Asia & the Pacific Policy Studies* 2 (1): 103–115.

Hoang, Thi Ha, Moe Thuzar, Sanchita Basu Das, and Termsak Chalermpalanupap. 2016. "Diverging Regionalisms: ASEAN and the EU." *ASEANFocus.* Special Issue, August, 4–13. https://www.iseas.edu.sg/images/pdf/ASEANFocus%20Issue%206%202016%20August%202016.pdf.

IRIN News. 2013. How to Reverse Buddhism's Radical Turn in Southeast Asia? Accessed January 3, 2019. http://www.irinnews.org/analysis/2013/07/16/how-reverse-buddhism%E2%80%99s-radical-turn-southeast-asia#.UqYO6PRDvTo.

ISEAS. 2017. "Trump in Southeast Asia." *ASEANFocus* 7: 4–7.

Moeller, Joergen Oerstroem. 2018. "US-China Trade War: Opportunities & Risks for Southeast Asia." *ISEAS Perspective* 64: 1–7.

Mohajan, Haradhan K. 2018. "History of Rakhine State and the Origin of the Rohingya Muslims." *Indonesian Journal of Southeast Asian Studies* 2 (1): 19–46.

Pardo, F. F. 2016. "Why ASEAN Matters to the EU." *ASEANFocus.* Special Issue, August, 17. https://www.iseas.edu.sg/images/pdf/ASEANFocus%20Issue%206%202016%20August%202016.pdf.

Pereira, Derwin. 2018. "How the US-China Trade War Will Make or Break ASEAN." *South China Morning Post.* Accessed January 3, 2019. https://www.scmp.com/comment/insight-opinion/asia/article/2173343/how-us-china-trade-war-will-make-or-break-asean.

The White House. 2017. *National Security Strategy of the United States of America*, Washington, DC: The White House.

United Nations Development Programme. 2018. *Human Development Indices and Indicators Statistical Update.* Accessed January 2, 2019. http://hdr.undp.org/sites/default/files/2018_summary_human_development_statistical_update_en.pdf.

Ware, Anthony. 2015. "Secessionist Aspects to the Buddhist-Muslim Conflict in Rakhine State, Myanmar." In *Territorial Separatism and Global Politics (War and Intrastate Conflict Series)*, edited by Damien Kingsbury and Costas Laoutides. London: Routledge.

Wilson, Jeffrey D. 2015. "Mega-regional Trade Deals in the Asia-Pacific: Choosing Between the TPP and RCEP?" *Journal of Contemporary Asia* 45 (2): 345–353.

Yeo, Lay Hwee. 2016. "Why the EU Matters to ASEAN." *ASEANFocus.* Special Issue, August, 16. https://www.iseas.edu.sg/images/pdf/ASEANFocus%20Issue%206%202016%20August%202016.pdf.

Yukawa, Taku. 2018. "The ASEAN Way as a Symbol: An Analysis of Discourses on the ASEAN Norms." *Pacific Review* 31 (3): 298–314.

2

ASEAN at 50: The Rise of China and the Emerging Regional Integration Architecture

Kee Cheok Cheong, Ran Li and Qianyi Wang

Introduction—A Half Century of Changing Relationships

As ASEAN celebrates its fiftieth anniversary in 2017, it is appropriate to review what has been and will be the most important relationship it has from multiple perspectives, including economic, political and geo-political. While Southeast Asia has historically been open to numerous external influences, from hosting Hindu kingdoms to colonization by the Western powers, this relationship is with China. China's association

---

K. C. Cheong (✉) · R. Li
Institute of China Studies, University of Malaya, Kuala Lumpur, Malaysia
e-mail: cheongkeecheok@um.edu.my

R. Li
e-mail: liran@um.edu.my

Q. Wang
Economic School, Shandong Technology and Business University, Shandong, China
e-mail: qianyiwang571@qq.com

© The Author(s) 2019   **13**
A. Idris and N. Kamaruddin (eds.), *ASEAN Post-50*,
https://doi.org/10.1007/978-981-13-8043-3_2

with Southeast Asia, of course, predates ASEAN. In the nineteenth and early twentieth centuries, a large number of sojourner migrants moved from China's southern provinces of Guangdong and Fujian to seek their fortunes in developing Southeast Asia. Cut off from their ancestral home after the Second World War, these migrants and their descendants became citizens in their host countries, many prospering but also viewed with mistrust by the local population.

ASEAN's relationship with China has evolved as a consequence of both China's transformation and ASEAN's own dynamics. During that period, China has moved from a closed economy aligned with and a key member of the Communist Bloc to one characterized by China itself as a "socialist market economy" in which market forces play a major role, albeit with extensive intervention from the state. ASEAN itself has gone from being (as the original ASEAN-5) a bulwark in the "free world" against the spread of Communism to a more neutral stance in which states with diverse political systems have been admitted to membership. Factors both domestic and external to these countries play important roles in these changes. So too are bilateral relations between the two territories.

It is worth remembering at the outset that ASEAN's founding at the height of the Cold War had little to do with China. It was established as a forum to resolve disputes between Malaysia and its neighbours Indonesia and the Philippines and to normalize relations with Singapore, which left the newly formed Malaysia just after two years. Yet China was material to the Western-aligned ASEAN because it was the major protagonist in the Cold War. Together with the Soviet Union, it supported Vietnam during the Vietnam War and was the rationale for the "Domino Theory" that powered Western efforts to contain the spread of Communism.

The Cold War brings also to the fore the role in Southeast Asia of the United States as the leader of "the free world". As the major driver of the Cold War, the United States was a leading participant in the only two "hot wars" of the Cold War era—Korea 1950–1953 and Vietnam 1955–1975. US impact on Southeast Asia was not limited to leading the war in Vietnam; it also established alliances and military bases in the Philippines and Thailand to support its war effort. While these alliances lasted, they served to divide ASEAN countries through the extent of affiliation with the United States. Interestingly, the existence of Communism did not define this affiliation. Both Indonesia and Malaysia had to deal with Communist insurgencies but were not closely affiliated with the United States. Most recently, with the rise of China, the United States has shifted its focus back to Southeast Asia to contain China's growing influence. In this sense, the emerging regional integration architecture in the form of the Trans-Pacific Partnership Agreement (TPPA) and its successor the Comprehensive and Progressive Agreement for Trans-Pacific Partnership (CPTPP) and the Regional Comprehensive Economic Partnership (RCEP) point to a vital role for China in the region's foreseeable future.

In reviewing China's rise to regional centre stage, this chapter also points specifically to the new regional agreements that are likely to impact ASEAN in the years ahead. Specifically, this chapter examines (a) the extent to which ASEAN is able to play a role independent of the great powers China and the United States, (b) the several areas of economic interaction between ASEAN and China that contrast with the latter's strategic and security posture, (c) China's regional role, both in promoting ASEAN centrality and in provoking responses from the United States and its allies, and (d) various manifestations of China's (and the US') recognition of ASEAN's standing in the region.

In the next section, we discuss whether ASEAN is able to carve for itself a role independent of the great powers which speaks to its "relevance". Section "ASEAN–China Economic and Security Relations" deals with the specific areas of interaction, both positive and negative, that have major consequences for ASEAN as an entity. Section "The Emerging Regional Integration Architecture and China" provides a commentary of the regional role China plays directly by promoting ASEAN and indirectly by provoking pushback against China's growing influence. Section "ASEAN's Standing as a Regional Entity" looks at the official standing that ASEAN has in relation to both China and the United States. Section "Conclusion" concludes with several observations.

Does ASEAN Have a Role Independent of China (and the United States)?

The failure of ASEAN to inject itself in the recent South China Sea dispute between China and ASEAN member countries has produced increasingly shrill voices criticizing ASEAN's ineffectiveness and questioning its relevance. The comment "leading ASEAN experts have begun to question the relevance of the regional organization, bemoaning its lack of resolve before China's repeated acts of provocation against ASEAN members, particularly the Philippines and Vietnam" (Heydarian 2015) exemplifies the narrative of the naysayers. Even more brunt is an editorial of the Manila Standard (2016) with the title "The Irrelevance of ASEAN" that lamented the inability of ASEAN to respond to China's South China Sea claims. While ASEAN'S "relevance" is not the theme of this paper, a fundamental question that can be asked is: Can ASEAN play a role independent of global powers, now increasingly China but still the reigning hegemon the United States?

Those who belong to the realist school of international relations argue that ASEAN's existence owes much to the accommodating stance of the global powers and that its successes and failures cannot be set apart from the actions or lack thereof of these great powers.[1] They argue that ASEAN's founding as a West-leaning organization was endorsed by Western powers and that their initial successes in dispute resolution owed much to their being left alone by the great powers. Successes in the two decades following its establishment were possible because the United States lost interest in Southeast Asia while China was just beginning to liberalize its economy and more focused on domestic reform than external diplomacy. When China, its economy strengthened by decades of heady growth, reemerged as a regional power, prompting a US response in the form of Obama's "pivot to Asia", ASEAN no longer found things so smooth sailing. The South China Sea issue is just one more example of ASEAN's inability to chart its own destiny.

Those from the constructivist school, however, give ASEAN credit for its successes and blame for its failures. Among ASEAN's boosters, Mahbubani and Severino (2014) declared that ASEAN "has dramatically raised living standards of the more than 600 million people residing within its ten-member countries and brought a host of indirect benefits to billions of others in neighboring states". They continued "ASEAN's three greatest contributions are peace, prosperity, and geopolitical stability for Southeast Asia. Each of these accomplishments is remarkable; considered in aggregate, they are astonishing". Former ASEAN Secretary General Severino (2014), in admitting that full economic integration is unlikely to be achieved by ASEAN any time soon, believed that "the ASEAN spirit is still going strong". Critics who blamed ASEAN's ineffectiveness on its so-called ASEAN Way of decision by consensus also belong to the constructivist school. While they arrived at a conclusion similar to that among the realists, they blamed ASEAN for its failure whereas realists believed ASEAN ineffectiveness was just in the nature of big power geopolitics.

The truth lies somewhere in between these extreme positions. ASEAN's ability not only to survive but to prosper in the face of major external changes—the United States withdrawal from Southeast Asia and the survival of Communist regimes despite the end of the Cold War—is testimony to its resourcefulness and survival skills. And, as will be seen later, while China's impact, for good or bad, will increase with time, it still sees ASEAN as an important institution representing Southeast Asia. On the ASEAN side, the pragmatism that had characterized the organization's founding and adaptation to changing circumstances will allow it to capture the benefits of this bilateral relationship while navigating through the challenges such a relationship poses.

ASEAN–China Economic and Security Relations

Not for the first time, ASEAN faces a changed geopolitical environment as the twenty-first century began—the rise of China. Since liberalization in 1978, China had enjoyed uninterrupted growth in the last two decades of the twentieth century, with no indication of a let-up as a new century began. It had dominated FDI flows, became "factory to the world", and was the destination for most global supply chains in which ASEAN countries participate. With China as its immediate neighbour,

ASEAN is clearly impacted by China's growth. This impact is felt in two areas. These are regional security and economic relations.

In terms of regional security, China's rise was benign—the Chinese leadership had from the very beginning pledged that it was committed to "peaceful development" (*he ping fa jan*), taking care even to avoid the term "peaceful rise". This has changed with China adopting a more muscular stance with respect to its claims over islands in the South China (and East China) Sea.

ASEAN finds great difficulty in responding to this security threat. Indeed, the lack of unity in confronting China's South China Sea claims has opened the floodgate to a spate of criticisms to the extent ASEAN's obituary has already been written (Bowring 2016). But it really is not hard to explain why. As explained elsewhere in this paper, ASEAN is a bloc of countries each driven by national self-interest as the bottom line. Thus, Beeson (2016, 18) argued that ASEAN's response to this security threat from China was muted by China's simultaneous deployment of charm and aggressiveness with some countries benefiting disproportionately from the former relative to other ASEAN members.[2] Even the Philippines, a major claimant of the disputed waters, has benefited economically from détente with China (Ho 2017). Countries like Indonesia and Thailand have no territorial claims and clearly see no merit in picking a fight with China. Confronting China would have greater adverse consequences for Myanmar for which China was for long the sole investor and purchaser of its resources when it was under an economic embargo imposed by the West (see Bolesta 2018).

ASEAN countries' response to China is based on a cost-benefit calculus that far exceeds the relevance of the maritime dispute. Some countries like Cambodia, Lao PDR and Myanmar have benefited substantially from Chinese trade and investment but also suffered environmental consequences. Countries like Vietnam experienced rising trade with China but are suffering from growing trade deficits. China–Malaysia trade, an important part of which are global supply chain-driven, are nearly in balance. Political realities are also important factors. Criticized by the west for its military takeover of government, Thailand's generals moved closer to China. And the previous government in Malaysia found China's adherence to non-interference of counterpart countries a good way, by inflating project costs, to hide debt repayment caused by massive embezzlement from the public eye (Sarawak Report 2016)

Notwithstanding critics' fixation with Chinese aggression, the South China Sea dispute is not the only example of the failure of ASEAN's operating principles. More serious are failures to deal with internal problems, the rationale for the formation of ASEAN in the first place. In 2014, a dispute broke out over the ownership of a temple located at the Thai Cambodian border. With ASEAN unable to resolve the dispute, it took the International Court to pronounce the final judgement. A second is the perennial blanket of smoke from fires to clear land for replanting in Indonesia that badly affects Singapore and Malaysia which Chander (2017) attributes to governance issues in Indonesia.

Economically, China's rise impacts ASEAN economic integration both positively and negatively. From the first perspective, ASEAN's economic integration has been spurred by the rise of China. In 1992, ASEAN leaders were sufficiently alarmed by the potential competition in trade and investment from China to launch the ASEAN Free Trade Area (AFTA). AFTA was to oversee "the reduction of tariffs on all intra-ASEAN trade in manufactures, processed agricultural products, and capital goods to a 0-5 percent range within fifteen years, starting in 1993" (Narine 2002, 127). Unlike for previous initiatives, this target was achieved in 2005 for the original ASEAN 5 plus Brunei. Sixty per cent of these have zero tariffs (Weber 2009, 8).

Despite this impetus to integrate, progress remains hostage to national self-interest, prompting Singapore's Prime Minister Lee Hsien Loong, to warn that with its limited achievements overshadowed by members' preoccupation with domestic affairs, ASEAN risked becoming irrelevant (ASEAN Affairs 2008). The slow advance of economic integration is reflected in the progress of the ASEAN Economic Community, launched in 2015. Even as tariffs are coming down and standardized through the ASEAN Single Window, a host of non-tariff measures continue to protect domestic industries and products (Tangkitvanich and Ratanakhamfu 2017). Concerns have also been expressed about the expected free flow of labour, with countries like the Philippines and Thailand expressing fears that they may experience

20   K. C. Cheong et al.

brain drain to Singapore (Cheong and Goh 2015). This lack of progress has resulted in demand–supply mismatches in ASEAN labour markets with adverse consequences for productivity (Vineles 2018, 2).

Failure to meet targets at appointed dates does not mean a complete lack of success in or no progress towards integration, however. As shown in Deloitte (2015, 3), small steps, although mostly in the form of declarations, have been taken since the formation of AFTA to foster greater integration with the AEC merely being the latest and arguably boldest step. It should also be noted that even if all the targets were met, the increase in intra-ASEAN trade and investment may not be substantially given the modest level of existing intra-ASEAN trade compared to trade with non-ASEAN countries, especially China. This has led Dosch (2015, 1) to observe: "Given the outward orientation for ASEAN trade, is the lack of an unhindered regional market really a problem?"

From the second perspective, although growing economic relations with China have revitalized an area that was almost moribund in terms of achievement in the first two and a half decades of ASEAN's existence, ASEAN's trade with China has far outstripped that among its own members. China is, as of 2013, the top trading partner for 6 and ranked second in another 3 of the 10 ASEAN countries (Table 2.1). How much of this trade is due to ASEAN is difficult to tell, but a measure of ASEAN's role can be seen from the China–ASEAN Free Trade

Table 2.1 China's importance in the trade of ASEAN countries, 2013

Country	China's rank as export destination	China's rank as import source	China's rank as trading partner[a]
Brunei	>5	4	>5
Cambodia	>5	1	2
Indonesia	2	1	1
Laos	1	2	2
Malaysia	2	1	1
Myanmar	2	1	1
Philippines	3	1	2
Singapore	2	1	1
Thailand	1	2	1
Vietnam	3	1	1

[a]Trade refers to the sum of exports and imports
Source Salidjanova and Koch-Weser (2015)

Agreement (CAFTA) signed in 2002 and which came into effect in 2010. China is also the sponsor of the RCEP Agreement that brings ASEAN together with China, Japan, Korea, India, Australia and New Zealand and has been touted as China's answer to the US-proposed Trans-Pacific Partnership, now stillborn. Thus, ever since the beginning of this century, China has been driving Asian integration, of course, with it in a leadership position.

China's FDI in these countries is also growing, initially the result of its "Go Out" Policy, in which Chinese enterprises expand their operations overseas, supported by Chinese financial institutions. In the early years of this policy, state enterprises were taking the lead, but the trend has caught on with non-state enterprises. Most recently, the massive One Belt One Road (OBOR) strategic initiative was announced by Chinese President Xi Jinping in Indonesia and Kazakhstan in 2013. While the growth in trade reflects market demand and supply between trading partners, the growth in Chinese FDI is a manifestation as much of China's strategic imperatives as of economics. ASEAN's role is as part the Maritime Silk Road that links China by sea to the Middle East and beyond. Funding for FDI, especially infrastructure, will come from the newly established Asia Infrastructure Investment as well as a $100 billion Silk Route Fund.

As is clear from Table 2.2, the data source being UNCTAD (2014), Chinese FDI in ASEAN countries was insignificant up to 2006. This had changed by 2008, with Singapore receiving US$1.5 billion, and

Table 2.2 China's outward FDI in ASEAN countries, 2004–2012, US$ Million

	2004	2006	2008	2009	2010	2011	2012
Cambodia	30	10	205	216	467	566	560
Indonesia	62	57	174	226	201	592	1361
Lao PDR	4	48	87	203	314	459	809
Malaysia	8	8	34	54	164	95	199
Myanmar	4	13	233	377	876	218	749
Philippines	–	9	34	40	244	267	75
Singapore	48	132	1551	1414	1119	3269	1519
Thailand	23	16	45	50	700	230	479
Vietnam	17	44	120	112	305	189	349

Source UNCTAD (2014)

that figure being maintained ever since. Indonesia, Myanmar and Vietnam also began to garner China's attention, primarily in the extractive and natural resource industries. By 2012, the last year for which data were available, Cambodia, with half a billion US$ of Chinese investment, Lao PDR with US$800 million and Myanmar with nearly as much had become major destinations for Chinese investment. Both Thailand and Vietnam received a moderate amount of Chinese FDI, with the Philippines the singular exception, having received little.

The data ending in 2012 left the story of Chinese FDI incomplete. The launch of the Belt and Road Initiative (see later) in 2013 would eventually see a major increase in Chinese FDI, especially in infrastructure, in ASEAN member countries. Malaysia presents an interesting example of how this FDI may materialize. From virtually nothing before 2013, China is now Malaysia's top source of FDI. The national railway company, China National Railway Corporation, is a strong contender for the high-speed rail link between Singapore and Kuala Lumpur. The Guangxi provincial government is involved in the development of Kuantan Port, while the Guangdong principal government is participating in the development of Melaka. Non-state real estate enterprises like Country Garden have also commenced major developments in Malaysia.

It bears reminding that the positive picture of trade and investment painted above should not be taken to mean that all ASEAN countries will benefit equally from ASEAN's economic interaction with China. Country-by-country analysis of the China relationship, as has been undertaken in a separate exercise recently, shows considerable variation in China's impact at the country level. In these analyses, Lao PDR (Kyophilavong et al. 2017) stood to reap short-term gains in economic growth, employment and poverty reduction, but at a potential long-term cost of environmental degradation and exposure to "Dutch Disease". Malaysia (Cheong and Wang 2017), although a major trading partner and an increasingly important FDI destination for China, faced domestic and non-China related external challenges that would have diluted any China impact. And the Philippines, though also counting China as a top trading partner, was not much affected by China because its share of trade in total GDP was not large and also falling (Lim 2017).

The Emerging Regional Integration Architecture and China

Since the beginning of this century, ASEAN has been signatory to a slew of free trade agreements (FTAs) both bilateral and multilateral. Almost all these have to do with China—directly as a signatory and indirectly as provoking a response to China's initiatives. The ASEAN–China FTA was the first, the trade in goods agreement signed in 2004 and coming into force in 2005, the trade in services agreement signed in 2008 and coming into force in 2009 and the Investment Agreement signed in 2009 and coming into force in 2010 (MITI, n.d.). Not to be outdone by China, both Korea and Japan signed FTAs with ASEAN in 2006 and 2008, respectively. FTAs with India and Australia–New Zealand followed in 2009. How much of ASEAN trade has been impacted (positively if trade creation resulted and negatively if trade diversion resulted) is hard to tell. With China at least, ASEAN countries have seen both trade and investment soar, as already shown.

ASEAN is also signatory to multilateral FTAs. Although the process was launched earlier than the above bilateral FTAs, in 1997, the ASEAN Plus Three (APT) Cooperation work plan was adopted only in 2007 (ASEAN 2017). The joint statement that launched this work plan "reaffirmed that the ASEAN Plus Three Process would remain as the main vehicle towards the long-term goal of building an East Asian community, with ASEAN as the driving force" (ASEAN 2017, 1). Just as with the bilateral FTAs, the centrality of ASEAN was preserved; although China is likely to play a major role, it is comfortable to have ASEAN leadership in this initiative.

The RCEP, consisting of the members of the APT and with the addition of Australia, New Zealand and India, represents a natural extension of all the bilateral FTAs and APT and has the strong endorsement of China (Chi 2018). Negotiations to launch the RCEP were begun in November 2012. The launch of the RCEP coincided with the US-backed Trans-Pacific Partnership (TPP) to which it has been unfavourably compared. President Trump's withdrawal from the TPP has put the RCEP back in the limelight. Still, obstacles remain that has so far delayed the successful conclusion of negotiations (Hunt 2017).[3]

When this occurs, ASEAN centrality will be assured over much of East and South Asia.

Unlike the FTAs discussed earlier, the TPP consisting of 12 member countries[4] had its origin outside Asia, did not include all members of ASEAN and excluded China. Established by former President Obama to counter China's growing influence through the RCEP, the TPP, according to Obama himself, was to be "a high-standard Trans- Pacific Partnership, a trade deal that puts American workers first and makes sure we write the rules of the road for trade in the 21st century" (Obama 2016). In encapsulating the real motivation for the TPP, this statement made it clear that the primary focus was America and that the "high standard" was for the benefit of American workers. It garnered both support and criticism,[5] but these became moot when Trump withdrew the United States from the TPP the first day he took office as President.

The remaining 11 countries were not prepared for the TPP's demise, however, and negotiated a revised TPP, officially the CPTPP Agreement (also referred to as TPP 2.0). This revised agreement shelved several difficult provisions, including liberalizing the state enterprise sector, but kept the remainder of the conditions intact. The suspension of these items, which are mostly for the US' benefit, lowers the bar compared to the original TPP, making CPTPP somewhat easier for these countries to accept (Helble and Xie 2017). At the same time, the departure of the United States has reduced considerably the economic heft of the CPTPP (13.4% of global GDP compared with 36% for the TPP, according to Torrey 2018), leaving Japan with the largest economy and poised to play a lead role (Mulgan 2018). As with the TPP, claims have been made of participating country gains (e.g. Sani 2018; World Bank 2018) and disputed (Jomo 2018). Given the diminished coverage of the CPTPP relative to the TPP, what is not disputed is that any gains realized would not be as large as from the original TPP.

What implications does the current state of play with the CPTPP have for ASEAN and China? Clearly, the CPTPP undermines the centrality of ASEAN since not all ASEAN countries are in the CPTPP, which is suggestive of the perceived differential benefits and costs of joining among ASEAN members.[6] At the same time, that only some ASEAN countries are participants of the CPTPP poses a threat to

ASEAN integration in that those countries that are in CPTPP may divert trade with other CPTPP countries, hurting those ASEAN countries that have not joined (Lim 2018).

As for China, which is the largest trading partner to many of the CPTPP countries, it has been argued that CPTPP would benefit from China joining (Hunt 2017). However, China's participation faces several challenges, not the least of which being that it is unlikely to countenance Japan leading the group. Nor does it share the enthusiasm of the CPTPP's 11 members in welcoming the United States back (Jomo 2018), given that all the agreements it backs exclude the United States. Although the high standards are likely to pose less of a barrier, given the rapid advances in technology China has achieved, other clauses such as state enterprise liberalization will also not sit well with China. With China pushing for the rival RCEP, it is also unclear how the CPTPP will fit into China's strategic thinking.

In 2017, on the sidelines of the ASEAN Summit, the United States, Japan, Australia and India discussed (re)starting the Quadrilateral Security Dialogue (the "Quad"). That this Quad included neither China nor ASEAN could hardly escape notice. As noted by Ng (2018), ASEAN's buy-in is essential to the organization's credibility. However, such buy-in is by no means certain. From ASEAN's perspective, there is concern that ASEAN's centrality would be jeopardized. Also, if the Quad is perceived as a means to contain China, ASEAN would not want to be seen as taking sides, especially since its economic relations with China are as important as, if not more important than, relations with the Quad combined. Finally, through its Belt and Road Initiative, China has had a major head start over the Quad's committed resources. Given especially the US' and Australia's current anti-China sentiments, the Quad will be a hard sell to convince ASEAN.

ASEAN's Standing as a Regional Entity

Inasmuch as it is important to determine the source of ASEAN's relevance (section "ASEAN–China Economic and Security Relations"), it is no less important to assess if ASEAN is recognized by China as representing the entire Southeast Asian region. As the discussion below shows, the answer is "yes, but…"

China's recognition of ASEAN is manifested in four ways. The first is the establishment of the China–ASEAN Free Trade Area (CAFTA), a China initiative the Agreement for which was signed in Phnom Penh, Cambodia, in 2002, and under which, when in full force, over 90% of traded goods between the signatories would be tax exempt. It was the first bilateral agreement signed by ASEAN (Wong 2010). That China was intent to cultivate good relations with ASEAN is clear. Bordered in the northeast by US allies Japan and Korea, it saw good relations with its southern neighbours as very important. Equally clear was China's intention of going beyond good relations to play a central role in ASEAN. It was no accident that both Japan and Korea followed suit in quick succession, with Korea signing in 2006 and coming into force in 2007 and Japan signing in 2008 and coming into force the same year.

The second is the high level of Chinese representation at ASEAN summits. Right from the beginning, China's Premier attends all ASEAN–China Summits. In contrast, "during the George W. Bush administration … the United States (did) not always attend at the highest-level regional gatherings of which it was a full participant" (Christensen 2015). In a region where "face" is important, ASEAN leaders likely appreciate this gesture more than what critics referring it as "charm offensive" realize. However, the perception is interpreted, ASEAN leaders cannot have failed to compare this with the US representation by lower-level functionaries until Obama's pivot to Asia. It has also not helped that some US strategists (e.g. Lohman 2015) have argued that the United States should just ignore ASEAN.

The third is China's development of the city of Nanning as the gateway for China–ASEAN economic exchanges.[7] Its joint development by the central, provincial and municipal governments attests to the importance the Chinese state attaches to this endeavour. The central government's role lies in developing human capital and promoting knowledge intensification (Wei 2015). The national government also developed Nanning's transport and border trade infrastructure. Nanning also enjoys tax privileges from the central government. At the provincial level, the Guangxi Autonomous Region's government

2 ASEAN at 50: The Rise of China and the Emerging ...   27

dovetails its initiatives into those of the national government. As part of the national Western Development Program in China's Eleventh Five-Year Plan,[8] the Guangxi provincial government planned the Beibu Gulf Economic Zone (BGEZ) in 2008 as the first regional cooperation zone with ASEAN. Nanning is a key city in the BGEZ, hosting the China–ASEAN International Logistics Base, the China–ASEAN Exposition, the China–ASEAN Business District and the China–Malaysia Qinzhou Industrial Park. Leveraging BGEZ's gateway status, the Guangxi government aims to promote the establishment of a China–ASEAN Free Trade Zone to benefit the Guangxi economy (Xia 2011). The Nanning City government's role is reflected in its extensive involvement in city spatial reorganization and infrastructure development in coordination with national and provincial development policies.

More recently, Guangxi's grand strategy was overtaken by an even grander one—the B&R initiative announced by Chinese President Xi Jinping. This was made up of the twenty-first-century Maritime Silk Road (the "Road") together with an overland route to Europe (the "Belt") (HKTDC 2015). ASEAN was to be central to B&R as the Maritime Silk Road is targeted to link major seaports along the coasts of Vietnam, Cambodia, Thailand and Myanmar. The launch of the China-led Asia Infrastructure Investment Bank (AIIB) in December 2015 gave further financial and institutional substance to this initiative.[9] Major highways and railroads were also to link China to ASEAN countries, with the AIIB providing financing, in addition to the establishment of a $10 billion China–ASEAN Investment Cooperation Fund and $15 billion China–ASEAN Loan Program (Wong and Chong 2010). All these strategies provide varied opportunities to Nanning, which already acts as the node China–ASEAN exchanges.

The fourth is the acknowledgement of the centrality of ASEAN in regional agreements like the APT and RCEP, currently under negotiation even though it is already playing a leading economic role in the region. In this sense, China has been much more proactive in promoting ASEAN as an institutional reality than ASEAN countries themselves which seek out alternative regional arrangements considered beneficial to them.

These economic positives, however, do not carry over to the strategic area. China has refused to recognize an ASEAN role in its South

China Sea dispute with its Southeast Asian neighbours, insisting that the dispute be resolved bilaterally. This contradictory behaviour clearly signals that China values its strategic interests above its economic interests, the latter of which, at least for now, represent a win-win situation. It also sees ASEAN countries, just like itself, prioritizing national vested interests over regional interests, and the unanimity that is required under "the ASEAN Way" for ASEAN to take a united stand difficult to achieve. As has already been explained, it is, therefore, able to prevent its achievement through the unequal award of benefits to dissuade countries like Cambodia, Laos and Myanmar, none of which has a stake in the dispute, from opposing China. Even for Malaysia, a claimant in the dispute, China had been able to deal with the previous government by buying the country's silence through the promise of substantial investments at a very time that other investors have shied away by the continuing saga of the scandal linked to its sovereign wealth fund. Even the new government that took over in May 2018 has not voiced open opposition to China's claim. Overall, then, China has been able to play a double role—even as it consolidates its territorial claims, it is able to simultaneously offer greater material benefits through investment, especially infrastructure to ASEAN member states while also enhancing regional connectivity. For their part, and despite ASEAN's critics recommending a united pushback against China, ASEAN leaders are pragmatic enough to realize that such a stance would just increase regional tension but do precious little to change China's resolve.

However, Malaysia's recent change in government sheds light on the limits of China's strategy of unquestioned reliance on the political status quo in China's bilateral relations with ASEAN countries. For China, this political change saw the unravelling, almost immediately, of major infrastructural projects commissioned by the old regime, and the end to the cosy political relationship that existed. As the new government reveals the previous regime's corrupt practices, China's carefully crafted reputation as a partner of development risks serious damage. Instead, it could be seen as abetting corruption and leaving Malaysia in serious debt. This is precisely what an already hostile Western media has seized on, accusing China of pursuing a "debt trap strategy" (Banyan 2018). While such arguments can be questions—borrowing countries themselves bear the responsibility for incurring debt—they are likely to lead to greater caution in China's dealings with host countries. As for ASEAN countries themselves, such fallout is likely to be temporary—China remains Malaysia's largest source of FDI in the first half of 2018 (Aziz 2018).

Conclusion

Whether by its absence or by its growing significance in Southeast Asia, China has had and will continue to have major implications for ASEAN as an entity and for its member countries. In the early years of its liberalization, its absence in the Southeast Asian theatre allowed, together with the US departure from the region, the breathing space to chart its own course. And even as China's pace of growth picked up, Chinese leaders had adopted a soft power stance with its Southeast Asian neighbours. This stance is no better exemplified by China, despite its growing might, ceding official leadership to ASEAN and promoting ASEAN centrality in APT. Its promotion of RCEP, although driven by its own strategic imperatives, has the same impact. The recent Belt and Road Initiative that incorporates ASEAN countries into the Maritime Silk Road will also boost ASEAN, although subjecting its countries to increasing Chinese influence.

As for ASEAN, it can boast of accomplishments first without and then with China playing a role, not least of which is its ability to survive but to play an expanding role through changing circumstances. Pragmatism and adaptability to change have been key to this success. However, this expanding role has posed increasing challenges to its loose institutional structure referred to as "the ASEAN Way", a structure largely unchanged since the Association's foundation. It should then be no surprise that setbacks have also being recorded, the most recent being failure to speak with a unified voice in the face of China's South China Sea claims. While the lack of a unified response does not say much about ASEAN's ability to resolve issues in its backyard, it also does not signify ASEAN's "irrelevance".[10] Of greater concern is the fact that this episode exposes, not for the first time and certainly not the

30 K. C. Cheong et al.

last, ASEAN leaders' prioritization of national over regional interest. Participation of some ASEAN countries in the TPP/CPTPP which has the potential to undermine ASEAN centrality is the latest manifestation of this lack of regional focus. The "ASEAN Way" may be alive and well, but the same cannot be said of the "ASEAN Spirit".

Finally, the ASEAN–China relationship speaks to the debate between realists and constructivists on ASEAN. As China rises and establishes itself as a global power, its geographic proximity to ASEAN invariably makes it the elephant in the ASEAN room to the delight of realists. However, ASEAN has survived through many changes and demonstrated the skills to move unevenly towards its stated goals, giving constructivists hope that it will be able to deal with China in its unique "ASEAN Way".

Notes

1. Beeson (2016) gives an account of these and opposing views with specific reference to China.
2. For instance, Cambodia and Laos have been major recipients of Chinese investment. Ho (2017) estimated that China's cumulative investment in Laos was US$5 billion, with a US$7 billion China–Laos high-speed rail project scheduled for completion in 2020. China also invested US$10 billion in Cambodia between 1994 and 2012.
3. India has been holding out against eliminating tariffs (Hunt 2017).
4. These are the United States, Australia, Brunei, Canada, Chile, Japan, Malaysia, Mexico, New Zealand, Peru, Singapore and Vietnam.
5. Both types of arguments have been well summarized by Davidson (2017). These arguments have been framed in terms of the gains and losses for America.
6. Countries like Cambodia, Laos and Myanmar, at an earlier stage of economic development compared to other ASEAN countries, may find the high standards too difficult to achieve.
7. A detailed account of Nanning's development into an ASEAN gateway is given in Wang et al. (2017).
8. Western Development Program, namely "Go West" or "Develop the West", was initially put forward by President Jiang Zemin in June 1999. It is embedded in China's Eleventh Five-Year Plan with the aim to develop Western regions to achieve the concept of "common prosperity".

9. ASEAN would be given priority in the AIIB, President Xi Jinping said in a speech to the Indonesian Parliament in October 2013 ASEAN-China Center (2013).

10. A united front, however principled, would not change China's resolve and likely heighten tensions in the region to the detriment of trade and investment.

References

ASEAN-China Center. 2013. *Speech by Chinese sident Xi Jinping to Indonesian Parliament*. October 3. http://www.asean-china-center.org/english/2013-10/03/c_133062675.htm.

ASEAN Affairs. 2008. "ASEAN in Danger of Going Irrelevant: Singapore PM." Accessed April 10, 2017. http://www.aseanaffairs.com/page/asean_in_danger_of_going_irrelevant_singapore_pm.

ASEAN Secretariat. 2017. "Overview of ASEAN Plus Three Cooperation." Information Paper, Jakarta.

Aziz, Adam. 2018. "Malaysia Received RM26.5b FDI in 1H2018, China Top Contributor, Says MITI." *The Edge Markets*, November 19. Accessed December 7, 2018. http://www.theedgemarkets.com/article/malaysia-received-rm265b-fdi-1h18-china-top-contributor-says-miti.

Banyan. 2018. "The Perils of China's 'Debt Trap' Diplomacy." *Economist*, September 6. Accessed December 7, 2018. https://www.economist.com/asia/2018/09/06/the-perils-of-chinas-debt-trap-diplomacy.

Beeson, Mark. 2016. Can ASEAN Cope with China? *Journal of Current Southeast Asian Affairs* 1: 5–28.

Bolesta, Andrzej. 2018. Myanmar-China Peculiar Relationship: Trade, Investment and the Model of Development. *Journal of International Studies* 11 (2): 23–36.

Bowring, Philip. 2016. "Obituary: Association of Southeast Asian Nations (1967–2016)." *Asian Sentinel*. Accessed April 29, 2018. http://www.asiasentinel.com/politics/obituary-association-southeast-asian-nations/.

Chander, Parkash. 2017. "A Political Economy Analysis of the Southeast Asian Haze and Some Solutions." Working Paper 303, S. Rajaratnam School of International Studies, Nanyang Technological University.

Cheong, Kee Cheok, and Kim Leng Goh. 2015. *The ASEAN Economic Community and the Brain Drain Threat: How Real Is It?* Paper presented at the FAEA 39 Conference on "Beyond AEC 2015", Bangkok, March 20, 2015.

Cheong, Kee Cheok, and Qianyi Wang. 2017. "China's Growth Deceleration—A New Normal for Malaysia Too?" Special Issue. *International Journal of China Studies* 8 (2): 199–220.

Chi, Dehua. 2018. "China Reiterates Support for RCEP Trade Talks." *gbtimes*, January 31. Accessed March 18, 2018. https://gbtimes.com/china-reiterates-support-for-rcep-trade-talks.

Christensen, Thomas J. 2015. *The China Challenge: Shaping the Choices of a Rising Power*. New York: Norton.

Davidson, Adam. 2017. "What the Death of the TPP Means for America." *The New Yorker*. Accessed March 19, 2018. https://www.newyorker.com/business/adam-davidson/what-the-death-of-the-t-p-p-means-for-america.

Deloitte. 2015. *The ABC of the AEC: To 2015 and Beyond*. Singapore: Deloitte.

Dosch, Jörn. 2015. The ASEAN Economic Community: What Stands in the Way? *Asia Pacific Issues* 119: 1–8.

Helble, Matthias, and Yizhe Daniel Xie. 2017. "Is the CPTPP a Risky gamble?" *East Asia Forum*, December 23. https://www.eastasiaforum.org/2017/12/23/is-the-cptpp-a-risky-gamble/.

Heydarian, Richard J. 2015. "Is ASEAN Still Relevant?" *The Diplomat*. Accessed October 26, 2016. http://thediplomat.com/2015/03/is-asean-still-relevant/.

Ho, Wah Foon. 2017. "China's Growing Influence in ASEAN." *The Star*, May 14. Accessed March 17, 2018. https://www.thestar.com.my/news/nation/2017/05/14/chinas-growing-influence-in-asean-asean-members-prefer-a-nonconfrontational-approach-towards-china-o/.

Hong Kong Tourist Development Council (HKTDC). 2015. "'One Belt One Road' Initiative: The Implications for Hong Kong." *HKTDC Research*. April 16. http://economists-pick-research.hktdc.com/business-news/article/Research-Articles/One-Belt-One-Road-Initiative-The-Implications-for-Hong-Kong/rp/en/1/1X000000/1X0A23WV.htm.

Hunt, Luke. 2017. "Does an ASEAN Agreement Mean Progress for RCEP?" *The Diplomat*, September 15. Accessed March 18, 2018. https://thediplomat.com/2017/09/does-an-asean-agreement-mean-progress-for-rcep/.

Jomo, Kwame Sundaram. 2018. "Japan-Led Pacific Rim Countries Desperate to Embrace Trump." Inter Press Service, March 8. Accessed March 19, 2018. http://www.ipsnews.net/2018/03/japan-led-pacific-rim-countries-desperate-embrace-trump/.

Kyophilavong, Phouphet, Xiong Bin, Bounlert Vanhnala, Piya Wongpit, Alay Phonvisay, and Phanhpakit Onphanhdala. 2017. "Impact of Chinese FDI on Economy, Poverty in Lao PDR." Special Issue. *International Journal of China Studies* 8 (2): 259–278.

Lim, Cherly. 2018. "How Will the CPTPP Pan Out for ASEAN?" *The ASEAN Post*. Accessed March 20, 2018. https://theaseanpost.com/article/how-will-cptpp-pan-out-asean-0.

Lim, Joseph A. 2017. "The Impact of China's New Normal on the Philippine Economy." Special Issue. *International Journal of China Studies* 8 (2): 221–258.

Lohman, Walter. 2015. "Why US Should Look Beyond ASEAN in the South China Sea." Heritage Foundation. Accessed March 17, 2017. http://www.heritage.org/global-politics/commentary/why-us-should-move-beyond-asean-the-south-china-sea.

Mahnubani, Kishore, and Rhoda Severino. 2014. "ASEAN: The Way Forward." McKinsey and Co. Accessed April 5, 2017. http://www.mckinsey.com/industries/public-sector/our-insights/asean-the-way-forward.

Manila Standard. 2016. "The Irrelevance of ASEAN." Accessed April 20, 2017. http://thestandard.com.ph/opinion/editorial/211659/the-irrelevance-of-asean.html.

Ministry of International Trade and Industry (MITI), Malaysia (n.d.). 2018. *Bilateral Free Trade Areas*. Accessed March 8, 2018. http://www.miti.gov.my/iti/resources/fileupload/ASEAN%27s%20Bilateral%20FTA%20(website).pdf.

Mulgan, Aurelia George. 2018. "CPTPP a Boost for Japan's Regional Trade Partnership." East Asia Forum, published on February 27. Accessed March 20, 2018. http://www.eastasiaforum.org/2018/02/27/cptpp-a-boost-for-japans-regional-trade-leadership/.

Narine, Shaun. 2002. *Explaining ASEAN: Regionalism in Southeast Asia*. Boulder: Lynne Rienner.

Ng, Joel. 2018. "The Quadrilateral Conundrum: Can ASEAN Be Persuaded?" Accessed March 2, 2018. http://www.rsis.edu.sg/profile/joel-ng/.

Obama, Barack. 2016. "The TPP Would Let America, Not China, Lead the Way on Global Trade." *Washington Post*, May 2. Accessed May 19, 2018. https://www.washingtonpost.com/opinions/president-obama-the-tpp-would-let-america-not-china-lead-the-way-on-global-trade/2016/05/02/680540e4-0fd0-11e6-93ae-50921721165d_story.html?utm_term=.1588085ce277.

Salidjanova, Nargiza, and Iacob Koch-Weser. 2015. *China's Economic Ties with ASEAN: A Country-by-country Analysis*, Staff Research Report, US-China Economic and Security Review Commission, Washington DC, March 15.

Sani, Ibrahim. 2018. "Malaysia Is Biggest Winner from TPPA2.0—Moody's." Astro Awani, March 9. Accessed March 19, 2018. http://english.astroawani.com/business-news/malaysia-biggest-winner-tppa2-0-moodys-169986.

Sarawak Report. 2016. "OUTRAGE! Najib's Secret Deal with China to Pay of 1MDB's (and Jho Low's) Debts! SHOCK EXCLUSIVE," July 26. Accessed December 6, 2018. http://www.sarawakreport.org/2016/07/outrage-najibs-secret-deal-with-china-to-pay-off-1mdb-and-jho-lows-debts-shock-exclusive/.

Severino, Rodolfo. 2014. "Let's Be Honest About What ASEAN Can and Cannot Do." East Asia Forum, January 31. Accessed November 17, 2018. http://www.eastasiaforum.org/2014/01/31/lets-be-honest-about-what-asean-can-and-cannot-do/.

Tangkitvanich, Somkiat, and Sawaoruj Rattanakhamfu. 2017. "Assessing the ASEAN Economic Community." East Asia Forum, March 21. Accessed March 6, 2018, http://www.eastasiaforum.org/2017/03/21/assessing-the-asean-economic-community/.

Torrey, Zachary. 2018. "TPP 2.0: The Deal Without the US." *The Diplomat*, February 3. Accessed March 19, 2018. https://thediplomat.com/2018/02/tpp-2-0-the-deal-without-the-us/.

United Nations Conference on Trade and Development (UNCTAD). 2014. *World Investment Report 2014*. New York: UNCTAD.

Vineles, Phidel Marion G. 2018. "Managing Labor Mobility? Stronger ASEAN Integration?" CO18043. RSIS Commentary, March 14. Accessed December 3, 2018. http://www.rsis.edu.sg/rsis-publication/cms/co18043-managing-labour-mobility-stronger-asean-integration/#.XBCjYmZRd9A.

Wang, Qianyi, Ran Li, and Kee Cheok Cheong. 2017. Nanning—Perils and Promise of a Frontier City. *Cities* 72: 51–59.

Weber, Katja. 2009. "ASEAN: A Prime Example of Regionalism in Southeast Asia." *Miami-Florida European Center of Excellence* 6 (5): 3–19.

Wei, Yehua. 2015. Zone Fever, Project Fever: Economic Transition, Development Policy, and Urban Expansion in China. *Geographical Review* 105 (2): 156–177.

Wong, John. 2010. The Nanning-Singapore Economic Corridor: Challenges for China and ASEAN. *East Asian Policy* 2 (3): 67–72.

Wong, John, and Catherine Siew Keng Chong. 2010. *The Nanning-Singapore Economic Corridor: Its Promises and Problems*. East Asian Institute: National University of Singapore.

World Bank. 2018. *Economic and Distributional Impacts of Comprehensive and Progressive Agreement for Trans-Pacific Partnership: The Case of Vietnam*. Washington, DC: World Bank.

Xia, Z. 2011. "Industrial Spatial Structure in Guangxi Beibu Gulf Economic Zone." PhD thesis, Southwestern University of Finance and Economics.

3

The ASEAN-ROK Economic Relations: Challenges and Opportunities

Nurliana Kamaruddin and Jan Vincent Galas

Introduction

In 2015, ASEAN member states made the commitment to create a regional community resting on three pillars; economic cooperation, political and security cooperation and sociocultural cooperation (ASEAN 2015a, 1). Arguably, of the three, economic cooperation has had the most success in terms of commitment and action by the governments of ASEAN member states. ASEAN's history of non-interference and the richly diverse culture within the region has complicated political and social unity; however, ASEAN leaders are generally driven-by-performance while ruling legitimacy has often been closely related to economic

N. Kamaruddin (✉)
Asia-Europe Institute, University of Malaya, Kuala Lumpur, Malaysia
e-mail: nurliana.k@um.edu.my

J. V. Galas
School of Business Administration, Chung-Ang University,
Seoul, South Korea
e-mail: jangalas@cau.ac.kr

© The Author(s) 2019
A. Idris and N. Kamaruddin (eds.), *ASEAN Post-50*,
https://doi.org/10.1007/978-981-13-8043-3_3

35

growth and achievements (Roberts 2012, 101). In order to encourage economic growth in the region, the ASEAN Economic Community seeks to pursue both internal integration within ASEAN and also integration to the global economy (ASEAN 2015b, 35).

ASEAN's effort for close integration is not something new. In the aftermath of the 1997 Asian Financial Crisis, ASEAN countries began to work more actively towards closer economic integration not only within the region but also with external partners. The Hanoi Plan of Action which was adopted during the Sixth ASEAN summit in December of 1998 included the Statement on Bold Measures. This statement set the path for ASEAN member nations to: "increase liberalization of trade in services, accelerate the implementation of the ASEAN Free Trade Area (AFTA) for the ASEAN-6 from 2003 and also sought to develop special incentives and privileges for foreign direct investment via the implementation of a framework agreement on an ASEAN Investment Area" (Roberts 2012, 94).

Alongside this effort, ASEAN has also begun to engage more actively with strategic economic partners, which include the Republic of Korea or South Korea. For many ASEAN countries, South Korea's impressive economic development has served as a lesson in their own development efforts.

After the Second World War and the devastation of the Korean War in the 1950s, South Korea was one of the world's poorest nations. In 1960, the gross domestic product (GDP) per capita of South Korea calculated to the current US$ was US$158.24. This was lower than the GDP of many Southeast Asian countries at the time (World Bank 2017a). However, this country that was once known as an "economic basket case" has gone on to achieve one of the most unprecedented experiences of economic growth (Rodrik et al. 1995, 55). South Korea achieved an average annual 7.9% of GDP growth from the 1960s to 2000, transitioning into a dynamic high-income nation within a couple of decades (Lee 2016, 3). Today the country is the 11th largest economy in the world with a GDP per capita of US$27,538.8 in 2016 (World Bank 2017a).

South Korea's economy has also proven resilient in the wake of economic crisis. The country was badly affected in 1997 Asian Financial

Crisis with some of its leading conglomerates becoming insolvent and the value of the South Korean Won crashing, forcing South Korea to request assistance from the International Monetary Fund (IMF). However, South Korea's economy was able to recover much faster and stronger compared to its Southeast Asian counterparts. The GDP which contracted by—5.471% in 1998 rebounded to 11.309% by 1999 (World Bank 2017b). In the more recent 2008 global financial crisis, South Korea also experienced a severe impact on its economy including a sharp fall in output as well as a severe depreciation of the Won. South Korea again demonstrated its ability to recover from the economic downturn. Lessons learnt from the 1997 economic crisis meant that this time South Korea had stable financial institutions and an effective policy response. By 2009, it was able to increase its export value by 10% and its GDP growth recovered from 0.708 to 6.497% in 2010 (OECD 2010, 23).

South Korea's output growth has slowed considerably from 2011, but the country continues to enjoy low inflation rates and a high government surplus (OECD 2016, 12). Its fast-paced economic development has also translated into positive social development outcomes as well. The country is ranked number 18 in the world with a very high human development level in the 2016 Human Development Index (HDI). Not only does the country have relatively low-income inequality, it has one of the highest life expectancy rates in the world (82.1) (UNDP 2016, 198). The country also has the highest tertiary enrolment rate of 93.179% of its population in 2015 (World Bank 2017c).

Although ASEAN countries today (with the exception of Singapore) have yet to achieve such high standards of living, its economic prospect has remained mostly positive. The economic growth rates for ASEAN countries between 1990 and 2012 was 5–6% even as the world's "economic growth rates were recorded at about 3 to 4 percent" (Lee 2017, 146). As the world faces economic uncertainty with the prospect of a US-China trade war, it has become more important than ever for ASEAN to improve its economic relations with other external partners. In this case, South Korea and ASEAN have and can continue to shape a mutually beneficial relationship in terms of both parties' economic cooperation.

This chapter traces the trends, challenges and prospects of economic cooperation between South Korea and ASEAN countries. As defined by Kahnert (1969), "economic cooperation is the process of removing progressively those discriminations which occur at national borders". Consistent with the principles of GAT and GATT 1994, ASEAN-Korea economic cooperation aims to enhance economic partnership through the elimination of barriers of goods, services, capital and labour. In sum, this chapter sets out to complete three tasks. First, it explores the growth and trends in ASEAN-Korea trade relations. Second, it examines the South Korea ODA history and identifies the top recipient countries in ASEAN. Lastly, it assesses the challenges and prospects for further economic cooperation.

ASEAN Economic Relations with South Korea

Bilateral relations between South Korea and individual ASEAN countries began much earlier that South Korea's relationship with the regional organization. For example, South Korea established formal diplomatic relations with Malaysia since 1960, the Philippines since 1969 and Singapore since 1975, and this had brought about an increasing presence of the Northeast Asian nation in the region. On the other hand, South Korea's relationship with ASEAN as a regional body only began in 1989. South Korea and ASEAN began with sectoral dialogue relations which were later upgraded to full dialogue partner status in 1991 during the 24th ASEAN Ministerial Meeting and later to summit level in 1997 (ASEAN 2017a, 1). Former Secretary General of ASEAN pointed out that ASEAN has also been positioning itself as an "extra-regional" organization that aimed at "promoting an open and inclusive regional architecture" (Minh 2017, 14–15).

ASEAN included South Korea in its effort at spearheading a more active regional community through ASEAN+3 in 1997 alongside Japan and China (ASEAN 2017b). This ASEAN-led initiative has also contributed to deepening economic ties with all three partner countries. Aside from the ASEAN+3 framework, ASEAN and South Korea continued to pursue closer partnership and South Korea signed the

Treaty of Amity and Cooperation in Southeast Asia in 2004. Relations between ASEAN and South Korea were also upgraded from a dialogue partner to a strategic partnership at the 13th ASEAN-ROK Summit held in Hanoi on 29 October 2010.

Similarly, economic agreements between ASEAN and South Korea were also pursued in order to enhance trade between the two parties. The Framework Agreement on Comprehensive Economic Cooperation was signed in 2005 followed by the Trade in Goods (AKTIG) Agreement in 2006, the Trade in Services Agreement in 2007 and the Investment Agreement in 2009. Culminating from these agreements was the ASEAN-ROK Free Trade Area (AKFTA) which came into effect on 1 January 2010 (ASEAN 2017a, 3). More recently, a new ASEAN-ROK Plan of Action to implement the Joint Declaration on Strategic Partnership for Peace and Prosperity was adopted on 5 August 2015 in Kuala Lumpur (ASEAN 2017a, 1).

In 2017, President Moon Jae-in of South Korea announced the New Southern Policy, declaring that the partnership status of South Korea and ASEAN would be elevated to the same level of importance as the four major powers (the United States, China, Japan and Russia) in order to mitigate the country's reliance on these powers (Whiteside 2017). For example, South Korea's recent diplomatic tension with China due to the deployment of a US anti-missile system, the THAAD or Terminal High Altitude Area Defence led to a boycott of Korean businesses in China (*The Economist* 2017). The subsequent economic fallout from the boycott reflected South Korea's dependency on the Chinese market. Not surprisingly, the South Korean government needed to step up the effort to diversify its market and its relationship with ASEAN provides it with said opportunity.

Growth and Trends of ASEAN-South Korea Economic Relations

Trade between ASEAN nations and South Korea has also seen positive growth in trend. As South Korea lacked in natural resources, ASEAN countries were able to fulfil this economic need. According to Yul

40   N. Kamaruddin and J. V. Galas

Kwon, as quoted by Choong Lyol Lee (2017, 140), 90% of South Korea's export and import from ASEAN since the 1990s were made up of raw materials and capital goods. More recently, electrical and electronic equipment, as well as mineral fuels, oils and distillation products, makes up most of the trade between South Korea and ASEAN in 2016 (ASEAN-Korea Centre 2017, 65).

The following table details the trade value of South Korea to ASEAN countries from 1989 to 2017. The numbers show that with the signing of AKFTA in 2010, trade value between ASEAN and South Korea went up significantly, increasing to over US$100 billion, showcasing the positive effect the free trade agreement has had for both parties. South Korea and ASEAN remain confident on being able to continue this positive trend in trade growth where country leaders agreed to the optimistic target of US$200 billion in two-way trade volume by 2020 during the ASEAN-ROK Commemorative Summit in 2014 (ASEAN 2014) (Table 3.1).

Alongside the growth in trade of goods and services, ASEAN's burgeoning market has also become attractive for foreign direct investment from South Korea. South Korea has increased its investment in ASEAN countries with its share of total investment inflow in ASEAN increasing from 3.5% in 2014 to 6.1% in 2016 (ASEAN-Korea Centre 2017, 74). As of 2016, South Korea is the fifth largest investor in ASEAN in comparison with other county and regional investors. However, foreign investment in ASEAN has mostly been channelled to Vietnam where FDI to Vietnam made up 63% of South Korea's overall investment in ASEAN countries (Table 3.2).

There has also been an increase in mobility between the citizens of South Korea and ASEAN nations especially in the form of tourism. South Korean travellers to ASEAN has significantly increased in numbers where "almost one out of nine Koreans visited one of the ASEAN member states in 2016" (Lee 2017, 137). From 2013 to 2016, Korean visitors to ASEAN countries make up about 30% of the overall visitors to ASEAN countries (ASEAN-Korea Centre 2018). In more recent years, as the quality of life improved in many of the ASEAN countries, tourism from these Southeast Asian nations has also increased.

South Korea has become a top destination for many of these tourists, partly influenced by the Hallyu (Korean Wave) phenomena. From 2015

Table 3.1 South Korea trade value with ASEAN (1989–2017)

Year	Export to ASEAN (US$ billion)	Increase rate (%)	Import to ASEAN (US$ billion)	Increase rate (%)	Total trade (US$ billion)
1989	4.04	28.9	4.19	21.7	8.23
1990	5.22	29.2	5.12	22.2	10.34
1991	7.33	40.5	6.16	20.3	13.49
1992	9.04	23.4	7.12	15.5	16.16
1993	10.11	11.8	7.31	2.7	17.42
1994	12.49	23.5	7.85	7.4	20.34
1995	17.98	44	10.14	29.2	28.12
1996	20.31	13	12.07	19.1	32.38
1997	20.37	0.3	12.55	3.9	32.92
1998	15.33	−24.7	9.14	−27.2	24.47
1999	17.71	15.5	12.25	34.1	29.96
2000	20.13	13.7	18.17	48.4	38.3
2001	16.46	−18.2	15.92	−12.4	32.38
2002	18.4	11.8	16.76	5.3	35.16
2003	20.25	10.1	18.46	10.2	38.71
2004	24.02	18.6	22.38	21.3	46.4
2005	27.43	14.2	26.06	16.4	53.49
2006	32.07	16.9	29.74	14.1	61.81
2007	38.75	20.8	33.11	11.3	71.86
2008	49.28	27.2	40.92	23.6	90.2
2009	40.98	−16.8	34.05	−16.8	75.03
2010	53.2	29.8	44.1	29.5	97.3
2011	71.8	35	53.12	20.5	124.92
2012	79.15	10.2	51.98	−2.1	131.13
2013	82	3.6	53.34	2.6	135.34
2014	84.58	3.2	53.42	0.2	138
2015	74.82	−11.5	45.03	−15.7	119.85
2016	74.52	−0.4	44.32	−1.6	118.84
2017	95.25	27.8	53.82	21.4	149.07

Source Korean International Trade Association, *K-Statistics* (2018)

to 2016, ASEAN travellers to South Korea increased from 1.8 million to 2.5 million (ASEAN-Korea Centre 2018). The increase in mobility results in increased currency flow between the two parties and would also impact positively on local tourism industries. South Korea has thus made significant effort to facilitate travel within the country with the Korean Tourism Organization (KTO) providing valuable resources for tourists including multilingual assistance for ASEAN travellers in Vietnamese, Thai and Malay (KTO 2018).

Table 3.2 South Korea's Foreign Direct Investment in ASEAN (2010–2016) (US$ million)

Year	2010	2011	2012	2013	2014	2015	2016
Brunei	0	0	0	0	0	0	0
Cambodia	46.73	138.55	161.75	178.16	106.33	71.95	139.59
Indonesia	339.89	724.51	691.96	980.84	952.8	227.56	189.6
Laos	1.67	2.04	0	0	12.55	45.69	77.27
Malaysia	1460.53	142.3	−58.21	−165.04	−254.38	152.35	358.88
Myanmar	0	0	0	0	11.1	36.97	35.34
Philippines	6.48	20.6	3.66	2.36	576.49	131	87
Singapore	948	−101.7	−282.5	773.5	−104.3	1027.20	1171.00
Thailand	180.23	97.16	131.07	716.25	141.49	529.45	47.03
Vietnam	1335.73	750.41	657.89	1766.81	3248.19	3488.01	3637.57
Total	4319.26	1773.87	1305.61	4252.90	4690.27	5710.41	5743.48

Source ASEAN Statistical Yearbook 2016/2017

Development Assistance from South Korea to ASEAN Countries

Alongside its impressive economic growth, South Korea has also successfully made the transition from an aid recipient nation to a donor nation. In its effort to establish itself as a middle power nation, South Korea is investing a considerable amount of resources towards consolidating this position in international society. A large part of this effort comes in the form of building good economic cooperation with key global partners not only through trade and investment but also development cooperation. South Korea also chose to concentrate on improving its influence within the Asian region through aid. The Asia Pacific region receives up to 49% of its total bilateral aid outflow (OECD 2017a, 230). Naturally, ASEAN member nations are some of the top beneficiaries, and Vietnam is the largest recipient of South Korean aid as seen in Table 3.3. Bilateral ODA with ASEAN countries has also seen a steady increase between 2011 and 2016 (Table 3.4).

A large part of South Korea's ODA (33%) is directed mostly at improving the economic infrastructure of its partner countries (OECD 2017a, 231). For example, the first project by the Economic Development Cooperation Fund (EDCF) managed by the Export-Import Bank of Korea completed in 1992 was with an ASEAN country,

Table 3.3 South Korea's top ten ODA partners of 2015 disbursement value received (2011–2015) (US$ millions)

Country	2011	2012	2013	2014	2015
Vietnam	139.49	200.32	234.56	178.84	217.16
Laos	33.48	23.52	27.07	28.98	87.63
Cambodia	62.23	56.15	60.54	68.62	65.85
Afghanistan	27.99	78.5	122.41	64.36	54.6
Bangladesh	80.02	46.76	44.71	68.06	52.16
Philippines	35.69	31.33	42.74	60.93	44.04
Indonesia	24.29	37.23	31.5	21.49	39.55
Sri Lanka	43.36	51.49	44.93	44.78	27.46
Mongolia	30.5	31.79	27.67	30.76	24.2
Myanmar	4.81	6.04	11.72	17.29	21.23
Nepal	20.97	20.77	17.09	14.44	17.56

Source OECD, *QWIDS* (2017b)

44 N. Kamaruddin and J. V. Galas

Table 3.4 South Korea's disbursement of ODA to ASEAN countries 2011–2016 (current price US$ millions)

	2011	2012	2013	2014	2015	2016
Brunei	–	–	–	–	–	–
Cambodia	62.23	56.15	60.54	68.62	65.85	53.15
Indonesia	24.29	37.23	31.5	21.49	39.55	41.66
Laos	33.48	23.52	27.07	28.98	87.63	36.58
Malaysia	1.85	0.43	0.14	0.34	0.49	0.37
Myanmar	4.81	6.04	11.72	17.29	21.23	44.42
Philippines	35.69	31.33	42.74	60.93	44.04	59.95
Singapore	–	–	–	–	–	–
Thailand	4.47	2.89	3.34	3.44	4.73	8.83
Vietnam	139.49	200.32	234.56	178.84	217.16	179.83

Source OECD, *QWIDS* (2017b)

Table 3.5 Projects approved by South Korea's EDCF in ASEAN countries for 2016

Country	Projects
Vietnam	Rehabilitation and Improvement of Bridges on National Highways Project (Phase 1) Khee Net Pass Railway Rehabilitation Project
Laos	The Mekong River Integrated Management Project (Phase 2) The Construction of Modern Hospital Project
Myanmar	Rehabilitation and Modernization of Mandalay-Myitkyina Rail Line Project (Gyohtaung-Me'za Priority Section)
Cambodia	Irrigation Development and Flood Mitigation Project in Banteay Meanchey Province Financial Accessibility Enhancement Project for Gender Equality in Cambodia Sewage System Development in Ta Khmau Town Project
Indonesia	Engineering Service Project for Multipurpose Dams, Rivers and Coastal

Source ECDF (2016, 7)

the Philippines (ECDF 2016, 2). Projects supported by South Korea's EDCF in Indonesia, Vietnam, Laos, Cambodia and Myanmar include infrastructure, sanitation and healthcare projects among others. Table 3.5 details the projects in ASEAN countries that were approved in 2016. The main goals of these projects are not only to lessen the infrastructure gap that these countries have with South Korea but with other

ASEAN member nations as well. This is important for both ASEAN and South Koreas as the trade of goods and services increase between the two parties the economic infrastructure of ASEAN countries would need to be able to keep up with demands.

Challenges and Prospects

The positive economic trends between South Korea and ASEAN paints an overall encouraging picture for future developments. However, despite ASEAN's increased importance to South Korea, as evident by President Moon Jae-in's New Southern Policy, the country faces some challenges its efforts to cultivate a comprehensive economic relationship with the region. First, in the form of competition with East Asia's bigger economic powers—China and Japan, second with ASEAN members own economic discrepancies. In both cases, South Korea needs to be able to play a strategic role in order to better position itself in its relationship with ASEAN.

Regional mechanisms such as ASEAN+3, the Asian Regional Forum (ARF) and the East Asian Summit also put South Korea with its other Northeast Asian counterparts—Japan and China, in forging ties with ASEAN member countries. South Korea's presence in the region, in contrast to the long historical relation China and Japan have had with ASEAN nations, is relatively new. It's smaller economy and market also means that trade is relatively much smaller in comparison with that of China and Japan. China's trade with ASEAN in 2016 valued at US$368 billion while trade with Japan valued at US$202 billion (ASEAN 2017a, 64). As Siegfrid Alegado (2018) from Bloomberg puts it, "Asia's two biggest economies are jostling to expand influence in the region".

Of the two, Japan has had a longer foothold in Southeast Asian economic partnership. The country is one of the ASEAN's largest investor, second to the United States, with 11.1% of ASEAN's net FDI inflow for 2016 coming from Japan (ASEAN 2017c, 149). Japan has Economic Partnership Agreements not only with ASEAN but also with almost all the member nations (with the exception of Laos, Cambodia and Myanmar) (MOFA 2018). Not only that, Japan continues to hold a favoured position in ASEAN countries. In a survey conducted by the ASEAN Studies Centre at the Institute of Southeast Asian Studies (ISEAS-Yusof Ishak Institute 2017, 14), most respondents viewed Japan as the most trusted major power in Southeast Asia.

However, China's size and dominance naturally put the country on a fast track to catch up. Unsurprisingly, many view China as the most influential major power in Southeast Asia, expecting China to "to fill the strategic vacuum vacated by the US" (Tang 2017, 38). China's recent initiative such as the "One Belt, One Road" which runs through Southeast Asia is a "grand strategy" meant to "rejuvenate" the Eurasian continent and has also brought about increased investment in Southeast Asia (Fallon 2015, 141). However, China's economic interest tends to clash with its security interest in the region. Ongoing tension in the South China Sea, for example, has impacted China's relationship with the Philippines and other Southeast Asian nations (Chan and Li 2015). China, unlike Japan, is less trusted in the role that it would play in "contributing to global peace, security, prosperity and governance" (ISEAS-Yusof Ishak Institute 2017, 14).

From this perspective, South Korea presents a compelling alternative as an economic partner to ASEAN. The relationship between ASEAN and South Korea is not only free from the historical baggage of colonialism (as in the case of Japan) but also hegemonic intent (as is the case of China). For ASEAN countries, Japan's technological advancement could also be too far for it to catch up to and the weight of China's massive market also provides too much competition for ASEAN's significantly smaller one. South Korea is, therefore, able to strategically place itself as a more-equal partner to ASEAN especially as it continues to pursue a two-way economic partnership.

Another challenge in building a comprehensive ASEAN-Korea relation is ASEAN's own level of integration. Although the organization has increased in complexity since the early days of its formation, it is still far from a cohesive economic community such as the European Union (EU). Admittedly, ASEAN member countries do not aspire to follow the same line of forming a single economic bloc as the EU; however, this would mean that ASEAN member countries have made relatively slower progress at ratifying economic agreements especially for the member countries with weaker economic capacities. As Yoon Ah Oh (2017, 157) rightly pointed out, the challenge remains as to how the lower-income countries can be assisted to achieve the economic level "where most member states can coordinate integration activities with minimal conflicts in interests and preferences".

Although ASEAN and South Korea have signed AKFTA, trade between South Korea and ASEAN is still more likely to focus on bilateral trade efforts with individual ASEAN countries. Similarly, the issue of negotiating the "noodle bowl" of individual FTAs that ASEAN member countries sign (such as South Korea's bilateral FTA with Singapore and Vietnam) remains complicated (ARIC 2017). Amidst rising regional FTAs, Korea can strategically manoeuvre AKFTA to boost economic relations with ASEAN by establishing a comprehensive and detailed plan that is mutually beneficial for both parties. This plan must involve a tripartite partnership among regulators, business sector and the academia. Korea can prioritize a 3-point agenda which are: (1) production and market development, (2) connectivity, and (3) ASEAN awareness campaign.

Market Entry and Production Partnership

The current initiatives of ASEAN-Korea Business Council (AKBC) in promoting cooperation among SMEs must cascade from national level to local government unit (LGU) level to widen scope and participation. The ASEAN Secretariat (2012) surveyed that SMEs make up 88.8–99.9% of enterprises in Southeast Asia which captures 51.7–97.2% of total employment. With these numbers, Korea can focus on policies assisting ASEAN's SMEs to explore and penetrate Korean markets which can then improve the current trade imbalance between the two parties.

Moreover, in promoting a more substantive regional value chain, Macaranas (2017) suggested the boosting financial and technical assistance is needed in upgrading ASEAN industrial structure to raise production and explore common grounds as partners. Korean business strategy on ASEAN must transition from an export destination to a production partner. As mentioned by ASEAN Secretary General Le Luong Minh, this can be done by increasing Korean businesses participation in public–private partnership projects (Kim 2016).

Technological Innovation and Connectivity

With South Korea's advanced information and communication technology (ICT), the government can take the lead and provide leverage in executing the Master Plan on ASEAN Connectivity (MPAC) 2025 as well as the Initiative for ASEAN Integration (IAI) Work Plan III. Providing technical and vocational education and training will enable South Korea to have a strong foothold in ASEAN's growing ICT industries.

Awareness and Cultural Exchange

Lastly, increasing awareness of ASEAN and its economic viability in South Korea is imperative. Currently, there are only five universities in South Korea that house Southeast Asian studies centre. These are Hankuk University of Foreign Studies (HUFS), Busan University of Foreign Studies (BUFS), Sogang Institute of East Asian Studies (Sogang IEAS), Seoul National University (SNU AC) and Korea University (KU Asiatic Research Institute).

The current lack of information about ASEAN society and culture in South Korea contributes to the lagging development of AKFTA. The availability of information and discourse on the current state, trends and outlook on ASEAN economies can entice new local players to trade and invest more in Southeast Asia. This can also be further addressed by boosting the role of ASEAN-Korea Centre (AKC) in raising public and private awareness on economic cooperation to accelerate economic and sociocultural cooperation between the ASEAN and Korea. Increasing academic research as well as fully utilizing the AKC can address this gap.

Conclusion

ASEAN-South Korea economic cooperation has shown positive growth over the years. The total number of trade value, FDI and ODA, as well as travellers, has significantly increased. This stable economic relationship has benefited both parties leading to an increase not only in economic cooperation but also in better diplomatic relations and mobility between the citizens of South Korea and the ASEAN region. However, these economic improvements face external challenges in the form of competition with China and Japan, and much-needed internal improvement on the level of economic cohesiveness within ASEAN.

As a country, South Korea also faces various new economic challenges. Chief among them is a slowing growth output, a rapidly ageing population, rising income inequality and the ever-present cost of possible conflict with North Korea. In contrast, ASEAN's relatively young workforce, untapped resources and expanding markets due to improving living standards can all be complementary assets that would benefit the increasing economic cooperation between the two parties. For ASEAN countries, South Korea's advance market, technological know-how, investments and ODA are all factors that could drive the region's continued economic expansion in the wake of South Korea's own economic growth.

References

Alegado, Siegfrid. 2018. "Japan Still Beating China in Southeast Asia Infrastructure Race." Bloomberg.com, published February 9. Accessed April 4. https://www.bloomberg.com/news/articles/2018-02-08/japan-still-beating-china-in-southeast-asia-infrastructure-race.

ASEAN. 2014. *Joint Statement of the ASEAN-ROK Commemorative Summit on the 25th Anniversary of the ASEAN-ROK Dialogue Relations: Our Future Vision of ASEAN-ROK Strategic Partnership.* ASEAN.org, published December 15. Accessed April 6, 2018. http://asean.org/storage/images/pdf/2014_upload/ASEAN-ROK_Joint_Statement-FINAL-15_Des_2014.pdf.

ASEAN. 2015a. *Fact Sheet: ASEAN Community.* Jakarta: ASEAN Secretariat, December. Accessed March 31, 2018. http://asean.org/storage/2012/05/7.-Fact-Sheet-on-ASEAN-Community.pdf.

ASEAN. 2015b. *ASEAN Economic Community Blueprint 2025.* Jakarta: ASEAN Secretariat.

ASEAN. 2017a. *Overview of ASEAN-Republic of Korea Dialogue Relations.* ASEAN.org, published June 15. Accessed March 29, 2018. http://asean.org/storage/2012/05/Overview-ASEAN-ROK-Dialogue-Relations-As-of-15-June-2017.pdf.

ASEAN. 2017b. *Overview of ASEAN Plus Three Cooperation.* ASEAN.org. Accessed March 30, 2018. http://asean.org/storage/2017/06/Overview-of-APT-Cooperation-Jun-2017.pdf.

ASEAN. 2017c. *ASEAN Statistical Yearbook 2016/2017.* Jakarta: ASEAN Secretariat.

ASEAN-Korea Centre. 2017. *ASEAN Korea in Figures.* Seoul: ASEAN-Korea Centre.

ASEAN-Korea Centre. 2018. *Key Indicators on ASEAN-Korea Relations.* ASEANKorea.org, published March 20. Accessed April 4, 2018. http://www.aseankorea.org/eng/Resources/statistics_view.asp?pageNum=50&page=1&boa_num=12619&boa_gubun=13&pageReturn=statistics&boa_cnt=1424.

ASEAN Secretariat. 2012. *SME Developments in ASEAN.* ASEAN.org. Accessed April 27, 2018. http://asean.org/asean-economic-community/sectoral-bodies-under-the-purview-of-aem/micro-small-and-medium-enterprises/overview/.

Asia Regional Integration Center (ARIC). 2017. *Free Trade Agreements.* Aric.adb.org, published June 8. Accessed April 4, 2018. https://aric.adb.org/database/fta.

Chan, Irene, and Mingjiang Li. 2015. "New Chinese Leadership, New Policy in the South China Sea Dispute?" *Journal of Chinese Political Science* 20: 35–50.

Economic Development Cooperation Fund (ECDF). 2016. *Annual Report 2016: Creating a Sustainable Future.* Seoul: Korea Economic Development Cooperation Fund.

Fallon, Theresa. 2015. "The New Silk Road: Xi Jinping's Grand Strategy for Eurasia." *American Foreign Policy Interest* 37: 140–147.

ISEAS-Yusof Ishak Institute. 2017. "Survey Report: How Do Southeast Asians View the Trump Administration?" In *ASEAN Focus: Issue 2/2017*, 12–14. Singapore: ISEAS-Yusof Ishak. Institute.

Kahnert, Friedrich. 1969. *Economic Integration Among Developing Countries.* Paris: Organisation for Economic Co-operation and Development (OECD).

Kim, Jae Kyoung. 2016. "ASEAN Seeks Korean Role in Economic Integration." *Korea Times*, published July 27. Accessed April 26, 2018. http://www.koreatimes.co.kr/www/biz/2018/04/488_210518.html.

Korea International Trade Association. 2018. *K-Statistics.* Accessed April 25, 2018. http://www.kita.org/kStat/byCountEcon_SpeCountBloc.do.

Korea Tourism Organization (KTO). 2018. "Travelers' Resources." Visitkorea.or.kr, last modified February 21. Accessed April 4, 2018. http://english.visitkorea.or.kr/enu/TRV/TV_ENG_3_1.jsp#.

Lee, Choong Lyol. 2017. "ASEAN-Korea Economic Relationship: A Road to More Active Future Cooperation." In *Partnering for Tomorrow: ASEAN-Korea Relations*, edited by Jim Kapsalis, Na-young Moon, Min-ji Kim, Chae-kyoun Ha, and Ji-hye Park, 132–156. Seoul: ASEAN-Korea Centre.

Lee, Jong Wha. 2016. *The Republic of Korea's Economic Growth and Catch-Up: Implications for the People's Republic of China*. ADBI Working Paper 571. Tokyo: Asian Development Bank Institute.

Macaranas, Federico. 2017. "ASEAN-Korea Economic Relations Through 2025." In *Partnering for Tomorrow: ASEAN-Korea Relations*, edited by Jim Kapsalis, Na-young Moon, Min-ji Kim, Chae-kyoun Ha, and Ji-hye Park, 101–131. Seoul: ASEAN-Korea Centre.

Minh, Le Luong. 2017. "Looking Back to Move Forward." In *ASEAN at 50: A Look at Its External Relations*, 9–18. Singapore: Konrad-Adenauer-Stiftung.

Ministry of Foreign Affairs (MOFA) Japan. 2018. *Free Trade Agreement (FTA) and Economic Partnership Agreement (EPA)*, last modified March 23. Accessed April 4, 2018. http://www.mofa.go.jp/policy/economy/fta/index.html.

Oh, Yoon Ah. 2017. "Discussion Paper." In *Partnering for Tomorrow: ASEAN-Korea Relations*, edited by Jim Kapsalis, Na-young Moon, Min-ji Kim, Chae-kyoun Ha, and Ji-hye Park, 157–162. Seoul: ASEAN-Korea Centre.

Organisation for Economic Co-operation and Development (OECD). 2010. *OECD Economic Survey: Korea 2010*. Paris: OECD Publishing.

Organisation for Economic Co-operation and Development (OECD). 2016. *OECD Economic Survey: Korea 2016*. Paris: OECD Publishing.

Organisation for Economic Co-operation and Development (OECD). 2017a. *Development Co-operation Report 2017: Data for Development*. Paris: OECD Publishing.

Organisation for Economic Co-operation and Development (OECD). 2017b. "Aid (ODA) Disbursements to Countries and Regions." *QWIDS Query Wizard for International Development Statistics*, last modified May 24. Accessed April 2, 2018. https://stats.oecd.org/Index.aspx?datasetcode=TABLE2A.

Roberts, Christopher B. 2012. *ASEAN Regionalism: Cooperation, Values and Institutionalization*. London and New York: Routledge.

Rodrik, Dani, Gene Grossman, and Victor Norman. 1995. "Getting Interventions Right: How South Korea and Taiwan Grew Rich." *Economic Policy* 10 (20): 53–107.

Tang, Siew Mun. 2017. "New Challenges in Search of Solutions." In *ASEAN at 50: A Look at Its External Relations*, 31–42. Singapore: Konrad-Adenauer-Stiftung.

The Economist. 2017. "A Geopolitical Row with China Damages South Korea Business Further." Economist.com, published October 19. Accessed March 30, 2018. https://www.economist.com/news/business/21730477-south-korean-industries-ranging-tourism-carmaking-are-being-badly-affected.

United Nations Development Programme (UNDP). 2016. *Human Development Report 2016: Human Development for Everyone.* New York: United Nations Development Program.

Whiteside, Darren. 2017. "South Korea's Moon Unveils New Focus on Southeast Asia." *Reuters,* published November 9. Accessed March 30, 2018. https://www.reuters.com/article/us-indonesia-southkorea/south-koreas-moon-unveils-new-focus-on-southeast-asia-idUSKBN1D90OC.

World Bank. 2017a. *GDP Per Capita (Current US$).* World Bank Databank, last modified July 1. Accessed April 3, 2018. https://data.worldbank.org/indicator/NY.GDP.PCAP.CD?locations=KR.

World Bank. 2017b. *GDP Growth (Annual %).* World Bank Databank, last modified July 1. Accessed April 3, 2018. https://data.worldbank.org/indicator/NY.GDP.MKTP.KD.ZG?locations=KR.

World Bank. 2017c. *Gross Enrolment Ratio, Tertiary, Both Sexes (%).* World Bank Databank, July 1. Accessed April 3, 2018. https://data.worldbank.org/indicator/SE.TER.ENRR?locations=KR.

4

Determinants of Chinese Overseas FDI in ASEAN Countries

Jie Zheng and Mohd Nazari Ismail

Introduction

The term "Foreign direct investments" (FDI) refers to business activities conducted by firms to obtain economic benefits by investing in another country, including mergers and acquisitions, establishing new overseas operations and reinvesting profits earned from overseas operations. It is one of the several ways for firms to be involved in international business.

This chapter elaborates the concepts and theories on FDI. The chapter also explains the growth trend of FDI by organizations from China as well as some of their unique features. Finally, the chapter will represent some findings on the possible factors that influence the growth of FDI from China.

J. Zheng (✉)
Sinohydro Bureau 8 Co., Ltd., Beijing, China

M. N. Ismail
FPP, University of Malaya, Kuala Lumpur, Malaysia
e-mail: mdnazari@um.edu.my

© The Author(s) 2019
A. Idris and N. Kamaruddin (eds.), *ASEAN Post-50*,
https://doi.org/10.1007/978-981-13-8043-3_4

Is FDI Beneficial or Not for Host Countries?

There are mixed opinions on the benefits of FDIs to the host country. The overwhelming majority are positive due to a number of reasons such as being a major contributor to job creation in host countries, promotion of higher productivity and building up competitiveness among host countries' firms as a result of spillover effects (Blomstrom et al. 1994; Caves 1996; Smarzynska Javorcik 2004).

But there are negative perceptions too. Some highlight the fact that there is no consistent relationship between FDI stock and economic growth of host countries. Furthermore, as the investing companies are often MNEs from developed countries, there is a higher possibility that local firms would be crowded out due to their technology backwardness and inferior management and marketing skills (Hanson 2001).

Although the views about FDI are mixed, as long as the competitive market is not perfect and there is the existence of trade barriers between countries, FDI will continue to develop (Denisia 1998).

Looking into the overseas FDI happened between China and ASEAN countries, we could see such a conclusion is well presented. ASEAN, an abbreviation for Association of Southeast Asian Nations, is an intergovernmental regional organization including ten Southeast Asian countries targeting at improving Pan-Asianism and intergovernmental collaboration and promotes educational, economic, military, political and cultural integration among its members and Asian states (The ASEAN Secretariat 2012). As emerging economies act as a more and more important role in the FDI activities, ASEAN is not an exception as against the trend. From a trade and growth perspective, ASEAN countries are very hard-core players in driving the global economy in recent years and have become more and more eye-catching on the stage of international trade and investment, both as a source and as the destination. Taking the year 2006 as a base, the percentage growth of inflow and outflow FDI of Southeast Asia has been maintained at a significant level (with the exception of the negative effect of a financial crisis) (The ASEAN Secretariat 2016) (Table 4.1).

Considering its comparatively stable political environment, rich resources endowment, diversified and compatible culture and society,

4 Determinants of Chinese Overseas FDI in ASEAN Countries

Table 4.1 Foreign direct investment: inward and outward flows and stock USD in millions

Year	World	ASEAN	Percentage of ASEAN to WORLD (%)	Increasing rate based on 2006 (%)
2006	1411171	63230	4.48	
2007	1909234	83801	4.39	32.53
2008	1499133	49867	3.33	−21.13
2009	1190006	46592	3.92	−26.31
2010	1383779	110531	7.99	74.81
2011	1591146	94819	5.96	49.96
2012	1592598	108057	6.78	70.90
2013	1443230	126098	8.74	99.43
2014	1323863	130378	9.85	106.20
2015	1774001	126596	7.14	100.21

Source Adapted from UNCTAD

and its high-speed development of infrastructure, ASEAN countries are destined to attract more FDI inflows. On the other hand, as it is true that till now most of China's OFDI still go to developed countries such as western European countries and the United States in seeking of strategic asset (Lv and Spigarelli 2016); however, we must notice the signal that China OFDI volume flows into ASEAN countries has been increasing hugely since the implementation of ASEAN–China free trade agreement signing in 2009 (Thi and Anh 2016). Stronger wave of FDI activities between ASEAN countries and China veiled in 2016 after the Belt and Road Initiative concept had been first brought out by Chinese President Mr. Xi Jinping for Silk Road Economic Belt (SREB) and Maritime Silk Road (MSR) in 2013 and then promoted enthusiastically and frequently by Chinese Prime Minister Li Keqiang during his visits to the countries along the Belt and Road (Liao 2015). From the below table, we could see that as world's FDI towards ASEAN decreased about 20% in 2016, ASEAN countries attracted large incremental in Chinese OFDI amount which displays a rise of 43.65% from 6412 million USD to 9211 million USD (Table 4.2).

As Dunning pointed out that the parameters in his OLI paradigm used to form a configuration to explain a specific FDI activity were influenced very much by the background and the contextual of a company or a country (Dunning 2000), the changing conditions of China's

Table 4.2 Comparison of ASEAN inward FDI from world and China

Host country	Source country	2010	2011	2012	2013	2014	2015	2016
ASEAN	Total countries (world)	1,08,174	87,664	1,17,545	1,20,051	1,33,057	1,21,621	96,723
	China [CN]	3489	7190	8168	6354	6185	6412	9211
ASEAN Percentage of China to world (%)		3.22	8.20	6.95	5.29	4.65	5.27	9.52

Source Compiled from data release by ASEAN stats

economy and society, as well as that of ASEAN countries, obviously need re-examination by applying the general theories of FDI.

And many scholars are indeed trying to develop general theories in various ways to explain China's OFDI behaviour. Most of them focused on pushing factors including China's domestic imperfect capital market, central-planned economy, natural resource inadequacy as per capita and technological backwardness which urged China to invest in overseas markets either highly developed with many technology advancements or least developed countries (LDCs) with abundant natural resources and weak institutional regulations (Buckley et al. 2007).

Therefore, a re-examination of traditional motivations is needed to find out whether they are suitable to be applied to the China–ASEAN context, designed to examine the aforesaid topic, traditional theories including Dunning's OLI (ownership-location-internalization para-digm) framework, Dunning's investment development path, institution-al-based view and resource-based view. Examining parameters cover the ASEAN countries' market size which is usually measured by GDP, GDP per capita, GDP growth; the ASEAN countries' institutional factors including the indicator of political stability, control of corruption and the government effectiveness; the ASEAN countries' natural resource rents to GDP; the ASEAN countries' annual patent application; and China's outward foreign direct investment volume in ASEAN countries from 2006 to 2015 measured in USD dollars.

Theories on Overseas FDI

Foreign direct investment is often considered as the representing mode of firm internationalization by establishing cross-border subsidiaries or affiliates (Zhang et al. 2012). The theoretical origin could be traced back to the late 1950s when the academic literature started to address the internationalization of US companies and their penetration into Japanese and European markets, which could be described as a north-to-north flow (Dunning 2001). During that academic developing process, the question about what factors contributed to a company's decision to set up business overseas came onto the stage.

OLI Paradigm and the FDI Motivations

Dunning's OLI (ownership-location-internalization paradigm) framework gave many hints. Dunning (1997) absorbed the previous studies and developed his eclectic paradigm which is composed of three factors, namely ownership advantages, locations advantages and internalization advantages.

Ownership advantages mean that firms possess certain competitive advantages which include privileged ownership, access to income generating assets and the ability to coordinate cross-border assets that bring benefit to them compared with their competitors (Dunning 2001). And such advantages are spatially transferrable and enable the firm to absorb its operational costs overseas.

Locational advantages are those non-transferrable/immobile characteristics that a firm owns and could benefit from when operating in its domestic country (Dunning 2000). The locational advantages include natural resource endowment, the supporting policies from the government of that location, the low-cost labours or materials, the bigger market size, etc.

Internalization advantages refer to the way and the extent of a firm opts to carry out overseas business by directly controlling an owned subsidiary rather than conducting exports, franchising or joint venture (Dunning 2000).

In his works, Dunning emphasized that although the OLI paradigm needed adjustment to be applied to different situations, a firm must have certain kind of ownership advantages to allow it to operate overseas (Dunning 2001).

Based on that OLI paradigm, three sets of motivations for multinational enterprises are deducted, which are market seeking, resource seeking, strategic asset seeking and efficiency seeking.

Natural resource seeking happens typically with countries of abundant quantities of minerals, raw materials and agricultural products. Market seeking considers the market size of the host countries, including factors such as a country's GDP, its GDP per capita and its GDP growth. Strategic assets include leading-edge technologies, brand and patent, while efficiency seeking considers the cost and quality of certain component endowments (Neary 2009; Franco et al. 2008; Kudina and Jakubiak 2008).

The Resource-Based View

The resource-based view posits that companies equipped with firm-specific resources which are of unique value, uncommon and not-ready to imitate by others possess sustainable competitive advantages. The resource-based view proposes that a firm's overseas business experience, its ability to utilize resources in new markets and its management capability played on international stage are valuable and imperfectly imitable (Yang et al. 2009). Although firms face difficulties in transferring their resources in dissimilar host country environments, as MNEs accumulate more of the above-mentioned tacit knowledge, they are more inclined to carry out foreign direct investment in overseas markets (Geringer et al. 2000).

Some scholars, such as Hoskisson et al. (2000), notice the importance of applying for resource-based framework in the background of developing countries with prosperous economic development. While MNEs as the first movers to harvest the economic and strategic benefits by deploying their management capability and accumulative international operating knowledge, companies from emerging economies are vigorously targeting at markets and leading-edge technologies to build up their own capabilities (Yang et al. 2009).

The Institutional-Based View

Institutions are usually explained as the "principles of the game". It was first defined by Douglass North (1991), an economist, as "the humanly devised constraints that structure human interaction", and defined by sociologist W. Richard Scott (1995) as "regulative, normative, and cognitive structures and activities that provide stability and meaning to social behaviour". The latest and most directly associated paper is Peng et al.'s (2008) *An Institution-Based View of International Business Strategy: A Focus on Emerging Economies*, which accentuated the institution-based view in international business strategy with the emphasis on developing economies.

The institutional-based view gives the conceptualization that the institutions of a country set the rules that influencing a company's strategic choices (North 1991). Government strategies including controls focused at the MNEs and changes in duty and non-tax obstructions in the host nation are formal institutional actions that influence FDI (Kudina and Jakubiak 2008). According to Peng and Pleggenkuhle-Miles (2009), institution-based view accommodates both factors from home country and the host country, including the industrial policies, international trading system, cultural distances and institutional norms. Institution-based view also stresses that multinational enterprises' ownership advantages are home country related (Dunning 2000).

Extension for General Theories of OFDI

However, as pointed out by Peter J. Buckley and many other scholars, the above-mentioned general theory of FDI is originated from and established on the experience of developed country's investors as they were the first movers (Buckley et al. 2007). And, as the deepening of globalization, more and more MNEs from emerging economies start their FDI activities worldly. Academic field started to question whether the extended theories concerning outward foreign direct investment suits emerging economies. While some say the traditional general theories are not suitable to be applied to companies from emerging economies, the majority provide that with extensions and adjustment, traditional theories/frameworks are still good explanations.

Among all the emerging economies, China's leaps and bounds style of economic growth and volume of OFDI greatly drew the attention of the academic field. Compared with developed countries' OFDI behaviour, China has its special features. Firstly, most of the OFDI players from China are state-owned enterprises (Investment News OECD 2008), especially at the initial stage. Only after 2003, private firms were officially permitted to engage in OFDI activities (China Statistical Press 2004). Closely connected with that phenomena is that China's OFDI is more for the political purpose, argued in many research papers. Secondly, China is a central planning country and its economic activities subject to the policy variation, which has a great influence on the pattern of China's OFDI. Thirdly, compared with westerners, Chinese have the living philosophy of "Guanxi", the networking skills that could exert influence to gain social benefits in a hierarchical society, which is also applied to business issues and leading to the inadequacy of regulation and policy transparency (Luo 1997). Therefore, China is often selected as a special case in the FDI research field. As Buckley found out that while China's OFDI exhibited some motivations were in line with traditional theories including marketing seeking, natural resources seeking and asset seeking (only after 2001), the "unprecedented finding" is that China's OFDI doesn't avoid political risk, which may because of the low cost of capital enjoyed by Chinese SOEs (Buckley et al. 2007). By reviewing most of the existing literature on China's OFDI, Ziyi Wei (2010) explains the behaviour of Chinese OFDI from two perspectives, namely the country-specific advantages and the firm-specific advantages. With thorough analysis, the author came up with the conclusion that the home country disadvantages such as the imperfection of capital market were actually converted into the firm-specific advantage of low cost of capital, thus making sense for the conformity of Chinese OFDI behaviour with Dunning's ownership advantage theory.

Research Methodology

Hypotheses Development

Based on the literature review conducted, a total of 8 hypotheses are formulated. These hypotheses are listed in the section below:

Market Seeking

Market features of host countries, especially the absolute market size, are usually perceived as a critical determinant of FDI flows. Because when the markets increase in size, the opportunities for better-utilizing resources and exploiting economies of scale and scope via FDI are much greater (Wheeler 1992). Other research (Chakrabarti 2001) shows

62 J. Zheng and M. N. Ismail

that FDI flow and market size are associated positively. Recent work mentioned the rise of vigorous market seeking motives steering Chinese MNEs (Buckley et al. 2007; Deng 2004; Taylor 2002; Zhang 2003) and that this trend may increasingly be guided towards large markets. Theory points out that market-hunting, horizontal FDI will be associated positively with growth in demand. The market growth hypothesis posits that rapidly growing economies provide more opportunities for creating profits than those which are growing more slowly or not at all (Lim 1983). We, therefore, derive the following three hypotheses:

H1 Host country GDP has a positive relationship with China's outward foreign direct investment flow to ASEAN countries,

H2 Host country GDP per capita has a positive relationship with China's outward foreign direct investment flow to ASEAN countries and

H3 Host country GDP growth has a positive relationship with China's outward foreign direct investment flow to ASEAN countries.

Strategic Asset

In Dunning's (2001) early works of developing his OLI paradigm, strategic asset seeking including leading-edge technologies, brand and patents is already viewed as an important factor of predicting FDI activities. Later combined with China's unique characteristic, FDI was considered as an instrument used by central government to access advanced technology and other immobile strategic assets to augment especially state-owned enterprises' competitive advantages (Taylor 2002; Zhang 2003). Therefore, China's OFDI is expected to flow into countries ranked high in terms of human and intellectual capital levels (Dunning and Fortanier 2008; Dunning et al. 1996). Buckley proposed that the level of intellectual capital could be proxied by the rate of patenting in the host country (Buckley et al. 2007). Therefore, the H4 is formulated as follows:

H4 Quantity of total annual patent application in host countries associated positively with China's outward foreign direct investment flow to ASEAN countries.

Natural Resource Endowment

The central government of China is alleged to use OFDI as a vehicle to bring back the supply of domestically inadequate resources to meet the demand of a growing Chinese economy (Gang 1992; Zhan 1995). Main sectors of natural resources include minerals, petroleum, timber, fishery and agricultural products (Wu and Sia 2002; Cai 1999). Examples included the acquisition of stakes in Australian mineral and food companies by CITIC and the purchasing of Canadian-based company PetroKaz by China National Petroleum Corporation (CNPC) (Wu and Sia 2002). Internalization theory addressed the importance of shared-based equity control in the exploitation of scarce natural resources, and therefore, a positive association between the natural resource endowment of host countries and Chinese OFDI is expected (Buckley and Casson 2003). Thus:

H5 The natural resource rents to GDP in host countries have a positive relationship with China's outward foreign direct investment flow to ASEAN countries.

Institutional Factors

Government strategies including controls focused on the MNEs and changes in duty and non-tax obstructions in the host nation are formal institutional actions that influence FDI (Kudina and Jakubiak 2008). And political stability and institutional maturity were listed as the key aspects in shaping the institutional context (Child and Marinova 2014), especially in consideration of Chinese conditions (Rugman et al. 2014). Buckley once obtained the conclusion that China's OFDI was negatively associated with political risks (Buckley et al. 2007). Political stability is connected with the legitimacy of the government's administrative system, the pattern alteration of governing and the coherence of policies implemented by the different government (Child and Marinova 2014). The maturity of institutions ought to be measured by having a transparent and clear legitimacy framework and regulated authority behaviour, which enables efficiently functioned and un-bureaucratic institutional agencies (Child and Marinova 2014). According to Worldwide Governance Indicators provided by World Bank, control of corruption and government effectiveness are sub-indicators of maturity of institutions. Accordingly, we hereby formulate H6, H7 and H8 as follows:

H6 Host country's control of corruption has a positive effect on China's outward foreign direct investment flow to ASEAN countries,
H7 Host country's government effectiveness has a positive effect on China's outward foreign direct investment flow to ASEAN countries,
H8 Host country's political stability has a positive effect on China's outward foreign direct investment flow to ASEAN countries.

Conceptual Model

The conceptual framework of this study is based on the literature review and previous related studies. The foundation of this study is the OLI framework of Dunning, the resource-based view and the institutional-based view (Fig. 4.1).

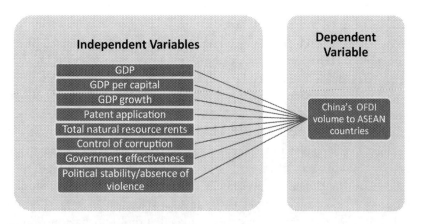

Fig. 4.1 Conceptual model

4 Determinants of Chinese Overseas FDI in ASEAN Countries   65

Table 4.3 Source of secondary data

Variable	Measurement	Function	Source
OFDI	Volume of China's OFDI	Dependent variable	The Ministry of Commerce of the People's Republic of China (MOFCOM)
GDP	Market size	Market seeking	World Bank's world development indicators
GDP_G	Host annual GDP growth rate	Market seeking	World Bank's world development indicators
GDP_C	Host GDP per capita	Market seeking	World Bank's world development indicators
TNR	Host total natural resource rent (% of GDP)	Natural resource seeking	World Bank's world development indicators
PA	Host patent application	Strategic asset seeking	world intellectual property organization
COC	Host control of corruption	Institutional factor	World Bank's governance indicator
GE	Government effectiveness	Institutional factor	World Bank's governance indicator
PSAV	Political stability/ absence of violence	Institutional factor	World Bank's governance indicator

Source Compiled by authors

Data Collection

The data comprise a panel of 10 ASEAN countries between 2006 and 2015. The sample host countries and time period are mainly decided by the extent to which collected information is capable of developing persistent measures of the selected variables over time. Details of the data source are described in Table 4.3.

Data Analysis and Findings

Panel data sets are called as a longitudinal data set or cross-sectional time series data set as well. A panel data set usually composes of time series observations on a number of cross-sectional units which are categorical to permit researchers to study the changing dynamics features of the data set (Seetaram and Petit 2012). As Driffield et al. (2007) argued, the application of panel estimation with fixed effect could control the heterogeneity of individual country and therefore reduce the probability of misspecification and yield more precise delivery of end results. With the data collected from the authority release, descriptive analysis, reliability analysis and regression are performed, and the results are presented.

Measurement Analysis

Descriptive Analysis

Data collected include China's outward foreign direct invest volume designated as the dependent variable, as well as a serial of independent variables including ten ASEAN countries' GDP, GDP per capita, GDP growth rate, total natural resource rents to GDP, annual patent application quantity, control of corruption, government effectiveness and political stability for a continuous period of ten years; therefore, we actually have 100 respondents. In order to increase the sensitivity of the data, here the amount of OFDI, GDP, GDP per capita and patent application quantity are converted into logarithmic value to be used in the data analysis. However, as the OFDI from China to Brunei was 0 and -3.28 million USD in 2006 and 2014, respectively, the OFDI from China to Malaysia was -32.82 million USD in 2007 and that to the Philippines was -27.59 million USD in 2015, the observed respondents for LOG_OFDI are 96 in total. Therefore, the total valid number is 96. In the following table, the min., max. and mean value, standard deviation, skewness and kurtosis are presented (Table 4.4).

Reliability Analysis

Checking the reliability, the most important parameter is the Alpha value. If the Cronbach's alpha coefficient is bigger than 0.7, the scale could be deemed as reliable (Pallent 2007). From the result presented

Table 4.4 Descriptive statistics

	N	Minimum	Maximum	Mean	Std. deviation	Skewness		Kurtosis	
	Statistic	Statistic	Statistic	Statistic	Statistic	Statistic	Std. error	Statistic	Std. error
LOG_OFDI	96	2.996	7.019	5.231	0.798	−0.785	0.246	0.398	0.488
LOG_GDP	100	6.52	8.957	7.922	0.674	−0.388	0.241	−1.247	0.478
GPD_C	100	0.268	56.007	10.866	16.546	1.653	0.241	1.199	0.478
GDP_G	100	−0.024	0.153	0.055	0.033	−0.348	0.241	0.73	0.478
PA	100	0	6155	883	1394	2.189	0.241	4.468	0.478
TNR	100	0	0.324	0.077	0.072	1.435	0.241	1.988	0.478
COC	100	0.005	0.986	0.397	0.285	0.633	0.241	−0.538	0.478
GE	100	0.024	1	0.523	0.288	−0.082	0.241	−0.978	0.478
PSAV	100	0.052	0.99	0.43	0.292	0.6	0.241	−0.853	0.478
Valid N (listwise)	96								

Table 4.5 Reliability analysis

Case processing summary			
		N	%
Cases	Valid	77	77
	Excluded[a]	23	23
	Total	100	100
Reliability statistics			
Cronbach's alpha	N of items		
0.69	9		

Item-total statistics				
	Scale mean if item deleted	Scale variance if item deleted	Corrected item-total correlation	Cronbach's alpha if item deleted
LOG_GDP	9.92	5.488	0.567	0.617
LOG_GDP_C	17.33	5.581	0.532	0.626
GDP_G	17.98	7.49	−0.065	0.701
LOG_PA	15.63	3.324	0.741	0.56
TNR	17.96	7.629	−0.397	0.71
COC	17.56	6.379	0.732	0.638
GE	17.42	6.459	0.773	0.641
PSAV	17.57	6.942	0.274	0.682
LOG_OFDI	12.82	5.964	0.193	0.725

[a]Listwise deletion based on all variables in the procedure

below, we found the reading of Cronbach's alpha is 0.69, a little bit lower than the required (Table 4.5).

Regression Analysis

In statistical modelling, regression analysis is an instrument used for estimating the relationships among variables, i.e. how well a group of independent variables could explain the dependent variable, which independent variable among a group of independent variables could best predict the outcome and when other variables are controlled whether a specific independent variable could still have the predicting capability (Berry 1993).

The outcome in the table below is calculated by the method of multiple regression generated by SPSS. Key elements including R squares, adjusted R squares, standard error of the estimates, ANOVA and Coefficient.

4 Determinants of Chinese Overseas FDI in ASEAN Countries   69

R-squared value and adjusted *R*-squared value measure the extent of the regression in predicting the values of dependent variable; while adjusted *R* square is used to modify the might-be overoptimistic estimation measured by *R*-squared value when the sample is small. Therefore, in our case, we will report the adjusted *R*-squared value since our respondents are only 100. From the table of model summary, we could see that the model explains the outcome very well as the *R*-squared value is 0.611, the adjusted *R*-square is 0.575, which means taking small sample size into consideration, the overall model still can explain 57.5% of the variance. What's more, from the table named ANOVA, we could see for the column "Sig.", short for significance, the value is 0.000, which means the p-value < 0.0005; therefore, we know the overall model is statistically significant.

Coefficient measures the marginal contribution of each independent variable to dependent variable OFDI. There are two values for coefficients, wherein one is B value of unstandardized coefficients which could be used to construct a regression equation, and the other is the Beta value of standardized coefficients which can be used to compare the contribution of each independent variable to dependent variable as different variables are converted into the same scale. T-statistic is the result of dividing coefficient estimate by its standard error, reporting whether the coefficient in that row equals zero. *P*-value is used to test whether the coefficient is statistically significant. If the p-value is less than 0.05, the variable makes a statistically significant contribution to explaining the dependent variable; if the p-value is larger than 0.05, it may overlap with other independent variables in the model. In the Coefficients table, we could see GDP per capita and GDP growth are not statistically significant; this may due to the fact that they are overlapping with absolute GDP. The same case goes to control of corruption variable which may overlap of government effectiveness. Therefore, as for each independent variable, GDP, patent application, total natural resources rents to GDP, government effectiveness and political stability and absence of violence make a statistically significant contribution to the dependent variable OFDI. Moreover, here we develop the equation for LOG_OFDI (Table 4.6):

Table 4.6 Regression analysis

Model summary

Model	R	R square	Adjusted R square	Std. error of the estimate
1	.782[a]	0.611	0.575	0.52006

ANOVA[b]

Model		Sum of squares	df	Mean Square	F	Sig.
1	Regression	36.958	8	4.62	17.081	.000[c]
	Residual	23.531	87	0.27		
	Total	60.489	95			

Coefficients[d]

Model		Unstandardized coefficients		Standardized coefficients	t	Sig.
		B	Std. Error	Beta		
1	(Constant)	0.525	1.285		0.409	0.684
	LOG_GDP	0.683	0.166	0.577	4.123	0
	GDP_C	−0.01	0.009	−0.209	−1.128	0.263
	GDP_G	−0.009	0.021	−0.039	−0.45	0.654
	PA	0	0	0.634	4.176	0
	TNR	−0.024	0.012	−0.221	−2.113	0.037
	COC	−0.004	0.01	−0.129	−0.375	0.708
	GE	−0.027	0.007	−0.97	−3.906	0
	PSAV	0.02	0.005	0.746	4.458	0

[a]Predictors: (Constant), PSAV, PA, GDP_G, TNR, GDP_C, GDP, GE, COC
[b]Dependent Variable: OFDI
[c]Predictors: (Constant), PSAV, PA, GDP_G, TNR, GDP_C, GDP, GE, COC
[d]Dependent Variable: OFDI

$$LOG\_OFDI = 0.525 + 0.683 \, LOG\_GDP\text{-}0.01GDP\_C\text{-}0.009GDP\_G + 0.000PA\text{-}0.024TNR\text{-}0.004COC\text{-}0.027GE + 0.02PSAV$$

Hypothesis Testing

This section summarizes the results of 8 hypotheses formulated in this study.

H1 Host country GDP has a positive relationship with China's outward foreign direct investment flow to ASEAN countries.

Host country GDP positively associated with China's OFDI and statistically significant with Beta $= 0.577$, p-value $= 0.000 < 0.05$.

H2 Host country GDP per capita has a positive relationship with China's outward foreign direct investment flow to ASEAN countries.

Host country GDP per capita has a negative relationship with China's OFDI volume but not statistically significant with Beta $= -0.209$, p-value $= 0.263 > 0.05$.

H3 Host country GDP growth has a positive relationship with China's outward foreign direct investment flow to ASEAN countries.

Host country GDP growth has a negative relationship with China's OFDI but not statistically significant with Beta $= -0.039$, p-value $= 0.654 > 0.05$.

H4 Host country's amount of patent application has a positive relationship with China's outward foreign direct investment flow to ASEAN countries.

Host country patent application positively associated with China's OFDI and statistically significant with Beta $= 0.634$, p-value $= 0.000 < 0.05$.

H5 Host country's total natural resource rents have a positive relationship with China's outward foreign direct investment flow to ASEAN countries.

Host country total natural resource rents negatively associated with China's OFDI and statistically significant with Beta $= -0.221$, p-value $= 0.037 < 0.05$.

H6 Host country's control of corruption has a positive relationship with China's outward foreign direct investment flow to ASEAN countries.

Host country control of corruption has a negative relationship with China's OFDI but not statistically significant with Beta $= -0.129$, p-value $= 0.708 > 0.05$.

H7 Host country's government effectiveness has a positive relationship with China's outward foreign direct investment flow to ASEAN countries.

Host country government effectiveness has a negative relationship with China's OFDI and statistically significant with Beta $= -0.97$, p-value $= 0.000 < 0.05$.

H8 Host country's political stability has a positive relationship with China's outward foreign direct investment flow to ASEAN countries (Table 4.7).

Host country political stability has a positive relationship with China's OFDI and statistically significant with Beta $= 0.746$, p-value $= 0.000 < 0.05$.

Discussion of the Results

From the table presented above, we could see that only a few motivations developed by general theories are still able to explain China's OFDI behaviour in ASEAN member countries, which includes market

4 Determinants of Chinese Overseas FDI in ASEAN Countries   73

Table 4.7 Overview of the study

Hypotheses	Variables	Results
H1	Host country GDP has a positive relationship with China's outward foreign direct investment flow to ASEAN countries	Supported and statistically significant
H2	Host country GDP per capita has a positive relationship with China's outward foreign direct investment flow to ASEAN countries	Not supported and not statistically significant
H3	Host country GDP growth has a positive relationship with China's outward foreign direct investment flow to ASEAN countries	Not supported and not statistically significant
H4	Host country's amount of patent application has a positive relationship with China's outward foreign direct investment flow to ASEAN countries	Supported and statistically significant
H5	Host country's total natural resource rents have a positive relationship with China's outward foreign direct investment flow to ASEAN countries	Not supported but statistically significant
H6	Host country's control of corruption has a positive relationship with China's outward foreign direct investment flow to ASEAN countries	Not supported and not statistically significant
H7	Host country's government effectiveness has a positive relationship with China's outward foreign direct investment flow to ASEAN countries	Not Supported but statistically significant
H8	Host country's political stability has a positive relationship with China's outward foreign direct investment flow to ASEAN countries	Supported and statistically significant

size measured by GDP, strategic assets measured by patent application and institutional factor measured by political stability percentile rank. The results indicate that under the ASEAN countries context which is a very mixed economy comprising developed country such as Singapore, semi-developed country of Malaysia and majority developing countries, market size, strategic assets and destinations of smaller political risks attract China's OFDI. These findings highlight the difference with Buckley et al. (2007)'s research paper whose major finding is that unlike MNEs of developed countries, Chinese enterprises are attracted by destinations of high political risks; however, in this research, we find Chinese companies do select countries of less political risks in ASEAN region to invest. What's more, the host country's total natural resource rents negatively associated with China's outward foreign direct investment volume, indicating Chinese companies are not hunting natural resources in the ASEAN region. Another thing need to mention is that contrary to general theories of OFDI, the government effectiveness is negatively associated with China's OFDI volume. To conclude, most of the traditional parameters selected in this study as proxies for motivations of market seeking, strategic asset seeking, natural resource seeking and institutional factors are making a unique contribution to explaining China's OFDI behaviour in ASEAN countries, wherein market seeking measured by GDP, strategic asset seeking measured by patent application and political stability are in conformity with traditional theories, while natural resource seeking and government effectiveness are contrary to traditional theories.

In terms of limitation, firstly, as the research is confined within ASEAN region which only have ten-member countries, the sample population of this study is small, which may influence the credibility of the results. Secondly, the generalizability of the findings is limited because the context of China's OFDI in ASEAN countries is quite different from China's OFDI in developed countries or LCDs countries. That means, the findings here are only suitable to be applied to ASEAN countries. Thirdly, in the reliability analysis, the Cronbach's alpha value is only 0.69, a little bit lower than required value of 0.7, suggesting that some other important predictors might be missing, and some adopted predictors should be removed.

One of the objectives of this study is to reconfigure the parameters nested in the general theories. ASEAN region has a diversified development level in terms of economy and technology. It has most developed countries like Singapore and Brunei Darussalam; it also has underdeveloped countries like Myanmar, Cambodia and Lao PDR, as well as other member countries having everything in between (ASEAN Secretariat 2018). Therefore, especially for those ASEAN countries not having a better situation than China, it is necessary to examine whether China's OFDI has a spillover effect in ASEAN countries, or whether China's OFDI activities are helpful for hosting countries' economy in ASEAN. Moreover, Dunning's IDP theories could be reexamined to see whether those emerging economies in ASEAN would have the same development path as countries like Japan or Malaysia with the spillover effects of FDI.

References

ASEAN Secretariat. 2018. *ASEAN Statistical Yearbook 2018*. https://doi.org/10.1017/CBO9781107415324.004.

Berry, William D. 1993. *Understanding Regression Assumptions*. Newbury Park, CA: Sage.

Blomstrom, Magnus, Robert E. Lipsey, and Mario Zejan. 1994. "What Explains Developing Country Growth?" National Bureau of Economic Research Working Paper Series. https://doi.org/10.3386/w4132.

Buckley, Peter J., and M. Casson. 2003. "The Future of the Multinational Enterprise in Retrospect and in Prospect." *Journal of International Business Studies* 34 (2): 219–222. https://doi.org/10.1057/palgrave.jibs.8400024.

Buckley, Peter J., L. Jeremy Clegg, Adam R. Cross, Xin Liu, Hinrich Voss, and Ping Zheng. 2007. "The Determinants of Chinese Outward Foreign Direct Investment." *Journal of International Business Studies* 38 (4): 499–518. https://doi.org/10.1057/palgrave.jibs.8400277.

Cai, Kevin G. 1999. "Outward Foreign Direct Investment: A Novel Dimension of China's Integration into the Regional and Global Economy Author(s): Kevin G. Cai Published by: Cambridge University Press on Behalf of the School of Oriental and African Studies Stable URL." *The China Quarterly* 160 (160): 856–880.

Caves, Richard E. 1996. *Multinational Enterprise and Economic Analysis*. 1st ed. Cambridge: Cambridge University Press.

Chakrabarti, Avik. 2001. "The Determinants of Foreign Direct Investment: Sensitivity Analyses of Cross-Country Regressions." *Kyklos* 54 (1): 89–113. https://econpapers.repec.org/RePEc:bla:kyklos:v:54:y:2001:i:1:p:89–113.

Child, John, and Svetla Marinova. 2014. "The Role of Contextual Combinations in the Globalization of Chinese Firms. 情境性组合在中国企业全球化中的作用." *Management and Organization Review* 10 (3): 347–371. https://doi.org/10.1111/more.12073.

China Statistical Press. 2004. "2003 Statistical Bulletin of China's Outward Foreign Direct Investment." http://hzs.mofcom.gov.cn/article/date/200409/20040900275799.shtml.

Deng, Ping. 2004. "Outward Investment by Chinese MNCs: Motivations and Implications." *Business Horizons* 47 (3): 8–16. https://doi.org/10.1016/S0007-6813(04)00023-0.

Denisia, Vintila. 1998. "Foreign Direct Investment Theories: An Overview of the Main FDI Theories." *European Journal of Interdisciplinary Studies* 2: 53–59.

Driffield, Nigel, Satomi Kimino, and David Saal. 2007. "Macro Determinants of FDI Inflows to Japan: An Analysis of Source Country Characteristics." *The World Economy* 30 (3): 446–469. https://doi.org/10.1111/j.1467-9701.2007.01001.x.

Dunning, John H. 1997. *Trade, Location of Economic Activity and the MNE: A Search for an Eclectic Approach.* Edited by Per Magnus Wijkman Bertil Ohlin, and Per-Ove Hesselborn. London, UK: Palgrave Macmillan.

Dunning, John H. 2000. "The Eclectic Paradigm as an Envelope for Economic and Business Theories of MNE Activity." *International Business Review.* https://doi.org/10.1016/S0969-5931(99)00035-9.

Dunning, John H. 2001. "The Eclectic (OLI) Paradigm of International Production: Past, Present and Future." *International Journal of the Economics of Business* 8 (2): 173–190. https://doi.org/10.1080/13571510110051441.

Dunning, John H., and Fabienne Fortanier. 2008. "Multinational Enterprises and the New Development Paradigm: Consequences for Host Country Development." Georgia Tech Center for International Business Education and Research Working Paper Series 2007–2008 (October 2006): 1–32.

Dunning, John H., Roger Van Hoesel, and Rajneesh Narula. 1996. "Explaining the New Wave of Outward FDI from Developing Countries: The Case of Korea and Taiwan." *MERIT Research Memoranda; 009.* Maastricht: Maastricht Economic Research Institute on Innovation and Technology (MERIT).

Franco, Chiara, Francesco Rentocchini, and Giuseppe Vittucci Marzetti. 2008. "Why Do Firms Invest Abroad? An Analysis of the Motives Underlying Foreign Direct Investments." *ETSG Forum,* 35. https://doi.org/10.2139/ssrn.1283573.

Gang, Ye. 1992. "Chinese Transnational Corporations." *Transnational Corporations* 1 (2): 125–133.

Geringer, J. Michael, Stephen Tallman, and David M. Olsen. 2000. "Product and International Diversification Among Japanese Multinational Firms." *Strategic Management Journal* 21 (1): 51–80. https://doi.org/10.1002/(SICI)1097-0266(200001)21:1<51::AID-SMJ77>3.0.CO;2-K.

Hanson, Gordon H. 2001. "Should Countries Promote Foreign Direct Investment." *G-24 Discussion Paper Series* 9 (9): 23. https://unctad.org/en/Docs/pogdsmdpbg24d9.en.pdf.

Hoskisson, Robert E., Lorraine Eden, Chung Ming Lau, and Mike Wright. 2000. "Strategy in Emerging Economies." *Academy of Management* 43 (3): 249–267.

Investment News OECD. 2008. "China's Outward Foreign Direct Investment." *Investment Division of the OECD Directorate for Financial and Enterprise Affairs.* https://doi.org/10.1016/j.bushor.2008.06.006.

Kudina, Alina, and Malgorzata Jakubiak. 2008. "The Motives and Impediments to FDI in the CIS Breakfast Session 1: New Frontiers in Investment Promotion." In *Global Forum on International Investment* 4: 1–32. www.oecd.org/investment/gfi-7.

Liao, Rebecca. 2015. "Rebecca Liao | How the AIIB Is Different Than Its Bretton Woods Counterparts." *Foreign Affairs.* https://www.foreignaffairs.com/articles/asia/2015-07-27/out-bretton-woods.

Lim, David. 1983. "Fiscal Incentives and Direct Foreign Investment in Less Developed Countries." *The Journal of Development Studies* 19 (2): 207–212. Routledge. https://doi.org/10.1080/00220388308421859.

Luo, Yadong. 1997. "Guanxi: Principles, Philosophies, and Implications." *Human System Management* 16 (1): 43–51.

Lv, Ping, and Francesca Spigarelli. 2016. "The Determinants of Location Choice." *International Journal of Emerging Markets* 11 (3): 333–356. https://doi.org/10.1108/IJOEM-09-2014-0137.

Neary, James Peter. 2009. "World Economy FDI: The OLI Framework." *The Princeton Encyclopedia of the World Economy* 1: 472–477. Princeton: Princeton University Press. https://doi.org/10.1017/CBO9781107415324.004.

North, Douglass C. 1991. "Institutions." *Journal of Economic Perspectives* 5 (1): 97–112. https://doi.org/10.1257/jep.5.1.97.

Pallent, Julie. 2007. *SPSS Survival Manual.* Milton Keynes: Open University Press.

Peng, Mike W., and Erin G. Pleggenkuhle-Miles. 2009. "Current Debates in Global Strategy." *International Journal of Management Reviews* 11 (1): 51–68. https://doi.org/10.1111/j.1468-2370.2008.00249.x.

Peng, Mike W., Denis Y. L. Wang, and Yi Jiang. 2008. "An Institution-Based View of International Business Strategy: A Focus on Emerging Economies." *Journal of International Business Studies* 39 (5): 920–936. https://econpapers.repec.org/RePEc:pal:jintbs:v:39:y:2008:i:5:p:920-936.

Rugman, Alan M., Quyen T. K. Nguyen, and Ziyi Wei. 2014. "Chinese Multinationals and Public Policy." *International Journal of Emerging Markets* 9 (2): 205–215. https://doi.org/10.1108/IJoEM-08-2013-0127.

Scott, W. Richard. 1995. *Institutions and Organizations: Ideas, Interests and Identities*. Los Angeles, London, New Delhi, Singapore, and Washington: Sage.

Seetaram, Neelu, and Sylvain Petit. 2012. "Panel Data Analysis in Tourism Research." *Munich Personal RePEc Archive (MPRA), Paper No. 75086*, no. 75086: 1–27.

Smarzynska Javorcik, Beata. 2004. "Does Foreign Direct Investment Increase the Productivity of Domestic Firms? In Search of Spillovers Through Backward Linkages." *American Economic Review* 94 (3): 605–627. https://doi.org/10.1257/0002828041464605.

Taylor, Robert. 2002. Globalization Strategies of Chinese Companies: Current Developments and Future Prospects. *Asian Business & Management* 1 (2): 209–225. https://doi.org/10.1057/palgrave.abm.9200011.

The ASEAN Secretariat. 2012. "About Asean." https://asean.org/asean/about-asean/.

The ASEAN Secretariat. 2016. "ASEAN Investment Report 2015." ASEAN Secretariat United Nations Conference on Trade and Development. http://unctad.org/en/PublicationsLibrary/unctad_asean_air2015d1.pdf.

Thi, Nguyen, and Tuong Anh. 2016. "Chinese Outward Foreign Direct Investment: Is ASEAN a New Destination?" SECO/WTI Academic Cooperation Project Working Paper Series 2016/06. Available at SSRN: https://ssrn.com/abstract=2794842 or http://dx.doi.org/10.2139/ssrn.2794842.

Wei, Ziyi. 2010. "The Literature on Chinese Outward FDI." *Multinational Business Review* 18 (3): 73–112. https://doi.org/10.1108/1525383X201000016.

Wheeler, David, and Ashoka Mody. 1992. "International Investment Location Decisions: The Case of U.S. Firms." *Journal of International Economics* 33 (1–2): 57–76.

Wu, F., and Y. Sia. 2002. "China's Rising Investment in Southeast Asia: Trends and Outlook." *Journal of Asian Business* 18 (2): 41–62.

Yang, Xiaohua, Yi Jiang, Rongping Kang, and Yinbin Ke. 2009. "A Comparative Analysis of the Internationalization of Chinese and Japanese Firms." *Asia Pacific Journal of Management* 26 (1): 141–162. https://doi.org/10.1007/s10490-007-9065-0.

Zhan, James Xiaoning. 1995. "Transnationalization and Outward Investment the Case of Chinese Firms." *Transnational Corporations* 4 (3): 61–93.

Zhang, Yongjin. 2003. *China's Emerging Global Business*. 1st ed. Basingstoke, UK: Palgrave Macmillan.

Zhang, Ying, Geert Duysters, and Sergey Filippov. 2012. "Chinese Firms Entering Europe." *Journal of Science and Technology Policy in China* 3 (2): 102–123. https://doi.org/10.1108/17585521211256973.

5

Empowerment for Economic and Human Capital Development Through Education

Wendy Mei Tien Yee and Serina Rahman

Introduction

Education is the foundation of human development. According to Tsunesaburo Makiguchi (1871–1944) a reformist educator, author and philosopher who founded The Theory of Value-Creating Pedagogy, "the purpose of education is not simply to transmit knowledge; it is to offer guidance on how to learn, enabling children to acquire the ability to pursue knowledge on their own" (Goulah and Gebert 2009). He adds, "It is not pouring knowledge into their minds. It is teaching students the methods with which they can acquire knowledge through their own efforts, presenting them with the key to unlocking the storehouse

---

W. M. T. Yee (✉)
CITra, University of Malaya, Kuala Lumpur, Malaysia
e-mail: wenyee2000@um.edu.my

S. Rahman
Regional Economic Studies, ISEAS—Yusof Ishak Institute,
Singapore, Singapore
e-mail: serina_abdul_rahman@iseas.edu.sg

© The Author(s) 2019
A. Idris and N. Kamaruddin (eds.), *ASEAN Post-50*,
https://doi.org/10.1007/978-981-13-8043-3_5

of knowledge" (Goulah and Gebert 2009). In Makiguchi's view, this is the type of education that will provide children with the keys to the "treasure house of knowledge" (Ikeda 2018).

Hence education builds on the capacity to enable and empower a person to continuously grow and unleash their limitless potential from within. When a person is able to open up the inner capacities of their lives through education, it will lead to effective transformation and influence on a global scale. Such human development of an individual paves the path for development and transformation at the community, national and the regional levels. Serious discussion on how education affects the transformation of an individual and creates a ripple effect to transformation at the regional level such as Association of Southeast Asian Nations (ASEAN) is thus timely. The challenge in the use of education to effect ASEAN regional economic and human capital development and integration would require the commitment to link micro-development of an individual and macro-development of the region to reinforce positive transformation on both planes.

Education for Human Capital Development

There is a close relationship between human capital development and economic growth. The literature has demonstrated the important role education has on human capital development; thus, educational development will also have an impact on economic growth both directly and indirectly. Among many economic theories, the human capital theory is the most influential economic theory of education which reiterates that investment in human capital creates the labour-force and skill-based labour that are indispensable for economic growth (Bouzekri 2015). This is because skills and knowledge are important tools for economic development. Many economists insist that investment in human capital development could influence future real income through embedding resources such as skills and knowledge in individuals (Bouzekri 2015). Studies proposed by Mankiw et al. (1992) and Lucas (1988) stressed the essential role of education as the most important production

5 Empowerment for Economic and Human Capital Development ...

factor in increasing human capital development as a determinant of economic growth. Education helps individuals acquire knowledge which encourages participation in groups, opens doors to job opportunities, develops social interactions, makes individuals aware of their rights, improves health, and reduces poverty (Bouzekri 2015). Nelson and Phelps (1966) and Benhabib and Spiegel (2005) emphasized that education can facilitate the sharing and transmission of knowledge needed for developing new technologies. Therefore, nations without enough human capital development cannot effectively manage their physical capital.

Although many arguments have pointed towards the powerful effects of education on human capital development and subsequently on the economic outcome, some studies do not support the conclusion that the correlation between education and economic growth is significant. These critiques found a negative relationship between human capital and economic growth (Pritchett 1996). This negative effect, however, was due to the lack of human capital measures in those studies. Most of such research on the economic aspects of schooling concentrates only on the quantity of schooling and neglects the importance of quality education because quality cannot be easily measured (Bouzekri 2015). This appears logical because quantity is easily measured, but at the same time it is very crude, and falsifies the reality of education and human capital development (Bouzekri 2015). In addition, research has been conducted based on a wide spectrum of countries from different social, political and economic backgrounds. For instance, education in Papua New Guinea is not the same as education in the US or Finland. The types and quality of education in developing, underdeveloped and developed nations differ. As such, it reflected the discrepancies in the earlier findings which suggested that education does not demonstrate any significant impact on human capital as well as economic development. It is evident that the debate on the impact of education on human capital development and economic development must be centred on the quality of education and the type of education, that is "people-centred education" to draw positive relationships between education, human capital development and economic development.

People Centred-Education for Development

What constitutes people-centred education? According to Nanda and Ikeda (2015), the essential foundation of education is to provide all students with the opportunity to learn and to guide all students to a life of happiness. It is important to realize that the motivation for education should lie in the humanitarian desire to help people in distress. An estimated 36 million people in the ASEAN region still live below the international poverty line (Lian 2017) and hence are still living in distress. The design and configuration of a people-centred education system and structure will affect how successfully education reaches the poorest and most vulnerable people, especially in underdeveloped and developing nations. In addition, there is also a great disparity in the social economic fabric among member states in ASEAN. In ASEAN Vision 2020, leaders of all ASEAN member states have committed to transforming these disparities, transforming ASEAN into a highly competitive region with equitable economic development and reduced poverty and socio-economic disparities. Hence, people-centred education also includes education for the practical side of life, which focuses on closing these disparity gaps through building human capital.

According to Makiguchi "The first aim of education should be to equip the student with the knowledge and skill for practical life. The second aim should be to develop his personality and to enable him to make the right use of this knowledge and skill" (Radhakrishnan 2006). A people-centred education system that focuses on knowledge and skills for practical life will enable and empower even the poorest and most vulnerable people to thrive and transform their lives. In his many years of experience as a teacher, Makiguchi observed widespread suffering and the tragic waste of human potential. For example, in his first posting as a teacher to a remote, rural region of Japan, the children there were very poor and the manners they brought from their impoverished homes were very rough. Makiguchi, however, insisted that:

> They are all equally students. From the viewpoint of education, what difference could there be between them and other students? Even though they may be covered with dust or dirt, but the brilliant light of life shines from their soiled clothes. Why does no one try to see this? (Ikeda 1996)

5 Empowerment for Economic and Human Capital Development ... 85

Makiguchi feels that the teacher and the cruel discrimination of society are all that stands between them. It is therefore necessary to emphasize that educational system and structures that measure only material progress will not benefit the marginalized, rural and poor communities. With the diverse social economic fabric among ASEAN countries, it is clear that "one size education" that only focuses on academic achievements cannot fit all. Unless the poorest and the most vulnerable people can transform their lives through an education system that provides opportunities for them to learn appropriate skills, education will fail to affect economic growth and narrow social economic developmental gaps in the region. As ASEAN moves towards the One Economic Community model, there will be cross-border trade and investment, which requires the support of appropriately skilled labour and mutual recognition arrangements to facilitate the mobility of skilled professionals. Hence, it is only through people-centred education, where every child is given an opportunity to develop skills according to their individual potential; there will always be inequitable development among the ASEAN member states, thus hampering the regional development and economic integration in ASEAN.

Both Mahatma Gandhi and Ikeda view education as a powerful tool in both individual and social transformation (Radhakrishnan 2006). The responsibility of education in social transformation is to make the lives of as many people as possible better, to help make sure no one gets left behind. To live up to this responsibility, the people-centred education system aims to ensure everyone is prepared to face the opportunities and challenges of economic development including employability. Employability here does not only refer to opportunities to be employed and equipped with skills ready for job markets but to be able to seek out opportunities as entrepreneurs and the ability to be self-employed. Being dependent on regional job markets created mainly by more developed nations within the region will not provide equitable opportunities for less economically developed ASEAN member states, especially marginalized communities. Poor communities from less economically developed states will become dependent on the more developed nations, and hence, equitable economic development and integration will remain a far-fetched idea.

This is a very important point to observe given disparities in national GDPs and the apparent disparity in the speed of social economic development among ASEAN member states. For example, current employment trends indicate that by 2025 more than half of all high-skilled employment in Cambodia, Indonesia, Laos, the Philippines, Thailand and Vietnam could be filled by workers with insufficient qualifications (Susantono 2015). The mismatch of skills will persist, and businesses cannot wait for the system to create a pool of skilled labour (Susantono 2015). If dependencies on such job markets persist, unskilled and incompetent workers especially from vulnerable and poor communities from underdeveloped and developing member states will be trapped in the low-income bracket. As such, the poor will remain within the vicious cycle of poverty.

The ASEAN One Economic Community model will be a good model of how nations with different social economic development statuses can leverage on people centred-education to develop knowledge and skills for equitable economic development and integration. The focus of a people-centred education system is on the shared goal of improving education and the quality of life for people in their respective countries within the region. Such an education system focuses on human capital development based on the available natural, social and environmental resources of the respective countries. Fundamentally, the people-centred education system is drawn from three main areas of learning such as the natural environment, the social environment and processes of productive work (Radhakrishnan 2006). Each one of those three sources is of equal importance and unique to their respective countries. These types of education are in support of resource-poor countries that comprise the majority of vulnerable and marginalized communities that cannot afford to leave their countries or villages to seek formal education.

When such communities learn through kinship with nature and the social environment, get training in skills, competencies and knowledge necessary for self-help, self-employment, and even self-assessment, they will progressively become empowered, find employment and become productive citizens of their society, eventually bringing about economic growth. Through such education, these communities will also be able to create their own jobs in their immediate social environment, become economically self-reliant and in turn provide opportunities for the younger generation to pursue higher formal education and break free from the continuous and vicious cycle of poverty. Schools thus need to become the starting point of this new social order. It is the vision of Gandhi and Ikeda to see a new world order (Radhakrishnan 2006), a world without exploitation or discrimination despite the disparity in developmental and economic gaps within the ASEAN region.

Global Citizenship Education

As the late great Nelson Mandela said: "Education is the most powerful weapon which you can use to change the world" (Strauss 2013). If people-centred education systems are established in all ASEAN countries, focusing on human capital development with the aim of not one person being left behind in regional economic development, there is little doubt that the education systems of the region will play a critical role in ASEAN integration. But the idea of achieving integration through education brings with it some apprehension about how ASEAN citizenship and identity will develop, given the broad and diverse cultural, political and economic dimensions that exist within the region.

This will perhaps require a more global educational programme such as global citizenship education to deepen the understanding of the challenges facing the region and humankind in general. While the people-centred education system can empower poor and marginalized communities from underdeveloped and developing ASEAN states to bridge the economic divide, broad global citizenship education helps to deepen understanding of the cultural diversity and challenges imposed across the different societies. Global citizenship education provides an understanding of the challenges facing humankind despite differences in cultural and ethnic background. It instils hope that problems, being of human origin, are amenable to human solutions (Ikeda 2014).

This will bring about an integrated perspective of commonality among all member states across different social, cultural, political and economic backgrounds. It is no doubt that global citizenship education will facilitate the development of solidarity with all ASEAN neighbours and the world. Global citizenship education also helps to identify early signs of impending global problems within local phenomena, empowering people to act (Ikeda 2014). Such awareness will foster the spirit of empathy and coexistence through awareness that actions that profit one's own country might have a negative impact or be perceived as a threat by other countries especially by those in the region.

Therefore, ASEAN integration requires ASEAN citizens to collaborate and unite as one community moving towards developing the ASEAN citizenship and identity. Political instability and territorial tensions as well as economic instability within the region often make integration difficult among ASEAN countries. However, global citizenship education with a strong emphasis on empathy for all member states and the importance of coexistence within the region will no doubt promote ASEAN integration with a common identity. Global citizenship education provides students with opportunities to learn about what it means to be responsible, active citizens, both in the classroom and in the diverse communities in which they belong. In the diverse ASEAN context, it is important to understand that they belong to many communities, and that they are also citizens of ASEAN and the wider global community.

Economic Integration and Development

Economic integration is commonly thought to refer to the interaction between nations or states for mutual economic benefit. Economic liberalization is expected to lead to economic growth and higher income levels, thereafter leading to available financial resources to address environmental problems. However, this is not always the case. In Southeast Asia, rapid economic growth and a desire to attract foreign investment have more often than not had severe impacts on the environment and human health. In areas where natural resources are seen to be of economic value, pristine ecosystems are opened up for development or mining, compromising habitats and threatening traditional livelihoods that depend on them. Indigenous people and local communities are often the most negatively affected by developments such as these, deepening economic inequalities that already exist both within and between states (Clémençon 1997).

5 Empowerment for Economic and Human Capital Development ... 89

Sustainable development is often lauded as the solution to a better balance between economic and environmental goals. There are many definitions of sustainable development. Some maintain that its elasticity contributes to its popularity; the concept can be applied with as little or as many intensities as suits those who wish to declare an environmental conscience (Bryant and Parnwell 1996). Many seem to forget, however, that the concept of sustainable development has a third aspect: social considerations such as equity, social mobility, participation and empowerment (UNESCAP 2004). True sustainable development should thus be inclusive.

Inclusive development takes sustainable development a step further in that it explicitly takes into account matters of social inclusiveness such as (but not limited to) human rights, inequality, redistribution, rural development, entitlement and capabilities concepts. Its goal is to empower the poorest (often in rural areas and involved in fishing, farming and other nature-based livelihoods), through investing in human capital and enhancing opportunities for participation in changing economies. In an extension of ecological inclusiveness, it aims to capacity-build local communities to participate in the protection of, access to and ownership of natural resources and ensure the sustainability of ecosystem services (Gupta and Vegelin 2016).

Poverty in the Midst of Development

While Southeast Asia is recognized as one of the fastest-growing regions in the world, there are great intra-state inequalities, with large numbers of "invisible" poor in what would otherwise be seen as successful countries. There is an irregular distribution of growth either because incomes are unable to keep pace with the general rate of growth or because impoverishment is created or amplified in the process of development. Growing inequality pushes these politically marginal poor (or those constructed to be marginal) out of sight; growth in these areas has harmed them (Rigg 2016).

There are several processes that lead to poverty: dispossession (of resources), displacement (from homes, work or social spaces), loss of security in employment or income, marginalization that excludes them from participation in social or economic life, and disempowerment through the reduction of agency, autonomy or the ability to control or shape their own lives. Rigg (2016, 174) sums it up as a situation in which the poor are "casualties of the violence of environmental changes shaped and driven by neo-liberalism and fast capitalism". In simpler terms, those who depend on natural habitats that might be damaged by development or industrialization suffer when there is pollution from industrial sources, when environmental protection measures are lacking or not enforced, and when human settlements increase in proportion to production and consumption levels (Clémençon 1997).

While all of this is taking place however, those in positions of power use sustainable development branding as a proclamation of their efforts for responsible stewardship of the environment, to solicit donor assistance and to neutralize popular criticism (Bryant and Parnwell 1996). Greenwashing of development projects and claims of green technology; sustainable construction and the use of environmentally friendly or recycled materials are common assertions.

Education to Empower the Poor

When sustainable development is the main maxim of national and business policy, the oft-touted tool to achieve it is education for sustainable development, an evolution of environmental education concepts that have long been in use. In Southeast Asia, the ASEAN has an ASEAN Environmental Education Action Plan (2014–2018) that outlines targets that should be achieved in schools, beyond schools (for sustainable cities, green economies, sustainable production and consumption), and for capacity-building and networking (ASEAN Secretariat 2014). However, the extent to which this policy document has been implemented on the ground is unclear. In a policy paper by the Institute of Global Conflict and Cooperation (IGCC), Clémençon (1997, 14) states:

5 Empowerment for Economic and Human Capital Development ... 91

> ... national sustainable development plans are only valuable to the extent
> that they are operationalised and are being implemented in the field.

This also applies to policies related to environmental education or education for sustainable development.

It has often been shown that conservation efforts on the ground are insufficient to counteract development pressures. Top-down directives such as regional policy documents and regulations are seen to be against local interests and do not engage trust or compliance of those who are directly impacted by both the policies and the development (Dupar and Badenoch 2002). While noble in its goal to improve environmental awareness and attitudes, policies such as the one above rarely translate into environmental action on the ground. They also do little to alleviate social problems that come about because of development pressures on those who depend on natural habitats and healthy ecosystems for their survival.

Education has always been used as an economic tool to build a highly skilled workforce that can help a nation meet its goals. Under inclusive development principles, education can be applied as a tool for social justice, ensuring improvements in rural societies, enabling access to opportunities and facilitating freedom from poverty and inequality (Lall and Vickers 2009). Education offers the poor a ladder up into a life of increased opportunities and the hope of more dignity (Hershock et al. 2007).

The 1977 Tbilisi Declaration for environmental education went beyond the need for environmental sensitivity, awareness, knowledge and attitudes to note the importance of skills acquisition to solve environmental problems. It also emphasized the need for active participation of all levels of society in this effort (Ponniah 1997). It is clear that for any environmental effort to succeed, it must involve local people as they are the ones who have an in-depth understanding of local biodiversity as their lives and livelihoods are directly affected by it (McCarthy 1997).

Clémençon (1997) recommends that public participation be broadened, NGO involvement strengthened and that local communities be made stakeholders in the protection of their natural heritage. In doing

Using Environmental Education as a Tool for Community Empowerment

The earlier section outlines how economic growth can result in the deepening of inequalities and an increase in marginalized poor. While education for sustainable development was a tool proclaimed to improve the ability of all sectors of society to achieve a balance between economic and environmental goals, there has either been little translation of these lofty plans and policies into truly impactful programmes on the ground, or the programmes have not adequately looked into the need to involve and collaborate with the marginalized poor. Economic integration and true inclusive sustainable development can only occur when all elements of society, economy and environment are taken into consideration.

The following section briefly describes a model of inclusive sustainable development that has been implemented over a period of 10 years (between 2008 and 2018). The programme has met several of these inclusive development requirements with some success. This programme (referred to here as KA) was run in a stretch of fishing villages in the southwest of Johor, Malaysia. While the programme did not in fact set out to achieve inclusive development goals, the evolution of the situation on the ground and the gradual empowerment of the local community led to the extent of its activities today.

KA began as an environmental education club for fishing village youth. The organization was set up by a local person with a vision for a better future for village youth, and a desire to see them does more than descend into vice, joblessness and aimlessness. The programme was facilitated by a visitor[1] who visited the local seagrass meadows and

5 Empowerment for Economic and Human Capital Development …

decided to teach local youth about the myriad marine treasures in their backyard. For four years the KA programme worked to combine these two visions and explicitly find ways to empower the local youth and by extension the wider community socially, psychologically, politically and economically.

Using environmental education as a tool, the KA programme worked to help the local community understand the value of their natural habitats through its youth. Experiential techniques were used to teach and garner interest, and also included coaching in speaking and presentation skills. Part of the marine science programme included citizen science training in which internationally recognized monitoring methods were used to document and monitor the coastal habitats. The knowledge gained in all these activities was enhanced by sessions with marine scientists, field trips to similar habitats and presentation opportunities at universities and other public fora. The youths' ability to partake in these activities awarded them with social and psychological empowerment as they were recognized as respected representatives of the village and local habitat experts.

The youth were then trained to adapt the knowledge they had into ecotourism guiding content, from which they were able to earn some pocket money as they shared what they knew with visitors and school groups. These small ecotourism efforts also provided additional income to the wider community through boat rental and catering services. This thus allowed them all to gain some economic benefits through sustainable activities. The natural habitats in this area, as with many other similar locations throughout Southeast Asia, face irreversible and unavoidable threats from coastal development and urbanization. Political empowerment came about for the youth when they were consulted by local adults and developers for information on local habitats and advice on the consequences of construction in the area.

This phase of the KA programme surpassed a number of the targets listed in the ASEAN Environmental Education Action Plan and encompassed many if not all of the stipulations listed in the Tbilisi Declaration. In 2014 however, extensive habitat damage from coastal development landed on the community and the KA co-founders decided to adapt their goals to ensure that the community could adapt to, participate in and benefit from the inevitable changes confronting them. The local vision took over the driving seat of the programme, and decisions made were based on consultations with other members of the community and the participating youths themselves; many of whom began to start work full-time for the KA programme.

The power to manage natural resources can be allocated beyond formal state structures (Dupar and Badenoch 2002). In this case, the KA programme actively resisted existing power structures by devising alternative sustainable incomes in the face of externally imposed habitat damage and loss of local livelihoods. Local people can be tapped as integral parts in conservation because they deal with the habitats daily and have a deep affinity with and knowledge of the ecosystems (Djohani 1996). In the case of KA, the community combined the scientific knowledge gained by the youth in the first phase of the programme with traditional ecological knowledge to create more holistic information that is now used in ecotourism and engagement with various other stakeholders (local businesses and developers, government agencies and the state port authority).

Ecotourism is often upheld as the epitome of sustainable and inclusive development activities, but the true success of ecotourism in terms of its ability to empower communities and protect the environment depends largely on who controls the ecotourism activity. Small-scale activities that provide long-term economic benefits to a community that is seen as stakeholders and decision-makers will have more positive impacts than an ecotourism effort that has been taken over by the tourism industry (Cochrane 1996). In the KA programme, the local community maintains control of local tourism and keeps it at a locally manageable level while engaging with external stakeholders such as the state tourism council, the regional development agency and surrounding property developers for support. This ability to engage beyond the grass-roots level further enhances their political and psychological empowerment.

Dupar and Badenoch (2002) state that decision-making powers must be given to local levels of society. Solving environmental problems and changing attitudes or behaviour can only come about when local communities are actively involved in identifying problems and

5 Empowerment for Economic and Human Capital Development …

devising necessary remedial actions (McCarthy 1997). Because local people have the best understanding of the context, conditions and issues on the ground, they are best-suited to contribute to effective problem-solving. In the KA programme, all decisions related to alternative income development, conservation efforts, tourism and capacity-building for jobs are made by the local community. Any outsiders involved in the programme are merely advisors and facilitators, assisting the community where necessary with the means to achieve their goals.

Empowerment of the community through the KA programme led to locally led initiatives for sustainable alternative livelihoods in the face of habitat damage and depreciation of traditional sources of incomes and increased social capital in terms of cooperation across social and political boundaries (Dupar and Badenoch 2002). The charisma and leadership of the local founder, as well as his vision for the KA programme helped otherwise antagonistic members of the local community to come together in a common goal of surviving the changes brought upon them by externally imposed plans for economic growth. Even as the KA programme supports capacity-building provides opportunities for alternative and supplementary incomes (through tourism and youth entrepreneurship), it maintains its goals of habitat documentation, monitoring and environmental education. Combining multiple objectives, the programme is now in the process of setting up a Nature and Heritage Centre to showcase local heritage so as to consolidate and strengthen ecotourism efforts to support the wider community. It is also currently in negotiations with the state government and other authorities to allow community management of local natural resources.

The Next Step: Economic Integration

As discussed earlier, macro-level economic integration has often led to ecological damage. ASEAN has several environmental education and sustainable development networks in place (Soerjani 1997), but the ability of these networks to enable the marginalized poor to benefit economically from environmental efforts and protect the natural habitats that they depend on is uncertain. Grass-roots networks, however, can

96   W. M. T. Yee and S. Rahman

enable the sharing of experiences and mutual learning for better application of environmental principles to inclusive and sustainable development. However, the establishment of grass-roots networks, not unlike those currently in existence for environmental youth leaders, can enable participants and drivers of programmes based on environmental education such as KA to widen their horizons, derive new ideas and solutions and spawn similar programmes in other parts of Southeast Asia.

Regional economic integration can only be truly effective if there is domestic economic integration and inclusivity. Facilitating and empowering the marginalized poor and rural communities to access and maximize opportunities will help them integrate economically with the rest of the country. Thereafter, the various local communities can come together in grass-roots economic integration efforts to lift the Southeast Asian economy as a whole by ensuring that economic growth reaches all corners of the region. Using tourism as the platform for this economic integration and promoting various sustainable community ecotourism localities through a holistic regional tourism offering can help to boost incomes, reduce poverty and facilitate economic integration. While it is clear that efforts such as the KA programme take time to reach fruition, the problem of partially obscured poverty and unequal economic growth must be dealt with immediately to ensure regional social and political stability and the long-term sustainability of growth itself. At the base of any effort to alleviate economic difficulties and inequalities is education. People-centred education that examines and meets individual needs enable rural, marginalized and disempowered communities a step up towards economic participation, thereafter paving the way to true ASEAN economic integration.

Note

1. This visitor is the second author of this paper. More information on this programme can be found at the following website: http://kelabalami. weebly.com.

References

ASEAN Secretariat. 2014. *ASEAN Environmental Education Action Plan 2014–2018*. Jakarta: ASEAN Secretariat.

Benhabib, Jess, and Mark M. Spiegel. 2005. "Humans Capital and Technological Diffusion." In *Handbook of Economic Growth*, edited by P. Aghion and S. Durlauf, 935–966. Amsterdam: North Holland.

Bouzekri, Dhikra. 2015. "The Role of Education as Human Capital and a Determinant of Economic Growth." *Morocco World News*. Accessed April 19, 2018. https://www.moroccoworldnews.com/2015/04/156723/role-education-human-capital-determinant-economic-growth/.

Bryant, Raymond L., and Michael J. G. Parnwell. 1996. "Politics, Sustainable Development and Environmental Change in Southeast Asia." In *Environmental Change in Southeast Asia: People, Politics and Sustainable Development*, edited by M. J. G. Parnwell and R. L. Bryant, 1–20. London: Routledge.

Clémençon, Raymond. 1997. "Economic Integration and Environment in Southeast Asia." Policy Paper No. 30. UC San Diego, CA: Institute of Global Conflict and Cooperation.

Cochrane, John. 1996. "The Sustainability of Ecotourism in Indonesia: Fact and Fiction." In *Environmental Change in Southeast Asia: People, Politics and Sustainable Development*, edited by M. J. G. Parnwell and R. L. Bryant, 237–259. London: Routledge.

Djohani, Rili Hawari. 1996. "The Bajau: Future Marine Park Managers in Indonesia?" In *Environmental Change in Southeast Asia: People, Politics and Sustainable Development*, edited by M. J. G. Parnwell and R. L. Bryant, 260–268. London: Routledge.

Dupar, Mairi Kristina, and Nathan Badenoch. 2002. *Environment, Livelihoods and Local Institutions: Decentralisation in Mainland Southeast Asia*. Washington, DC: World Resources Institute.

Goulah, Jason, and Andrew Gebert. 2009. "Tsunesaburo Makiguchi: Introduction to the Man, His Ideas, and the Special Issue." *Educational Studies* 45 (2): 115–132.

Gupta, Joyeeta, and Courtney Vegelin. 2016. "Sustainable Development Goals and Inclusive Development." *International Environmental Agreements: Politics, Law and Economics* 16: 433–448.

Hershock, Peter D., Mark Mason, and John N. Hawkins, eds. 2007. *Changing Education: Leadership Innovation and Development in a Globalising*

Asia-Pacific. Studies in Comparative Education No. 20. Hong Kong: Springer.

Ikeda, Daisaku. 1996. *Thoughts on Education for Global Citizenship*. Lecture delivered at Teachers College, Columbia University, June 13, 1996. Accessed December 20, 2018. http://www.daisakuikeda.org/sub/resources/works/lect/lect-08.html.

Ikeda, Daisaku. 2014. "Value Creation for Global Change: Building Resilient and Sustainable Societies." *2014 Peace Proposal. Shinjuku: Soka Gakkai International*. Accessed January 8, 2016. http://www.sgi.org/content/files/about-us/president-ikedas-proposals/peaceproposal2014.pdf.

Ikeda, Daisaku. 2018. "john-dewey-and-tsunesaburo-makiguchi | Center for Dewey Studies | SIU." *Center for Dewey Studies*. Accessed May 31, 2018. https://deweycenter.siu.edu/publications-papers/john-dewey-and-tsunesaburo-makiguchi.php.

Lall, Marie, and Edward Vickers, eds. 2009. *Education as a Political Tool in Asia*. New York: Routledge.

Lian, Buan. 2017. "Southeast Asia's Poorest Mostly Filipinos, Indonesians—ASEAN Report." *Rappler*. Accessed March 12, 2018. https://www.rappler.com/world/regions/asia-pacific/188918-asean-report-poverty-philippines-indonesia.

Lucas, Robert E. 1988. "On the Mechanics of Economic Development." *Journal of Monetary Economics* 22: 3–43.

Mankiw, N. Gregory, David Romer, and David N. Weil. 1992. "A Contribution to the Empirics of Economic Growth." *Quarterly Journal of Economics* 107: 407–437.

McCarthy, J. 1997. "Bringing the Environment Back to the Village: Some Thoughts on Environmental Education in Indonesia." In *Environmental Education for Biodiversity and Sustainable Development*, edited by M. Soerjani and M. Hale, 267–270. Jakarta: University of Indonesia.

Nanda, Ved P., and Daisaku Ikeda. 2015. *Our World to Make: Hinduism, Buddhism and the Rise of Global Civil Society*. 1st ed. Cambridge, MA: Dialogue Path Press.

Nelson, Richard R., and Edmund S. Phelps. 1966. "Investment in Humans, Technological Diffusion and Economic Growth." *The American Economic Review* 56: 69–75.

Ponniah, Wimala. 1997. "Environmental Education for Sustainable Development in Post-Unced Process." In *Environmental Education for Biodiversity and Sustainable Development*, edited by M. Soerjani and M. Hale, 2–32. Jakarta: University of Indonesia.

Prichett, Lant. 1996. "Where Has All the Education Gone?" Policy Research Working Paper No. 1581. The World Bank.

Radhakrishnan, N. 2006. *The Living Dialogue: Socrates to Ikeda*. 1st ed. New Delhi: Gandhi Media Centre.

Rigg, Jonathan. 2016. *Challenging Southeast Asian Development: The Shadows of Success*. Abingdon and New York: Routledge.

Soerjani, M. 1997. "ASEAN Region Network on Environmental Education (ARNEE): Preliminary Ideas to Promote Mutual Cooperation." In *Environmental Education for Biodiversity and Sustainable Development*, edited by M. Soerjani and M. Hale, 473–484. Jakarta: University of Indonesia.

Strauss, Valerie. 2013. "Nelson Mandela on the Power of Education." *Washington Post*, December 5. Accessed September 30, 2014. https://www.washingtonpost.com/news/answer-sheet/wp/2013/12/05/nelson-mandelas-famous-quote-on-education/?noredirect=on&utm_term=.ab79406c6429.

Susantono, Bambang. 2015. "Stopping Asean's Brain Drain: Philippine Daily Inquirer." *The Straits Times*. Accessed February 22, 2017. https://www.straitstimes.com/asia/se-asia/stopping-aseans-brain-drain-philippine-daily-inquirer.

United Nations. 2004. "Integrating Economic and Environmental Policies: The Case of Pacific Island Countries." Development Papers No. 25. New York: United Nations Economic and Social Commission for Asia and the Pacific (UNESCAP).

6

ASEAN Qualification Reference Framework: Harmonization of ASEAN Higher Education Area

Zita Mohd Fahmi, Usharani Balasingam and Jake M. Laguador

History of Association of Southeast Asian Nations (ASEAN)

ASEAN was formed on 8 August 1967 by means of Bangkok Declaration (ASEAN Declaration) to foster trust among the five founder states, Indonesia, Malaysia, Philippines, Singapore and Thailand through meetings of the foreign ministers known as ASEAN Ministerial Meetings. It was a reaction to the issues of territorial boundaries, the Cold War, peace and security of the new fledging independent

---

Z. Mohd Fahmi
Former Secretary to ASEAN Quality Assurance Agency (AQAN),
Quest International University Perak, Ipoh, Malaysia

U. Balasingam (✉)
University of Malaya, Kuala Lumpur, Malaysia
e-mail: usha@um.edu.my

J. M. Laguador
Lyceum of the Philippines University, Batangas City, Philippines

© The Author(s) 2019
A. Idris and N. Kamaruddin (eds.), *ASEAN Post-50*,
https://doi.org/10.1007/978-981-13-8043-3_6

states from colonial powers (save for Thailand).[1] The objectives emphasized growth and social development of the members, the promotion of regional peace and stability and the development of mutual cooperation in various fields (Woon 2015, 4).[2] Brunei (1987), Vietnam (1995), Laos (1997), Myanmar (1997) and Cambodia (1999) (the latter four referred to by the acronym CLVM) were later additions as full members pursuant to ASEAN ideals of inclusiveness (Woon 2015, 8).[3] The ASEAN Secretariat is housed in Jakarta, Indonesia.

The ASEAN Heads of States/Governments, at their summit in Kuala Lumpur in December 1997 in the 30th anniversary promulgated Vision 2020 (later accelerated to 2015 at the 12th ASEAN summit in the Philippines) which envisioned a concert of Southeast Asian nations, outward looking, living in peace, stability and prosperity, bonded together in partnership in dynamic development and in a community of caring societies. The Ninth ASEAN Summit in Bali (2003) adopted the Declaration of ASEAN Concord 11 (Bali Concord 11) where the vision of ASEAN community three pillars namely political and security, economic and sociocultural cooperation was initiated. The ASEAN Charter came into force on 15 December 2008 which created five councils ASEAN Political-Security Community Council (APSC), ASEAN Economic Community Council (AECC) and the Socio-Cultural Community Council (ASCC), ASEAN Coordinating Council (ACC) and the Committee of Permanent Representatives (CPR) established. The other landmark is the ASEAN Human Rights Declaration (AHRD) which was adopted in 2012 in Phnom Penh, Cambodia (Woon 2015, 14).

The importance of the right to education is such that, according to the United Nations' Committee on Economic, Social and Cultural Rights (CESCR, 20th Session 1999), it *"epitomizes the indivisibility and interdependence of all human rights"*.[4]

ASEAN Education: The Backbone of the Three Pillars

The area of education that includes skills and training is invariably linked to human resource capital development. It is an undercurrent that runs across all three pillars of the ASEAN community. The intrinsic value of the education is significant in that provides the means of economic prosperity that is the cornerstone of political-security and translates to a caring and humane community in the sociocultural context.

Hence, education is the crucial integration mechanism that cut across the divides and provides a link through all three pillars of the ASEAN community. This is reflected by the statement in ASEAN Ministers of Education First Meeting (Singapore, 2006) that education *"permeates through all the three pillars of the ASEAN Community in enhancing competitiveness of the individual member states as well as ASEAN as a region"*. The Cha-am Hua Hin Declaration on the Roadmap of ASEAN Community (2009–2015) emphasized the importance of the education sector *"to achieving enduring solidarity and unity among the nations and peoples of ASEAN"*. The initiatives were to promote regional integration and cooperation in higher education.

Charter of the Association of Southeast Asian Nations (2007), (Chapter I, Article 1, paras. 5 and 10).

The ASEAN Charter (2007) aims to: "create a single market and production base which is stable, prosperous, highly competitive and economically integrated with effective facilitation for trade and investment in which there is free flow of goods, services and investment; facilitated movement of business persons, professionals, talents and labour; and free flow of capital" and *"develop human resources through closer cooperation in education and life-long learning and in science and technology, for the empowerment of the peoples of ASEAN and for the strengthening of the ASEAN Community" (Chapter I, Article 1, paras. 5 and 10).*

The ASEAN Charter recognizes the interrelationship of education (human capital development), the economy cum the labour market, peace and social inclusiveness. To enable and empower the creation of a single market from an economic and education standpoint, there is a need for transferability and recognition of levels knowledge and skills associated with desired learning outcomes, namely a key instrument being a regional qualification framework arising from the national qualification framework (NQF) which is to be quality assured by trusted accreditation and quality assured processes.

A qualification framework has been defined as *"An instrument for the development and classification of qualifications (e.g. at national or sectoral level) according to a set of criteria (e.g. using descriptors) applicable to specified levels of learning outcomes".*

ASEAN Economic Ministers endorsed the Asian Qualifications Reference framework in August 2014; the ASEAN Education Ministers in September 2014; and the ASEAN Labour Ministers through Ad-referendum from November 2014 to May 2015.

The harmonisation of higher education infrastructure is reflected in the Kuala Lumpur Declaration 2015 which is directed to create a common space as well as the implementation framework. This framework focuses on quality assurance, qualifications framework, student mobility and technical and vocational education and training (TVET) (Lythe 2009). There are already early steps taken towards understanding various national systems particularly to explore the issue of harmonisation. It is to be recognized that the traditional academic pathway has traditionally been more developed while the TVET pathway is more recent in terms of the development of common standards and levels and the receiving formal recognition and accreditation. The High Official Meeting (23–26 August 2015, Chiangmai Thailand) on "SEA (Southeast Asia)-TVET: Working towards Harmonization and Internationalisation" set out strategies for cooperation of TVET in SEA: firstly to cooperate, share and review NQF to that of the ASEAN Qualification Framework, secondly to develop a SEA-TVET consortium and thirdly to have four (4) regional priority areas, namely hospitality and tourism, agriculture and fisheries, electronics, mechatronics and manufacturing and construction with a common competency standard which is being realized.

This lead to the formation of SEA-TVET consortium which comprises TVET institutions in SEAMEO member countries that agree to work together to harmonize and internationalize their programmes through curriculum harmonisation, student and staff exchange, industrial attachment and resource sharing (Paryono 2016).[5] ASEAN countries are in different stages of development and maturity. The TVET scope and means of delivery are tied to economic needs and challenges.

In March 2016, the ASEAN Socio-Cultural Community Blueprint was launched that advocates the promotion of an innovative ASEAN approach to higher education *"which will promote greater people to people interaction within and outside ASEAN"*. This includes mobility programmes which are intended to facilitate free flows of ideas, knowledge and skills to inject dynamism within the region.

It is envisaged that regional and global cooperation will enhance the quality and competitiveness of ASEAN higher education institutions. The tie into international higher education cooperation within the Asia Pacific and European Union regions are also within the vision to make ASEAN citizens valued, mobile and recognized internationally.

ASEAN Ministerial Meeting on Education (ASED), Work Plan, Linkages and Support

The ASED website underscores the fact that education underpins ASEAN community building. Its core is to create a knowledge based society and to enhance the regional cooperation in education.[6] This contributes to the understanding of the richness of ASEAN's history, languages, culture and common values to create the "we feeling" in the ASEAN community. ASEAN leaders during the summit in Dec 2005 set new directions for regional education collaboration when they welcomed the decision of the ASEAN Education Ministers to convene the ASEAN Education Ministers' Meetings (ASED) on a regular basis.

The ASEAN Education Ministers identified four priorities that ASEAN cooperation on education would address, namely (i) promoting ASEAN awareness among ASEAN citizens, particularly youth; (ii) strengthening ASEAN identity through education; (iii) building ASEAN human resources in the field of education; and (iv) strengthening ASEAN university networking. To this end, various projects and activities have been or are being developed or organized to fulfil the directives.

The collaboration and complementary arrangement of respective programmes and activities of ASEAN and SEAMEO forums on education were agreed by the Education Ministers in order to address the priorities on ASEAN. SEAMEO has contributed to human resource development in the region since 1965.

ASEAN cooperation on education is overseen at the ministerial level by an ASEAN Education Ministers' Meeting—which meets annually—and the implementation of the programmes and activities for education matters is carried out by the ASEAN Senior Officials on Education (SOM-ED), which reports to the ASEAN Education Ministers' Meeting. SOM-ED also oversees cooperation on higher education. The AUN was established to serve as an ASEAN mechanism to (i) promote cooperation among ASEAN scholars, academicians and scientists in the region; (ii) develop academic and professional human resource in the region; (iii) promote information dissemination among the ASEAN academic community; and (iv) enhance the awareness of regional identity and the sense of "ASEANness" among members.

Julio Amador III, an Asia Studies Visiting Fellow at the East–West Center in Washington (2013), listed down in a policy brief eight issues the country, Philippines and others must ponder on as ASEAN member state (AMS): the member state policy framework for commitment to ASEAN and the role of higher education to contribute to it; expansion of AUN membership; the mutual recognition of university degrees; synchronization of academic calendar; the state of the ASEAN studies with the member states; student and faculty mobility; the regional scholarships; and collaboration in research and extension (Geronomic 2013).[7]

Following on the ASEAN Socio-Cultural Community Blueprint 2025, the ASEAN Work Plan on Education 2016–2020 includes as key priorities strengthening the implementation of quality assurance mechanisms in the higher education sector as well as the socio-economic development through university-industry partnership (ASEAN 2018e). The Work Plan on Education expands education cooperation in ASEAN towards the development of a more coordinated, cohesive and coherent ASEAN position and its links to global education goals.

In 2015, the ASEAN leaders acknowledged higher education as a catalyst in achieving economic and sociocultural goals of ASEAN and welcomed the adoption of the Kuala Lumpur Declaration on Higher Education at the 27th ASEAN Summit. Cooperation on higher education in ASEAN has gained momentum with the full swing implementation of the European Union Support to Higher Education in ASEAN Region (SHARE) on the same year for a four-year period. The SHARE is a flagship project of the ASEAN Education Sector that aims to promote harmonisation of higher education and introduce an ASEAN scholarship inspired by the EU's Erasmus Mundus to create space for higher education in ASEAN.

The ASEAN Education Sector is governed by and under the purview of the ASEAN Ministers of Education Meeting (ASED) which convenes bi-annually and the ASEAN Senior Officials Meeting on Education (SOM-ED) which meets annually. Chairmanship of both meetings rotates alphabetically between the AMS and was held by Malaysia in the period 2016–2017. The ASEAN Secretariat supports coordination of sectoral activities through the Education, Youth and Sports Division (EYSD) and liaises with the SEAMEO Secretariat as well as with ASEAN Dialogue Partners and international organizations. Two ASEAN bodies focus specifically on education, the ASEAN University Network (AUN), headquartered in Bangkok, Thailand, and the ASEAN Quality Assurance Network (AQAN), headquartered in Kuala Lumpur, Malaysia.[8]

The Kuala Lumpur Declaration on Higher Education (2015) agrees to: (i) acknowledge higher education as one of the catalysts in accelerating ASEAN's economic, political and sociocultural development agenda; (ii) uphold quality in the provision of higher education across all member states; (iii) enhance the academic contribution of ASEAN higher education within the global academic community; (iv) embrace diversity and solidarity of the ASEAN Community through enhanced intra-ASEAN mobility of students and scholars; (v) contribute to the promotion of peace, prosperity, resilience and vibrancy of ASEAN through synergized collaboration between the academia, industry, government and community; (vi) foster sustainable local community development through participation of youth, professionals and volunteers in entrepreneurial endeavours; (vii) build an innovation-driven ASEAN Community with critical thinking capability and skill through capacity building offered by higher education institutions within ASEAN, such as opportunities for lifelong learning, TVET, online and blended learning, postgraduate education, transnational education and other flexible learning options; (viii) contribute to sustainable development through academic programmes, research, community development and stakeholder engagement; (ix) increase the visibility of ASEAN globally through increased thought leadership in various disciplines of higher education at regional and international levels. The ASEAN Ministerial Meeting on Education (ASED) is tasked to report to regularly through the ASEAN Socio-Cultural Community Council on the progress of the implementation (ASED 2016).[9]

Taking two year's term from May 2016 to May 2018, Malaysia's chairmanship focuses on the theme "*Fostering ASEAN Community of Learners – Empowering Lives Through Education*" which underscores the potential of education to ensure sustained economic growth, shared prosperity, political stability and social progress in ASEAN (ASEAN 2018g).

At the ASED meeting in 2016, the ASEAN Education Ministers have also directed the alignment of the plans under the ASEAN Plus Three Cooperation on Education and East Asia Summit Cooperation on Education, with the ASEAN Work Plan on Education 2016–2020. In support of the efficient implementation of said work plan, the ASEAN Education Ministers approved three key documents on education, namely the ASEAN Declaration on Strengthening Education for Out-of-School Children and Out-of-School Youth, the ASEAN Qualifications Reference Framework (AQRF) Governance and Structure and the revised Charter of the AUN.

Existing and new partners pledged support to ASEAN and the implementation of the ASEAN Work Plan on Education 2016–2020, namely UNESCO, UNICEF, SEAMEO and Teach for All Network as regards learning outcomes and metrics, teacher training and promotion of shared values. The progress of ongoing ASEAN projects was reported including those on higher education, TVET, qualifications frameworks, quality assurance, student mobility, credit transfer, university collaboration and people-to-people connectivity.

The ASEAN Education Ministers commended efforts of project implementers and their efforts through existing ASEAN frameworks including the AUN, the AUN Southeast Asia Engineering Education Development Network, the ASEAN-EU Cooperation on Education on Support to Higher Education in ASEAN Region, the GIZ Regional Cooperation Programme to Improve the Training of TVET Personnel, the Fulbright US-ASEAN Initiative and Connecting the Mekong through Education and Training Project.[10]

ASEAN Qualification Reference Framework (AQRF)

History

It is to be acknowledged that economic consideration was the underlying push for an AQRF. Further that this was a push supported by New Zealand and Australia in furtherance of an ASEAN-Australia-New Zealand Free Trade Area (AANZFTA).

The driver concept paper *Project on Education and Training Governance: Capacity Building for National Qualifications Frameworks* was supported by the Agreement Establishing the AANZFTA Economic Cooperation Support Programme (AECSP). Under the programme's services component, the concept proposal was considered at the 1st Meeting of the AANZFTA FTA Joint Committee (FJC) in May 2010 in Manila, the Philippines and approved inter-sessionally in July 2010.

The AQRF was developed in 2014 by a task force (TF-AQRF) comprising officials from ASEAN ministries of trade, labour and manpower development, education, as well as other relevant qualification agencies.

The AQRF was endorsed by the ASEAN Economic Ministers (AEM) in August 2014; the ASEAN Education Ministers (ASED) in September 2014; and the ASEAN Labour Ministers (ALMM) through ad-referendum in May 2015 (ASEAN 2018b).

Following the endorsement, the TF-AQRF continued to develop the implementation mechanism of AQRF which the task force had begun to discuss in the 4th TF-AQRF meeting in March 2014 in Yangon, Myanmar. The discussion and development of the implementation mechanisms of AQRF continued until the official final meeting of the TF-AQRF (7th meeting held in October 2015, in Bangkok, Thailand).

Once this is completed, the focus shifts to the future wherein a governance structure and interim governance mechanism need to be factored into play. The stated development above and the governance structure and mechanism are as provided in the AQRF Governance and Structure.[11]

It is also stated in the same document that pending formalization and the setting up of the ASEAN Committee, the AMS agreed at the 7th meeting. The work of TF-AQRF leading up to the formal establishment of the AQRF Committee to oversee the implementation of AQRF would be supported by an interim committee. The activities and establishment of the AQRF would be supported externally by Australia and New Zealand from June 2016 to June 2018 as endorsed by the AANZFTA FJC at their 8th meeting, 13–18 March 2016, Melbourne, Australia.

During this transition period, the fourth phase of the AQRF project would support the establishment of the AQRF Committee and the referencing to the AQRF of at least two AMS, and Australia and New Zealand would be invited as nonvoting members and/or experts.

Structure and Function: AQRF Committee

The structure reflects the link between education, work and the economy bringing the relevant players and stakeholders into the framework. There is a three-tier level of hierarchical relationship. At the highest level are the three ministerial meetings of the Education, Economics and Labour of the ASEAN region. The next level is the AQRF Committee and below that is the NQF Committees. The objective is to ensure there is trust in the AQRF. This is by ensuring that the qualification framework is validated by the outcomes ascribed, namely.

To consider whether or not a referencing report submitted by each National AQRF Committee meets the AQRF referencing criteria and advises the National AQRF Committee on how all the criteria could be met.

To promote the use of the AQRF among AMS to enable support for lifelong learning.

To promote the quality assurance processes that underpin the AQRF and to foster the use of quality assurance frameworks as a benchmark.

To facilitate the AQRF process in addressing emerging regional and international qualifications framework issues in the regional and international arena, including linkages to qualifications recognition.

To enhance the effectiveness of the AQRF by monitoring and evaluating its implementation, including a review of the AQRF Committee's membership, operations and its TOR.

To periodically report to the three ASEAN Ministerial bodies on progress and activities and on further strategic steps to improve regional and national consistency and relevance.

To provide information and advice on the AQRF to interested parties.

To share approaches for further capacity building related to AQRF among AMS.[12]

It has been reported that four (4) AMS states have announced their intention to reference in 2018. The four states are Indonesia, Malaysia, Philippines and Thailand.[13]

The Framework of ASIAN Qualification Reference Framework (AQRF)

AMS are varying uniquely with different population sizes, composition, development levels, sizes of the economy and without a common language that could cut across the divides. This, in turn, has its effect and is reflected in the varying maturity of the NQF. Some AMS has established comprehensive NQFs, others have sectoral frameworks in place, and others have yet to develop or implement qualifications frameworks. The AQRF factors this in as well as the facet of education encompassing training and skills and lifelong learning within its framework.[14]

The purpose of the AQRF as articulated in the document is namely to support recognition of qualifications; encourage the development of qualifications frameworks that can facilitate lifelong learning; encourage the development of national approaches to validating learning gained outside formal education; promote and encourage education and learner mobility; promote worker mobility; lead to better understanding of qualifications systems; and promote higher quality qualifications systems (CEDEFOP 2017).

It is noted that the AQRF is the second regional framework after the European Qualification Framework (EQF) to attain operational

112   Z. Mohd Fahmi et al.

Table 6.1 AQRF level descriptors

	Knowledge and skills	Application and responsibility
	Demonstration of knowledge and skills that:	The contexts in which knowledge and skills are demonstrated:
Level 8	Is at the most advanced and specialized level and at the frontier of a field	Are highly specialized and complex involving the development and testing of new theories and new solutions to resolve complex, abstract issues
	Involve independent and original thinking and research, resulting in the creation of new knowledge or practice	Require authoritative and expert judgment in management of research or an organization and significant responsibility for extending professional knowledge and practice and creation of new ideas and or processes
Level 7	Is at the forefront of a field and show mastery of a body of knowledge	Are complex and unpredictable and involve the development and testing of innovative solutions to resolve issues
	Involve critical and independent thinking as the basis for research to extend or redefine knowledge or practice	Require expert judgment and significant responsibility for professional knowledge, practice and management
Level 6	Is specialized technical and theoretical within a specific field	Are complex and changing
	Involve critical and analytical thinking	Require initiative and adaptability as well as strategies to improve activities and to solve complex and abstract issues
Level 5	Is detailed technical and theoretical knowledge of a general field	Are often subject to change
	Involve analytical thinking	Involve independent evaluation of activities to resolve complex and sometimes abstract issues
Level 4	Is technical and theoretical with general coverage of a field	Are generally predictable but subject to change
	Involve adapting processes	Involve broad guidance requiring some self-direction and coordination to resolve unfamiliar issues

(continued)

Table 6.1 (continued)

	Knowledge and skills	Application and responsibility
	Demonstration of knowledge and skills that:	The contexts in which knowledge and skills are demonstrated:
Level 3	Includes general principles and some conceptual aspects Involve selecting and applying basic methods, tools, materials and information	Are stable with some aspects subject to change Involve general guidance and require judgment and planning to resolve some issues independently
Level 2	Is general and factual Involve use of standard actions	Involve structured processes Involve supervision and some discretion for judgment on resolving familiar issues
Level 1	Is basic and general Involve simple, straightforward and routine actions	Involve structured routine processes Involve close levels of support and supervision

Source AQRF

status in 2017 (CEDEFOP 2017).[15] The framework is structured in ensuring that the learning outcomes of the qualification descriptors of which there are eight (8) levels are quality assured in the context of the domains of knowledge and skills and application and responsibility. While there is no stated credit value in the AQRF, it is encouraged within the national framework for reason of comparison between member states.

The linking of the levels of the member states to that of the AQRF is the process to ensure comparability of qualifications in AMS states. The process in which this is done is detailed in the AQRF document. The year 2018 will see the four (4) member states as previously mentioned undergo the referencing process and report. The 8 levels described in the AQRF (sourced from AQRF) is reproduced as follows (Table 6.1).

The movement towards an AQRF has hastened the progress of the NQF framework in some countries. However, the realities in the differing stages of development within the 10 ASEAN are noted in the study conducted by Bateman and Coles (2015).[16]

NQF Level of Establishment

Each ASEAN country is at a different stage of planning or implementation of an NQF. The development of an NQF can be categorized according to the following general categories.

1. No intent;
2. Desired but no progress made;
3. Background planning underway;
4. Initial development and design completed;
5. Some structures and processes agreed and documented;
6. Some structures and processes established and operational;
7. Structures and processes established for five years; and
8. Review of structures and processes proposed or underway.

Table 6.2 outlines the level of establishment of NQFs in the region in a study by Bateman and Coles (2016).

The same study summarized the ASEAN national qualification framework architecture as reproduced in Table 6.3 (Bateman and Coles 2015).

Table 6.2 National qualification framework (NQF) summary

Country	Level of establishment	Stage
Brunei Darussalam	Inaugurated 2013, implemented	6
Cambodia	Inaugurated 2012, initial stages of implementation	5
Indonesia	Inaugurated 2012, initial stages of implementation	6
Lao PDR	Planned	3
Malaysia	Inaugurated 2007, fully implemented and at review stage	8
Myanmar	Planned	3
Philippines	Inaugurated 2012, initial stages of implementation	5
Singapore	Sector QF—Workforce Skills Qualifications system, Inaugurated 2003	7
Thailand	Inaugurated 2014, initial stages of implementation, 3 established sub-frameworks (i.e. skills, professional, and higher education)	4
Vietnam	Planned	3

Source Bateman and Coles (2015)

6 ASEAN Qualification Reference Framework … 115

Bateman and Coles (2013)[17] came up with tables of comparison between the regional and national framework and also between four regional frameworks which are reproduced in Tables 6.4 and 6.5.

Table 6.3 Summary of ASEAN national qualification framework

Summary of NQF architecture source			
Country	Level	Domain	Credit
Brunei Darussalam	8	• Knowledge and skills (the types of knowledge and skills involved) • Practice: Applied knowledge and understanding (the context in which the knowledge and skills are applied) • Generic cognitive skills • Communications, ICT and numeracy skills • Autonomy, accountability and working with others (the level of independence)	H Ed—40 hours of national learning = 1 TVET—10 hours of national learning = 1
Cambodia	8	• Knowledge • Cognitive skills • Psychomotor skills • Interpersonal skills and responsibility • Communication, information technology and numerical skills	Varies depending on methodology
Indonesia	9	Consists of 2 parts: • General—characteristics, personalities, working attitudes, ethics and morality • Specific: 1. Skills in fulfilling the job and competence 2. Science/knowledge 3. Methods and level of competence in applying science/knowledge 4. #Management skills	Yes—in Higher Education+
Lao PDR*	8	• Knowledge • Skills application • Social skills	–

(continued)

116   Z. Mohd Fahmi et al.

Table 6.3 (continued)

Summary of NQF architecture source

Country	Level	Domain	Credit
Malaysia	8	• Knowledge • Practical skills • Social skills and responsibilities, values, attitudes and professionalism • Communication, leadership and team skills • Problem-solving and scientific skills • Information management and lifelong learning skills • Managerial and entrepreneurial skills	40 hours = 1 credit point
Myanmar*	8	• Knowledge and skills • Application and competence • Responsibility	–
Philippines	8	• Knowledge, skills and values application • Degree of independence (autonomy and responsibility)	–
Singapore	6	Level of knowledge and skills involved • Level of application of the knowledge and skills • Level of accountability, independence, self-organization or organization of others that is required to solve problems or complete tasks • Cognisant of the occupational levels and range and depth of the knowledge and skills required of the jobs which the qualifications relates to	1 WSQ credit value (cv) is equivalent to 10 recommended training and assessment hours (1 cv = 10 hours)
Vietnam	8	• Knowledge, skills and values • Application • Degree of independence (autonomy and responsibility)	1 = 30 hours of notional learning

Note *proposed, #Directorate General of Higher Education 2012, +not included in decree
Source Bateman and Coles (2015)

6 ASEAN Qualification Reference Framework ... 117

Table 6.4 Types of qualification framework functions

Differences between the types of frameworks	National qualification level	Regional qualification framework level
Main function:	To act as a benchmark for the level of learning recognized in the national qualifications system and possibly an indication of volume and type of learning	To act as a translation device to enable comparisons of levels of qualifications and therefore qualifications across member countries
Developed by:	National governments, national agencies, regional and bodies and education and training bodies	Member countries acting jointly
Sensitive to:	Local, regional and national priorities (e.g. levels of literacy, labour market needs)	Collective priorities across member countries (e.g. enabling mobility and learners and workers across borders)
Currency/value depends on	Factors within national context	The level of trust between member countries
Quality is guaranteed by:	The practices of national bodies and learning institutions	The common application of the referencing criteria and guidelines as well as the robustness and transparency of the national referencing process and national quality assurance systems
Levels are defined by reference to	National benchmarks which may be embedded in different specific learning contexts, e.g. school education, work or higher education	General progression in learning across all contexts that is applicable to all countries

Source Mike Coles and adapted from Bateman and Coles (2013)

118   Z. Mohd Fahmi et al.

Table 6.5 Key characteristic of regional qualifications framework

Framework	Levels	Domains
ASEAN Qualification Reference Framework[a]	8–10	• Knowledge and skills: the kind of knowledge and skills involved • Application: the context in which the knowledge and skills are applied • Responsibility and accountability: the level of independence
Carribean Community (CARICOM)[b]	5 TVET	Broad statements related to job roles: semi-skilled, entry-level worker (supervised); skilled worker (unsupervised); technician/supervisor, Master Craftsman/Technologist; advanced professional/senior manager
European Qualifications Framework[c]	8	• Knowledge—knowledge is described as theoretical and/or factual • Skills—cognitive (involving the use of logical, intuitive and creative thinking) and practical (involving manual dexterity and the use of methods, materials, tools and instruments) • Competence—responsibility and autonomy
Pacific Qualifications Framework[d]	10	• Knowledge and skills—the kind of knowledge and skills involved • Application—the kind of issues or problems to which the knowledge and skills are applied • Degree of independence—the amount of independence or organization that is required to solve problems or complete tasks.
Southern African Development Community[e] (SADC)	10	To be defined

(continued)

Table 6.5 (continued)

Framework	Levels	Domains
Transnational Qualifications Framework for the Virtual University or Small States of the Commonwealth[f]	10	The number of domains vary with the levels but generally address: • Knowledge • Skills • Level of autonomy

[a]ASEAN members includes Brunei Darussalam, Cambodia, Indonesia, Lao PDR, Malaysia, Myanmar, Philippines, Singapore, Thailand and Vietnam

[b]22 member states includes: Antigua and Barbuda, Bahamas, Barbados, Belize, Dominica, Grenada, Guyana, Jamaica, Montserrat(Br.) St. Kitts and Nevis, St. Lucia, St. Vincent and the Grenadines, Suriname, Trinidad and Tobago

[c]Austria, Belgian FL, Bulgaria, Croatia, Czech Republic, Denmark, Estonia, France, Germany, Iceland, Ireland, Latvia, Lithuania, Luxembourg, Malta, the Netherlands, Portugal, England/Northern Ireland, Scotland and Wales

[d]The 15 member states includes Cook Island, Federated States of Micronesia (FSM), Fiji, Kiribati, Nauru, Niue, Marshall Islands, Palau, Papua New Guinea, Samoa, Solomon Islands, Tonga, Tuvalu and Vanuatu plus Tokelau

[e]Member states includes Angola, Botswana, Democratic Republic of Congo, Lesotho, Madagascar, Malawi, Mauritius, Mozambique, Namibia, Seychelles, South Africa, Swaziland, Tanzania, Zambia and Zimbabwe

[f]Member countries are Antigua and Barbuda, Barbados, Belize, Botswana, Cyprus, Dominica, Grenada, Guyana, Jamaica, Lesotho, Maldives, Malta, Mauritius, Papua New Guinea, Samoa, Seychelles, Sierra Leone, St. Kitts and Nevis, St. Lucia, St. Vincent and the Grenadines, Swaziland, The Bahamas, The Comoros (non-Commonwealth), The Gambia, Tonga, Trinidad and Tobago, Tuvalu and Vanuatu

Source Bateman and Coles (2013)

The aspect of the qualification frameworks with regard to skills is also being developed. The stages between the countries differ in progression. The ASEAN qualification framework requires the member state to have reference ASEAN Quality Assurance Framework, East Asia Summit Technical Vocational Education and Training Quality Assurance Framework (EAS, TVET, QAF) and the INQAAHE Guidelines of Good Practice in Quality Assurance. This is also reiterated in other documents of relevance in regard to certification of skills, the ASEAN Guiding Principles for Quality Assurance and Recognition of Competency Certification Systems.[18]

Quality Assurance

The National Qualification Framework (NQF) of any state will be valuable and trusted if it meets or exceeds the measure of the level of the outcome objectives assigned under the level descriptors. The NQF of a member state being validated to be able to match the AQRF levels will enhance the trust and the confidence in the NQF of the member state. This is important to allow for credit transfers and global mobility for recognition and accreditation of qualifications. This is also of importance in the referencing exercise where the level of the NQF is matched with the AQRF levels based on the attainment of the level outcomes of the AQRF level descriptors.

Quality assurance of education and training generally centres on:

* Approval and monitoring of the product, such as curriculum or programme design;
* Approval and monitoring of the provider, such as universities and other higher education providers;
* monitoring of assessment, certification and graduation procedures and outcomes;
* System-wide evaluations of quality; and
* provision of public information on the performance of providers[19] (Bateman et al. 2012).

It is recognized that integral to the credibility, acceptance, recognition and transferability of the qualifications within the region and across the different regions internationally is a trusted quality assured system and mechanism. The alignment to UNESCO sustainable development goals and plans of actions as well as other regional and international framework should be a driving consideration.

The second meeting of the AQRF Committee was held in Manila, the Philippines from 12 to 13 July 2017 to discuss the important role of quality assurance in the process of referencing national qualification frameworks (NQFs) of participating AMS to the AQRF. The quality

6 ASEAN Qualification Reference Framework ...

assurance of the referencing process is an important aspect of the harmonisation process.

The referencing process envisaged by Bateman and Coles (2015) following that from the European Union experience includes the criteria that each country has to meet (and justify this to the other member countries) the following:

* All competent bodies are involved and sign up to the referencing outcome (level to level match) and the referencing process (meeting these criteria);
* A full justification to an external audience of the level to level matches;
* An explanation of the use of learning outcomes, credit and validation;
* A full explanation of the allocating of qualifications to NQF levels;
* A description of QA processes in the country to an external audience;
* An explicit sign up to the report from all QA bodies;
* Proof that international experts were involved in the process;
* The country provides one unanimously accepted report of the referencing;
* Steps are taken to give visibility to regional framework levels on certificates;
* The level to level match is published on a public portal (Bateman and Coles 2015).

Referencing

The AQRF describes referencing as a *"process that results in the establishment of a relationship between the national qualification framework (NQF) and that of a regional qualification framework"*. The aim of the referencing process is to describe a common structure (or criteria) for linking the NQF to AQRF. It is to ensure that the linking process undertaken is robust and transparent and to provide a common reporting structure for the referencing report. It is to be recognized that the referencing is a nested process, and there are bigger circles of referencing from the national, regional and international context that qualification and skills are desired to be transferred into a borderless world. Hence, referencing in the immediate broader context will consider the frameworks mentioned earlier, ASEAN Quality Assurance Framework, East Asia Summit Technical Vocational Education and Training Quality Assurance Framework (EAS, TVET, QAF) and the INQAAHE Guidelines of Good Practice in Quality Assurance and the ASEAN Guiding Principles for Quality Assurance and Recognition of Competency Certification Systems.

The AQRF with regard to referencing process has provided:

* *For member states with an NQF*, identify in a broad sense, the best fit of levels of the national frameworks to that of the AQRF.
* *For the member states without an NQF*, identify for national qualification types or for key qualifications, the best fit to the level of the AQRF.

The AQRF has set out the criteria for referencing as reproduced here which seeks to comply with international expectations. These are that the structure of the education and training system is described. The responsibilities and legal basis of all relevant national bodies involved in the referencing process are clearly determined and published by the main public authority responsible for the referencing process. The procedures for inclusion of qualifications in the NQF or for describing the place of qualifications in the national qualifications system are transparent.

There is a clear and demonstrable link between the qualifications levels in the NQF or system and the level descriptors of the AQRF. The basis in the agreed standard of the national framework or qualification system and its qualification described. The national quality assurance system(s) for education and training refer(s) to the NQF or systems are described. All of the bodies responsible for quality assurance state their unequivocal support for the referencing outcome. The process of referencing has been devised by the main public authority and has been endorsed by the main stakeholders in the qualification system. Foreign experts with relevant qualifications are involved in the referencing process and its reporting.

A comprehensive report, setting out the referencing and the evidence supporting it shall be published by the competent national bodies and shall address separately and in order each of the referencing criteria. The outcome of the referencing is published by the ASEAN Secretariat and by the main national public body. Finally, after the referencing process all certification and awarding bodies are encouraged to indicate a clear reference to the appropriate AQRF level on new qualifications certificates, diplomas issued.[20]

International Linkages and MRA

ASEAN while working within its region to harmonise higher education in academic and vocational areas is mindful of the larger picture of a need to interconnect higher education and labour cum economic mobility in a global arena. In this regard, regional and international benchmarks serves as a guide.

For example, for vocational standards East Asia Summit Technical and Vocational Education and Training Quality Assurance Framework (EAS TVET QAF), the participating countries are ASEAN, Australia, China, India, Japan, Korea, New Zealand, Russia and the United States. The framework comprises of a set of principles, guidelines and tools to assist EAS committee to develop, improve and assess their quality of their TVET systems (Regional Perspective—Existing approach in developing quality and qualification framework in Asia) (Regional Perspective 2018). ASEAN has also in collaboration with the German government developed the RECOTVET programme since 2014 aimed to support regional harmonization and quality improvement in TVET (ASEAN to advance vocational education and training) (ASEAN 2018e). The UNESCO (2016) report enhancing relevance in TVET also reviews the progress and development in TVET.[21]

A core purpose of a regional qualifications framework is "*enabling NQFs and national qualifications systems to align with or 'talk to' each other*" (Burke et al. 2009).[22]

Bateman and Coles (2013) also said that "*a common reference framework aims to: deepen integration and harmonisation; create a common identity; facilitate: transparency of multiple complex systems; mobility of workers and students; recognition and credit transfer; and support economic imperatives such as removal of barriers to trade. Regional qualifications frameworks are different to bilateral, trilateral and multilateral agreements between national qualifications agencies, professional bodies and education providers for qualifications standards and recognition. Regional qualifications frameworks do not replace or undermine these agreements, but should support and enhance them*".

The areas which mutual recognition agreement has been made include accounting services, dental practitioners, medication practitioner, engineering services, nursing services, surveying qualifications, architectural services and tourism (Bautista 2018).[23]

The Asia Pacific Regional Convention on the Recognition of Qualifications in Higher Education (UNESCO 2012) aims to "*ensure that studies, diplomas, and degrees in higher education are recognised as widely as possible, considering the great diversity of educational systems in the Asia- Pacific region and the richness of its cultural, social, political, religious, and economic backgrounds*".[24]

Credit Transfers and Student Mobility

The underlying framework of a regional qualification framework that is referenced is to build a space of trust and assurance of the value and credibility of the accredited qualifications and the corresponding outcomes. It enables cross-border transfer of qualification and enables the linking of and combination of qualifications from different institutions and sub-systems. Credit transfers to be realized require a common referenced framework where the pathways and equivalencies need to be defined, and credit assignment can be made clear between national, regional and international institutions. Taiji Hato (2014) has referred to the need for a permeable (comparable and compatible) framework to assist this end.[25]

The AUN has established the ASEAN Credit Transfer System (ACTS). It is a student-centred system applied to student mobility among AUN member states. This system was developed to facilitate student mobility under AUN Student Exchange Program. ACTS has been designed to accommodate differences in the implementation of a credit system among the member universities without any requirement to modify the existing institutional or national credit system.

ACTS (since 2011) mainly focuses on promoting people-to-people linkage with its three aims: enrichment of purpose, enhancement of students' soft skills and exposure of international experience. ACTS also benefits students in three ways: credit earning, intellectual exchange and networking of ASEAN friends. However, the limitation to this arrangement is that it is limited to a maximum of two semesters, and the system does not have the function of measuring equivalency levels of the credit transfers. This is left to the collaborating universities. The ACTS had expanded under Phase 2 the collaboration to credit transfer with Kyoto University (Kyoto University, Scholarship Programme).

According to Taiji Hota (2014) cited above, the Asian Cooperation Dialogue (ACD) is moving towards an Asian Credit Transfer System (ACD-ACTS). However, like the ACTS, there is no measuring of equivalency levels. The suggestion to increase trust and quality assurance to ensure transferability of credits includes joint teaching and exchange of staff aside from student exchange, credit transfers of optional and eventually core subjects, improvement of transparency of education with substantive details of content and level of study with measured outcomes to assure quality and a study plan of student with home and host university to ensure comparable and measurable levels and outcomes of learning. The current development is one by spearheaded by SHARE that in a given time, the maturity of the framework and credit transfer systems is expected to evolve into an ASEAN credit system via the SHARE credit transfer handbook easily transferable within the region of ASEAN (SHARE [2018] Boosting ASEAN Student Mobility Towards a Comprehensive Approach in Credit Transfer) (SHARE-ASEAN 2018).[26]

Challenges and Issues

In the study conducted by Bateman and Coles (2015), the countries identified challenges and barriers related to the implementation of NQF and referencing to AQRF . It solicited responses that covered the NQF, the higher education sector and the TVET sectors. The issues highlighted included that the preconditions were not in place (not have a fully implemented NQF), lack of coordination and connections between different sectors education of that of higher education and TVET, limited staff (educational and ministerial staff) and stakeholders (providers, students and industry) capacity and awareness in relation to the NQF, the standards, the outcome-based curriculum development, programme and institution accreditation, audit and monitoring of higher education providers and of financial limitations. It is recognized the countries are also limited by the varying stages of economic development that would have an impact on issues of funding.

Challenges

1. The difference of the maturing of capacity building of the different ten states will have an effect on the progress and ability to reference of each country. It is to be recognized that flowing into higher education are the primary and secondary levels that need to be developed to be aligned to International Standards of Classification of Education that would be able to ensure connectivity into the levels envisaged for higher education.
2. The differing levels of maturity and complexity in the national academic and vocational and skills qualification framework and capacity building. The need to incorporate within the same the national and ASEAN framework the UNESCO sustainability influence in education. The recognition of prior learning, formal and informal learning in relation to the framework is an ancillary challenge.
3. The need to establish and ensure continued independence and impartiality of the public governing authority in all sphere of education dimension (academic and skills) in relation to higher education

within the country in terms of accreditation, registration, licensing, audit and quality assurance of education by the providers.

4. The need to ensure quality teaching is carried out by appropriately qualified personnel. The need for recruitment and training policies that are aligned with the national and international qualification framework.

5. The need to ensure capacity building in terms of educational resources and facilities across all regions. In this regard, the opening learning platform may assist to provide access to education.

6. The lack of a common language as the method of communication, education and research that would bind the region of ASEAN.

7. The mobility of staff (teaching and research) and student exchanges in building the circle of trust. This would involve creativity, coordination and overcoming of hurdles that like a common language, schedule, level of descriptors, curriculum modification and credit transfers arrangements may present.

8. The development of a regional framework is invariably tied to other frameworks of a region that is sought to be penetrated. Over periods of time, the regional grouping is spiral in nature and there are many frameworks within regions and a global framework that may overlap. This would require a strategic recognition, alignment and mapping across the different frameworks.

9. The scales and method of evaluation of standards meeting the level descriptors and the appropriateness to the levels should be uniform, consistent, transparent, objective and impartial. The evaluation must be made by impartial experts. There should be an audit required under the auspices of UNESCO or external independent trusted bodies that would act to safeguard the sanctity of the same. This is anticipated more so in event of global higher education framework.

10. The credibility and validity of supporting evidence that translates beyond paper requirements to manifest in visible forms should be measurable and measured. It is a concern that alongside knowledge, skills and competencies which may have mechanism devised for measurement, there are soft skills and values that are not as defined or readily measurable.

11. The robustness of the detailed support and evidence that learning outcomes are translated into industry effectiveness (stakeholder input) needs to be the link that ultimately is the test that the learning outcomes are quality assured and level appropriate. In this regard, further evidence of tracer studies of graduate and the impact whether within and outside areas of studies within the industry should be monitored and measured for translation of education to the economy or valued output.

The Way Forward

It is envisaged that an ASEAN Higher Education Space (supported among others by frameworks of academic and vocational qualifications, standards, benchmarks, processes, internal and external quality assurance) would be the aim. The way forward would need a continued journey of collaboration and cooperation, working towards common agreements and consensus, alignment and convergence of the higher education systems, the building of trust and confidence (integrity) among external assurance bodies, mutual recognition of accrediting decision and endorsement from the ASEAN Ministers of Education. In this regard, higher education harmonisation, regionalisation within ASEAN and beyond ASEAN are the key considerations.

Notes

1. It was signed in Thailand by Foreign Minister Indonesia (Mr. Adam Malik), Philippines (Mr. Narcisco Ramos), Singapore (Mr. S. Rajaratnam), Thailand (Mr. Thanat Khoman) and Malaysia (Tun Abdul Razak, Deputy Prime Minister).
2. Woon, W. *The ASEAN Charter: A Commentary* (Singapore: NUS Press, 2016), 4.
3. Woon, W. *The ASEAN Charter: A Commentary* (Singapore: NUS Press, 2016), 8.

4. UNESCO Committee on Economic, Social and Cultural Rights, General Comment 11, Plans for primary education (Twentiethsession, 1999).
5. Paryono, Overview of the TVET movement in SEA. http://seatvet. seameo.org/download/13_China%20Networking%20Programme% 2C%201-3%20Aug%202016/Dr_Paryono_VOCTECH_ Overview_of_TVET_Movement_in_Southeast_Asia.pdf. Accessed May 26, 2018.
6. ASED. http://asean.org/asean-socio-cultural/asean-education-minister-meeting-ased. Accessed April 14, 2018.
7. Geronimo, J. Y. "8 Ways PH Higher Education Can Prepare for ASEAN 2015" [online]. *Rappler* 2013. https://www.rappler.com/move-ph/issues/education/44519-higher-education-sector-asean-2015-preparation. Accessed April 14, 2018.
8. European Union Support to Higher Education in the ASEAN region (SHARE). http://share-asean.eu/about/welcome-message-from-asean. Accessed April 8, 2018.
9. ASED Joint Statement of the Ninth ASEAN Education Ministers Meeting (9th ASED). http://asean.org/strorage/2016/05/Joint-Statement-of-the-9th-ASED. Accessed May 25, 2016. See also ASEAN concludes Work Plan on Education 2016–2020. http://asean.org/asean-concludes-work-plan-education-2016-2020. Accessed April 14, 2018.
10. Malaysia assumes chairmanship of ASEAN Education Ministers Meeting; sets direction for next five years, available at: http://asean.org/malaysia-assumes-chairmanship-of-asean-education-ministers-meeting-sets-direction-for-next-five-years. Accessed April 14, 2018.
11. *ASEAN Qualifications Reference Framework: Governance and Structure* [online]. http://asean.org/storage/2017/03/ED-01-AQRF-Governance-and-Structure-document.pdf, p. 6. Accessed April 15, 2018.
12. *ASEAN Qualifications Reference Framework: Governance and Structure* [online] http://asean.org/storage/2017/03/ED-01-AQRF-Governance-and-Structure-document.pdf, p. 6. Accessed April 15, 2018.
13. Bautista, C., n.d. "ASEAN Qualifications Reference Framework (AQRF): Context, Development and Implementation" [online]. https://www.share-asean.eu/sites/default/files/SHARE-01_AQRF-and-CQF_Prof-Dr-Cynthia-Bautista.pdf. Accessed April 14, 2018.
14. See also 2007 on APQN Project No. 2 on Qualifications Framework in the Asia Pacific Region. https://www.apqn.org/media/project_group_reports/pg2_project_report_Oct2007.pdf. Accessed April 15, 2018.

15. CEDEFOP Global Inventory of Regional and National Qualifications Framework. (2017). The European Centre for the Development of Vocational Training (Cedefop): http://www.cedefop.europa.eu/en/publications-and-resources/publications/2221. Accessed April 14, 2018.
16. Bateman, A., and Coles, M. (2015). ASEAN Qualifications Reference Framework and National Qualifications Frameworks: State of Play.
17. Bateman and Coles Qualifications frameworks and quality assurance of education and training Report Prepared for the World Bank (2013), 21. https://olc.worldbank.org/sites/default/files/Qualifications%20frameworks%20and%20quality%20assurance%20of%20education%20and%20training_final.pdf. Accessed August 17, 2018.
18. ASEAN Guiding Principles for Quality Assurance and Recognition of Competency Certification Systems Jakarta, ASEAN Secretariat, August 2016. http://asean.org/resources_cat/asean-publications-3. Accessed April 14, 2018.
19. Bateman, A., Keating, J., Gillis, S., Dyson, C., Burke, G., and Coles, M. Concept Paper: East Asia Summit Vocational Education and Training Quality Assurance Framework, Volume II, Australian Government, Canberra. 2012.
20. Bautista, C., n.d. "ASEAN Qualifications Reference Framework (AQRF): Context, Development and Implementation" [online]. https://www.share-asean.eu/sites/default/files/SHARE-01_AQRF-and-CQF_Prof-Dr-Cynthia-Bautista.pdf. Accessed April 14, 2018.
21. UNESCO Asia Pacific Regional Bureau of Education. (2016). Enhancing Relevance in TVET. http://www.unesdoc.unesco.org/images/0024/002433/243365E.pdf. Accessed April 17, 2018.
22. Burke, G., Keating, J., Vickers, A., Fearnside, R., and Bateman, A. Mapping Qualifications Frameworks Across APEC Economies. APEC Secretariat. www.apecknowledgebank.org/file.aspx?id=2029. Accessed April 14, 2018.
23. Bautista, C., n.d. "ASEAN Qualifications Reference Framework (AQRF): Context, Development and Implementation" [online]. https://www.share-asean.eu/sites/default/files/SHARE-01_AQRF-and-CQF_Prof-Dr-Cynthia-Bautista.pdf. Accessed April 14, 2018.
24. Asia-Pacific Regional Convention on Qualifications Recognition. http://www.unescobkk.org/education/promotion-of-academic-mobility/asia-pacific-regional-convention-on-the-recognition-of-qualifications-in-higher-education-an-overview. Accessed April 14, 2018.

25. Taiji Hota. (2014). The Proceedings of the ASEM Dialogue on Quality Assurance and Recognition 25–26 August 2014, Sunway Putra Hotel, Kuala Lumpur Malaysia, Malaysian Qualification Agency 2015. http://www.aqan.org/aqanv2/document/pdf/I%20-%20Proceeding%20 2014%20-%2022Sept2015.pdf. Accessed April 15, 2018.
26. SHARE European Support to Higher Education in ASEAN. (2018). Boosting ASEAN Student Mobility Towards a Comprehensive Approach in Credit Transfer Policy Brief Number 8. August 8, 2018. https://www.share-asean.eu/sites/default/files/PB%208_FINAL.pdf. Accessed August 14, 2018.

References

ASEAN (Association of South East Asian). 2016. *ASEAN Guiding Principles for Quality Assurance and Recognition of Competency Certification System*. Jakarta: ASEAN Secretariat. https://asean.org/storage/2012/05/ASEAN-Guiding-Principles-for-Quality-Assurance-and-Recognition-of-Competency-Certification-Systems1.pdf.

ASEAN. 2018a. "ASEAN Education Ministers Meeting (ASED)." Accessed April 14. http://asean.org/asean-socio-cultural/asean-education-ministers-meeting-ased/.

ASEAN. 2018b. "ASEAN Qualification Reference Framework." Accessed April 14, 2018. http://asean.org/storage/2017/03/ED-02-ASEAN-Qualifications-Reference-Framework-January-2016.pdf.

ASEAN. 2018c. "ASEAN Qualifications Reference Framework: Governance and Structure". Accessed April 15, 2018. http://asean.org/storage/2017/03/ED-01-AQRF-Governance-and-Structure-document.pdf.

ASEAN. 2018d. "ASEAN Quality Assurance Framework for Higher Education (AQAFHE)." Accessed April 15. https://www.chea.org/userfiles/.../ASEAN%20Quality%20Assurance%20Final-CIQG.p.

ASEAN. 2018e. "ASEAN to Advance Vocational Education and Training." Accessed May 25, 2018. http://asean.org/asean-to-advance-vocational-education-and-training/.

ASEAN. 2018f. "Concludes Work Plan on Education 2016–2020." Accessed April 14, 2018. http://asean.org/asean-concludes-work-plan-education-2016-2020/.

ASEAN. 2018g. "Malaysia Assumes Chairmanship of ASEAN Education Ministers Meeting; Sets Direction for Next Five Years." *ASEAN Secretariat News*. Accessed April 14, 2018. http://asean.org/malaysia-assumes-chairmanship-of-asean-education-ministers-meeting-sets-direction-for-next-five-years.

ASED. 2016. "Joint Statement of the Ninth ASEAN Education Ministers Meeting (9th ASED)". May 25. Selangor, Malaysia. Accessed April 14, 2018. http://asean.org/storage/2016/05/Joint-Statement-of-9th-ASED_25-May-2016_ADOPTED-2.pdf.

UNESCO. 2012. "Asia-Pacific Regional Convention on the Recognition of Qualifications in Higher Education." Accessed 14, 2018. http://www.unescobkk.org/education/higher-education/promotion-of-academic-mobility/asia-pacific-regional-convention-on-the-recognition-of-qualifications-in-higher-education-an-overview/.

Bateman, Andrea, and Mike Coles. 2013. *Qualifications Frameworks and Quality Assurance of Education and Training*. Washington, DC: World Bank Group. Accessed August 17, 2018. https://olc.worldbank.org/sites/default/files/Qualifications%20frameworks%20and%20quality%20assurance%20of%20education%20and%20training_final.pdf.

Bateman, Andrea, and Mike Coles. 2015. *ASEAN Qualifications Reference Framework and National Qualifications Frameworks: State of Play.* Jakarta: SHARE-ASEAN Secretariat. http://asean.org/storage/2018/03/Guiding-Principles-for-Quality-Assurance-and-Recognition-of-Competency-C....pdf.

Bateman, Andrea, Jack Keating, Shelley Gillis, Chloe Dyson, Gerald Burke, and Coles Mike. 2012. *East Asia Summit Vocational Education and Training Quality Assurance Framework*. Vol. II. Canberra: Australian Government.

Bateman, Andrea, and Mike Coles. 2016. *ASEAN Qualifications Reference Framework and National Qualifications Frameworks State of Play Report Commissioned by SHARE (European Union Support to Higher Education in the ASEAN Region).* The implementation of SHARE is entrusted to a consortium of British Council (leader), Campus France, DAAD, EP-Nuffic, ENQA, and EUA.

Bautista, Maria Cynthia Rose Banzon. 2018. "ASEAN Qualifications Reference Framework (AQRF): Context, Development and Implementation." Accessed April 14, 2018. https://www.share-asean.eu/sites/default/files/SHARE-01_AQRF-and-CQF_Prof-Dr-Cynthia-Bautista.pdf.

Burke, Gerald, Phillip McKenzie, Chandra Shah, Jack Keating, Alison Vickers, Rob Fearnside, and Andrea Bateman. 2009. "Mapping Qualifications Frameworks Across APEC Economies." *APEC Secretariat.* Accessed April 14, 2018. www.apecknowledgebank.org/file.aspx?id=2029.

CEDEFOP. 2017. "Global Inventory of Regional and National Qualifications Frameworks". The European Centre for the Development of Vocational Training. Accessed April 14, 2018. http://www.cedefop.europa.eu/en/publications-and-resources/publications/2221.

Geronimo, Jee Y. 2013. "8 Ways PH Higher Education Can Prepare for ASEAN 2015." *Rappler.* Accessed April 14, 2018. https://www.rappler.com/move-ph/issues/education/44519-higher-education-sector-asean-2015-preparation.

Lythe, David. 2009. "Qualification Frameworks in Asia and the Pacific." International Labour Office. Accessed April 14, 2018. http://apskills.ilo.org/resources/qualification-frameworks-in-asia-pacific.

Paryono. 2016. "Overview of the TVET Movement in SEA." Accessed May 26, 2018. http://seatvet.seameo.org/download/13_China%20Networking%20Programme%2C%201-3%20Aug%202016/Dr_Paryono_VOCTECH_Overview_of_TVET_Movement_in_Southeast_Asia.pdf.

Regional Perspective. 2018. "Existing Approach in Developing Quality and Qualification Framework in Asia." Accessed April 14, 2018. www.regional-tvet-conference-laos.org/kontext/controllers/document.../481903.pdf.

SHARE-ASEAN. 2016. Qualification Reference Framework and National Qualification Framework State of Play Report 2015 Commission by SHARE Consortium Partner DAAD. Accessed April 10, 2018. www.share.asean.edu.

SHARE-ASEAN. 2018. "European Union Support to Higher Education in the ASEAN Region." Accessed April 8, 2018. http://share-asean.eu/about/welcome-message-from-asean.

SHARE Europe Support to Higher Education in ASEAN. 2018. "Boosting ASEAN Student Mobility Towards a Comprehensive Approach in Credit Transfer Policy Brief Number 8." Accessed August 14, 2018. https://www.share-asean.eu/sites/default/files/PB%208_FINAL.pdf.

Taiji Hota. 2014. "The Proceedings of the ASEM Dialogue on Quality Assurance and Recognition." Sunway Putra Hotel, Kuala Lumpur Malaysia, Malaysian Qualification Agency 2015. Accessed April 15, 2018. http://www.aqan.org/aqanv2/document/pdf/I%20-%20Proceeding%202014%20-%2022Sept2015.pdf.

UN Economics and Social Council. 2006. "Committee on Economic, Social and Cultural Rights, General Comment 11, Plans of Action for Primary Education (Twentieth session, 1999)." Accessed April 10, 2018. http://www.refworld.org/docid/4538838c0.html.

Woon, Walter. 2015. *THE ASEAN Charter: A Commentary*. Singapore: NUS Press.

7

Representing Migration in ASEAN: Challenges to Regional Integration

Charity Lee

Migration Within the ASEAN Community

ASEAN is a thriving region with 635 million residents, the third largest collective population in the world after China and India, and a collective gross domestic product of over US$2.5 trillion as of 2016. However, the economic prosperity of the region remains significantly unbalanced between the 10 member states. An estimated 15% of the population, mostly coming from Laos, Cambodia, Indonesia and the Philippines, continues to live on less than US$2 per day (Association of Southeast Asian Nations [ASEAN] 2016) and the wage gap that exists between ASEAN countries is large. For example, workers in Myanmar earn on average US$91 per month (MOLES and ILO 2016), while those in Singapore earn US$2859 (MOM 2016). Average wages in Malaysia and Thailand are over three times those in Indonesia and Cambodia, respectively.

C. Lee (✉)
Faculty of Languages and Linguistics, University of Malaya,
Kuala Lumpur, Malaysia
e-mail: charity.lee@um.edu.my

© The Author(s) 2019
A. Idris and N. Kamaruddin (eds.), *ASEAN Post-50*,
https://doi.org/10.1007/978-981-13-8043-3_7

136   C. Lee

This socio-economic disparity between the member states, along with the ageing labour force in the more developed ASEAN countries, is push factor for international labour migration within the region and is likely expected to continue expanding (ILO 2014). Docquier et al.'s (2014) analysis using Gallup World Poll data reported that more than 12% of ASEAN's population over the age of 25 wanted to migrate in 2010 (2016). International migration is challenging to classify into neat categories. International migrants, who consist of people who change their usual country of residence, can generally be divided into labour migrants and forced migrants. Labour migration movement is usually motivated by economic and employment-related factors, while forced migration movement involves an element of coercion and threats to life or livelihood and includes the movement of asylum seekers, refugees and internally displaced people (IOM, n.d.). However, regular migration flows often occur alongside irregular migration flows, with the latter referring to migrants, who move "outside the regulatory norms of the sending, transit and receiving countries" (ibid.). Many migration flows within the larger Asia Pacific region are considered mixed flows, involving not just regular and irregular migrants, but also smuggled migrants, trafficked persons, refugees and asylum seekers (UNESCAP 2017). It is, therefore, important to note that many migrants may meet more of the above-mentioned categories of migration or even transition between them.

The Asian Development Bank and International Labour Organization estimated that intra-ASEAN labour migration increased from 1.5 million in 1990 to 6.5 million in 2013 (International Labour Organization [ILO] and Asian Development Bank [ADB] 2014). This migration flow is mostly concentrated along five corridors involving 90% of migrants: (i) Indonesia to Malaysia, (ii) Malaysia to Singapore, and (iii) Laos PDR, Cambodia and Myanmar to Thailand (UN Population Division 2017). Labour-receiving ASEAN states comprise Singapore and Thailand, while labour-sending states comprise Cambodia, Indonesia, Laos PDR, Myanmar and the Philippines. With an equal stock of inward and outward migrants in ASEAN, Malaysia is the exception (ibid.). However, the migration movement is primarily high-wage to Singapore. As such, Malaysia has often aligned with labour-recipient instead of labour-sending states on the issue of migrant labour rights. Table 7.1 presents the migrant flow according to the destination country and country of origin within ASEAN.

International labour migrants in ASEAN are usually divided according to three main economic activities or domains, in which they are employed, as can be seen in Table 7.2 based on the latest available data from the ILO. The economic domains are agricultural (including

Table 7.1 Bilateral migration matrix World Bank estimates, ASEAN member states, 2013

Origin	Destination				
	Brunei	Cambodia	Indonesia	Lao PDR	Malaysia
Brunei		0	0	0	976
Cambodia				1201	17,226
Indonesia	352	108		0	1,074,737
Lao PDR	0	265	0		0
Malaysia	643	175	1979	0	
Myanmar	0	53	0	282	79,691
The Philippines	3468	156	3517	0	410,149
Singapore	2285	125	19,681	0	42,474
Thailand	25,451	31,472	19,681	1652	93,635
Vietnam	0	37,225	0	11,447	28,223
Total	32,199	69,579	44,858	14,582	1,747,111

Origin	Destination				
	Myanmar	The Philippines	Singapore	Thailand	Vietnam
Brunei Darussalam	N/A	82	0	0	121
Cambodia	N/A	40	0	750,109	2485
Indonesia	N/A	3325	152,681	2952	7671
Lao PDR	N/A	0	0	926,427	4284
Malaysia	N/A	798	1,044,994	8199	0
Myanmar		424	0	1,892,480	9783
The Philippines	N/A		14,176	17,581	292
Singapore	N/A	825		2962	466
Thailand	N/A	342	17,644		512
Vietnam	N/A	416	0	17,663	
Total	N/A	6252	1,229,495	3,618,373	25,614

Source ILO 2015

138   C. Lee

Table 7.2 Employed migrants by economic domain, ASEAN member states, latest year

Member State	Economic domain			
	Agricultural	Industry	Services	Total
Brunei Darussalam (2014)	394	15,462	36,305	52,161
Cambodia (2013)	18,700	8500	22,000	49,200
Indonesia (2015)	24,686	9752	31,180	65,618
Lao PDR (2006)	600	6500	6500	13,600
Malaysia (2014)	646,400	764,800	715,900	2,127,100
Myanmar	N/A	N/A	N/A	N/A
The Philippines	N/A	N/A	N/A	N/A
Singapore (2014)	4600	645,100	706,000	1,355,700
Thailand (2012)	44,756	127,258	973,145	1,145,159
Vietnam	N/A	N/A	N/A	N/A

Source International Labour Organization (ILO). "Migration in ASEAN in Figures: The International Labour Migration Statistics (ILMS) Database in ASEAN". Bangkok: International Labour Organization, 2015

forestry and fishing), industry (including mining, manufacturing and construction) and services (including retail, food and beverage, finance, technical, administration, education, entertainment and social work).

A large majority of labour migrants in ASEAN are low-skilled with primarily lower levels of education. According to the classification by the International Standard Classification of Education, these migrants have mostly basic (primary to lower secondary) and intermediate (upper secondary to non-tertiary post-secondary) levels of education (ILO 2018), as illustrated in Table 7.3.

Alongside labour migrants, the Asia Pacific region is home to around 7 million persons of concerns including 3.5 million refugees (UNHCR, n.a.), which is an estimated 30% of the global refugee population (Petcharamesree 2016). The UNHCR has noted in its 2014 Factsheet on Southeast Asia that there are 2.7 million persons of concern within the ASEAN region (UNHCR 2014). Historically, forced migration first emerged as a significant regional issue during the Indo-China crisis in the 1970s, and since then, Cambodia, Lao PDR, Myanmar and Vietnam have been the main source of the region's forced migrants. Recent forced migration trends in the region have seen an increase in the number of non-ASEAN refugees, who mostly originate from West and

Table 7.3 Employed migrants by level of education, ASEAN member states, 2013 Member States, latest year (%)

Country	ISCE level of education		
	Basic	Medium	Advanced
Brunei Darussalam (2014)	19.82	60.25	19.92
Cambodia (2013)	93.22	3.05	3.74
Indonesia (2015)	54.33	30.41	15.26
Lao PDR	N/A	N/A	N/A
Malaysia (2016)	27.81	44.53	27.65
Myanmar	N/A	N/A	N/A
The Philippines (2017)	0.4	97.9	1.7
Singapore	N/A	N/A	N/A
Vietnam	N/A	N/A	N/A

Source International Labour Organization (ILO). "Migration in ASEAN in Figures: The International Labour Migration Statistics (ILMS) Database in ASEAN". Bangkok: International Labour Organization, 2015; ILO. "International Labour Migration Statistics Database in ASEAN", edited by International Labour Organization (ILO), 2018

South Asian as well as certain African regions (Andika Ab. Wahab 2017). Legislation on migration in ASEAN states focuses primarily on documented or legal labour migrants, while forced migrants and displaced people, such as asylum seekers and refugees, are largely absent.

The signing of the Declaration of ASEAN Concord II (Bali Concord II) in Bali, Indonesia, on 7 October 2003 paved the way for efforts to establish the ASEAN Community by 2020, and this commitment was further affirmed through the signing of the Cebu Declaration on the acceleration of an ASEAN Community by 2015 and the ASEAN Charter both in 2007. The latter in particular provided the legal and institutional framework for the establishment of the ASEAN Community, which comprised three pillars, the ASEAN Political-Security Community (APSC), the ASEAN Economic Community (AEC) and the ASEAN Socio-Cultural Community (ASCC), each with their own blueprints that establish how the goals are to be achieved. The key tenets of the ASEAN Community are improving economic growth, promoting peace and stability and establishing an ASEAN identity. As migration has been and will continue to be an important part of ASEAN's development as a region, this chapter aims to explore how intra-ASEAN migration is represented in the main ASEAN Community blueprints and other regional declarations and instruments that address migration-related issues.

Data and Methodology

The data set used in this analysis comprised the following ASEAN documents: the AEC, APSC and ASCC Blueprints, the 1999 Bangkok Declaration on Irregular Migration, the 2007 Declaration on the Protection and Promotion of the Rights of Migrant Workers, the 2017 Consensus on the Protection and Promotion of the Rights of Migrant Workers, the 1997 ASEAN Declaration on Transnational Crime and the ASEAN Declaration Against Trafficking In Persons Particularly Women And Children. The Vientiane Action Programme (VAP) and Hanoi Plan of Action (HPA) were included and mentioned only where relevant but were not part of the main analysis due to its lack of focus on migration.

The analysis was informed by corpus-assisted discourse analysis, which combines corpus linguistics (CL) with in-depth linguistic analysis. Discourse analysis holds the view that language is the means by which social practices and actions are enacted and is concerned with what is being accomplished by using language in particular ways and in particular contexts (Fairclough and Wodak 1997). When applied to an examination of the representation of social actors, the study of discourse can offer insights into the language used to construct, uphold, maintain, resist or subvert particular perspectives on groups of people. To this end, CL has been used by discourse analysts to analyse large bodies of texts, including written, spoken, formal and informal texts.

The data set was prepared for analysis using the concordance software, AntConc, to search for word frequencies and collocations. The most frequent words used usually indicate statistical significance in a large data set, but the data set in this analysis was not large and therefore was utilized to identify potentially significant collocations or word associations. Collocations can be defined as "the occurrence of two or more words within a short space of each other in a text" (Sinclair 1991) and are useful for exploring the discursive presentation of people or groups of people (Baker 2006). There are two basic kinds of collocations: grammatical and lexical collocations. The former includes naturally occurring word associations in grammatical constructions, while the latter refers to the co-occurrence of any two lexical items. The analysis here was concerned with the lexical collocations surrounding the representation of migration found in the data set. Examining lexical features that occur together in its context allows for the analysis of how particular messages may be conveyed implicitly in texts (Hunston 2002; Baker et al. 2008).

The ASEAN Community Blueprints

The analysis begins by looking at the ASEAN Community blueprints. In both AEC blueprints, migrants are always referred to impersonally as "labour", more specifically the noun phrase "skilled labour", rather than as "migrants" or "migrant workers". "Labour" is also collocated with other nouns, such as "market", "productivity" and "mobility", with the focus here being primarily on high-skilled migrant workers as well as people involved in business and trade. These social actors are named in the AEC 2015 as "natural persons engaged in (cross-border) trade in goods, services and investments" and in the AEC 2025 as "natural persons and business visitors engaged in the conduct of trade in goods, trade in services, and investment".

There was also mention of mobility and educational opportunities for workers involved in "priority service sectors" as well as students and academic staff. One of the ways this is to be achieved is through mutual recognition agreements (MRAs), intended to facilitate the movement of high-skilled workers and professionals by ensuring regional acknowledgement of their qualifications. This representation supports the general representation of the workforce as high-skilled "human resource" and "human capital" development with a focus on "labour productivity" that can be found throughout the AEC blueprints.

142   C. Lee

Bangkok Declaration on Irregular Migration 1999

The roots of the 1999 Bangkok Declaration can be traced back to the 1993 Bangkok Declaration, which arose out of international interest in the 1990s in irregular migration, particularly the trafficking of migrants (Kneebone 2011). The Declaration has been widely acknowledged as being a breakthrough in multilateral efforts in ASEAN to address the issue of irregular migration (Kneebone 2011; Song 2015; Wongboonsin 2006) despite it not being a legally binding document. The Declaration concerns itself with the management of irregular migration flows and includes a description of the probable causes of irregular migration within ASEAN.

Of note is the lack of any clear definition of "irregular migration" or "irregular migrant", although the reference to the contributions of the Asia Pacific Consultations on Refugees, Displaced Persons, and Migrants, and the Manila Process does indicate the inclusion of asylum seekers, refugees and displaced people. Article 18, advocating the dissemination of the document to involve government and private sectors and civil society "in a collective regional effort to alleviate the adverse effects of irregular migration and to prevent and combat trafficking of human beings, especially women and children", is telling as it foregrounds the issue of trafficking. The word "trafficking" appears seven times. The causes or "push factors" for irregular migration given include human trafficking as well as poverty, unequal levels of development between nations and natural disasters leading to rising unemployment.

"Regular migration" is differentiated from "irregular migration" but "migrants", which occurs twice with "irregular", once with "undocumented/illegal" and once in the noun phrase "outflow of migrants", is not defined or further differentiated. These references specific to migrants as social actors concern their involvement in migration flows, their repatriation ("Concerned countries… should enhance cooperation in ascertaining the identity of undocumented/illegal migrants… with a view to accelerating their readmission") and their treatment ("Irregular migrants should be granted humanitarian treatment, including appropriate health and other services"). With regard to repatriation, undocumented migrants are also referred to as "those without the right to enter and remain".

Apart from the examples given above, all other references to migrants employed the nominalization "migration". Linguists have long argued that *nominalization*, defined as "a transformation that reduces a whole clause to its nucleus, the verb, and turns that into a noun" (Fowler et al. 1979), can have reifying effects that present social processes and qualities as impersonal, objective and unchangeable things rather than a result of human actions (Billig 2008). "Irregular migration" is used 18 times in the Declaration and represented as a "cost" that needs reducing and a problem that should be prevented and combatted. The occurrences of "irregular migration" could also be seen to be activating the ASEAN member states and passivating "migration" through the use of active verbs, e.g. "Recognizing a need for international cooperation to promote sustained economic growth and sustainable development in the countries of origin as a long-term strategy *to address irregular migration*", and prepositional circumstantial *of*, e.g. "The orderly *management of migration* and *addressing of irregular migration*". The result of these discursive strategies is that the complexities of irregular migration are obscured, and the individual migrants' experiences are collectivized to represent an anonymous mass movement of people.

2007 Declaration and 2017 Consensus on the Protection and Promotion of the Rights of Migrant Workers

The 2007 Declaration and the 2017 Consensus on the Protection and Promotion of the Rights of Migrant Workers advocate information sharing, best practices, opportunities and recommended safeguards in relation to protection and promotion of migrant workers' rights. The 2007 Declaration was a direct result of the VAP 2004–2010, in which an instrument to protect migrant workers was placed on the list of working items. Following the establishment of the 2007 Declaration, a drafting team consisting of receiving states, Malaysia and Thailand, and sending states, the Philippines and Indonesia, was tasked to oversee the implementation of the Declaration. However, after a long and arduous process of multilateral negotiations, the sending states both changed their position from advocating for the instrument to be legally binding to merely morally binding, with the final outcome, the 2017 Consensus being described as a "living and evolving document" (ASEAN 2017). The main difference between both documents is that the Declaration consists of the ASEAN member states' expressed commitment to establishing an instrument to protect migrant workers, while the Consensus provides details of how this is to be accomplished.

The main social actors identified in both the Declaration and Consensus are the member states, receiving states, sending states and migrant workers. The "migrant worker" is defined in Article 3 of the Consensus as someone, "who is to be engaged or employed, is engaged or employed, or has recently been engaged or employed in a remunerated activity in a State of which he or she is not a national" and the document explicitly states that only documented migrant workers and "those who become undocumented through no fault of their own" are covered by the Consensus (Article 2). This group of migrant workers are differentiated from the "undocumented migrant worker", defined in Article 4 as those who enter any receiving state by illegal means and fail to secure proper work permission, as well as those who are no longer legally employed.

These definitions are further expanded in Article 57, which state that the definition of undocumented migrant workers does not imply that the Consensus is taking responsibility for regularizing this group of migrants. Furthermore, Article 58 underlines the commitment of the member states in striving to "prevent and curb the flow of undocumented migrant workers". Here, undocumented migrant workers are represented with a water-related metaphor "flow" that is threatening and therefore needs to be prevented. Water metaphors are common metaphors used in anti-immigration discourses to justify exclusionary or punitive measures against migrants (Charteris-Black 2006; Hart 2008;

Gabrielatos and Baker 2008; Baker et al. 2008; Baker and McEnery 2005), and its use in this instance accomplishes the same thing.

Chapters 3 and 4 of the Declaration consist of all rights accorded to documented migrant workers including those that relate to their recruitment in and return to the sending states, arrival and treatment in receiving states, and access to employment benefits, health care and legal recourse among others. Although most of the statements in Chapters 3 and 4 of the Declaration were written in the active form, e.g. "migrant workers have the right to fair treatment in the workplace", the repeated use of the phrase "subject to national laws, regulations and policies of the Receiving State" throughout these sections does not imply genuine but rather conferred agency on the part of the migrants. The sending, receiving and other member states were activated and made responsible parties in protecting migrant workers in Chapters 5–7, respectively, as can be seen by the statements that begin primarily with active verbs, e.g. "*Enforce* laws, regulations and policies related to the protection of migrant workers" (Article 51). Kneebone (2011) argued in her analysis of the 2007 Declaration that some of the obligations particularly for receiving states expressed therein were somewhat vague and circular and there was uncertainty over how it was fulfilling the conditions expressed in the International Convention on the Protection of the Rights of All Migrant Workers and Members of Their Families (ICRMW). The Consensus does provide more in-depth details as to the actual implementation of the obligations expressed in the Declaration, but the non-binding nature of the Consensus leaves the actual extent of its implementation fully to the discretion of member states.

Declaration on Transnational Crime and Declaration Against Trafficking in Persons Particularly Women and Children

As discussed above, one of the main discourse topics found in the ASEAN documents was human trafficking, particularly of women and children. Both the 1997 Declaration on Transnational Crime and the 2004 Declaration Against Trafficking In Persons Particularly Women

146   C. Lee

And Children were drafted before the ASEAN Charter but nonetheless lay the groundwork for discussion on trafficking in the APSC and ASCC. Interestingly, the word "migrant" does not appear at all in both documents. "Illegal migration" is mentioned once in the Declaration on transnational crime as one of the transnational issues, "which transcend borders and affect the lives of the people in the region". Migration is referenced in the Declaration on trafficking on two occasions in relation to the need for understanding the causes of migration movement that make women and children particularly vulnerable to being trafficked.

Discussion

The representation of migration was articulated through engagement with several discourse topics. Firstly, the issue of human trafficking or smuggling was a salient topic that appeared in all the documents within the data set except the AEC blueprints. Ibrahim (2005) noted the *1994 United Nations Development Report* as the impetus for a change in the international discourse surrounding migration. Moving away from human rights, the term "human security" was introduced to highlight the concern with potential risks and vulnerabilities that threaten human populations. These threats included human trafficking and "excessive international migration" alongside other illicit problems. Ibrahim argued that the human security perspective was a paradox to the people-centred approach to development that the UN was purportedly advocating, as migrants, who are people themselves, are seen to be threatening to a receiving state's population, thus legitimizing discriminatory beliefs and xenophobia (ibid., 169).

The dangers of such a perspective are particularly obvious when it comes to forced migration. Displaced people, asylum seekers and refugees have been known to enter transit or destination countries through illegal means, and at times, it is the only way they are able to escape and seek refuge (Koser 2001). The inclusion of all forms of irregular migration and the focus on the trafficked nature of their journeys places the threat to security above their immediate humanitarian needs.

The link to the illicit nature of trafficking also perpetuates unfounded fears and beliefs that migrants bring social and security problems to a host population. A case in point is Nieuwenhuys and Pécoud's analysis of anti-trafficking information campaigns in central and Eastern Europe, which revealed similar messages and methods found in negative campaigns against irregular migration (2007).

Secondly, another discourse topic that is often discussed within human trafficking advocacy and international discourse on irregular migration is victimhood. As the analysis showed, the language used to refer to migrants was constructed using passivating strategies, with the member states taking on active roles to protect and manage migrants. Furthermore, the victim representation was often linked to women and children, which creates a "special kind of helplessness" (Rajaram 2002) that has long been part of the feminization of international discourse on migrants (Johnson 2011). Without attempting to downplay the human rights violations generated by trafficking, this victimizing perspective is problematic. It risks viewing all potential migrants as helpless, "dehistoricized" and "depoliticized" victims (Malkki 1996) requiring help in an unequal relationship of "trusteeship" (Musarò 2011) rather than as social actors' agentive capacity. In other words, it reduces the capacity of migrants to determine their own interests and tends to legitimize their external management (Pupavac 2006).

Another feature of the data set is the general lack of mention to forced migrants. Apart from the APSC, which mentions displaced people and refugees once, the other ASEAN documentation is silent on how forced migration is to be dealt with within the region. The fact that "regular" and "irregular" migration are not clearly defined and differentiated from one another as seen in the Bangkok Declaration, for example, points to a problematic conflation of migrant categories. The ASEAN states generally view forced migrants as illegal or irregular migrants and frame them only within the border control or security discourse (Petcharamesree 2016). This practice of conflating migrants into a single threatening category enables states to legitimize exclusionary policies against them (Don and Lee 2014) and can often negatively impact the way residents of the receiving country perceive migrants (Hoewe 2018).

148   C. Lee

Although the Bangkok Declaration was hailed as a progressive and forward-looking instrument to facilitate the management of irregular migrants, it has not proven to lead to consistent state-led protection norms, as illustrated by the 2015 Rohingya crisis in the Bay of Bengal and the Andaman Sea. The initial "push back" and refusal to take responsibility for the 5000 Rohingya refugees stranded at sea on fishing boats by Malaysia, Thailand and Indonesia, eventually led to the three states softening their stance on "humanitarian grounds" and agreeing to temporarily shelter the Rohingyas. The resolution to this crisis was a result of the initiative taken by individual states rather than ASEAN-led action and to this day, no durable solution or solidarity exists in the region with regard to the Rohingya crisis. Of the 10 member states, only Cambodia and the Philippines have ratified the UN 1951 Refugee Convention and its 1967 Protocol. Other states have so far given no indication of their intention to ratify the convention, despite previously showing positive commitment to this issue.

The representation of migration in AEC focused on the labour market as it referred exclusively to "skilled labour" instead of "migrants". This is, of course, unsurprising given that the purview of the AEC is in creating a single market and production base. Thus, the desirable migrant is one who fits into the AEC description of being highly skilled and involved in the business. Unskilled foreigners do not appear to be the desired part of "ASEAN's cultural heritage" and "ASEAN identity" despite the region's long reliance on such migrants to fulfil its labour needs. ASEAN's intra-regional labour migration has comprised mostly low-skilled migrants during its main expansion in the first two decades of the twentieth century (Kaur 2018) and continues to consist of disproportionally more medium- and low-skilled migrants (International Labour Organization [ILO] and Asian Development Bank [ADB] 2014). It is estimated that high-skilled occupations (e.g. professionals, managers and technicians) accounted for only 10.2% of the overall flow to Malaysia and 3.1% of that to Thailand in 2012 (ibid.). However, evidence from the AEC indicates that low-skilled migrants are no longer a priority. The AEC calls for the removal of barriers to enable "freer flow of capital, skilled labour and professionals", while including provisions for skilled migrants or exceptional talents to benefit from educational

Implications for Migration Policies

The ASEAN Community, which was inspired to some degree by the regional integration achieved in the European Union, is an expression of the region's aspirations not just towards socio-economic progress but also towards a set of normative standards and obligations that affect its people. However, observers have noted the gap between these aspirations and its actual implementation particularly in regard to human rights standards (Rathgeber 2014) as governance in most ASEAN states is guided mainly by the understanding of public order, state stability, rule of law and the spirit of non-interference between states. Despite progress on the instruments relating to the protection of migrant workers, only the Philippines and Vietnam have signed the ICRMW. None of the key ASEAN receiving countries has ratified the Discrimination (Employment and Occupation) Convention, which prohibits exclusion or preferences based on ethnicity, gender, religion, political opinion, national or social origin. Other instruments that deal directly with migrant workers' rights, including the Migration for Employment Convention (Revised), the Migrant Workers (Supplementary Provisions) Convention, the Equality of Treatment (Accident Compensation) Convention, Equality of Treatment (Social Security) Convention and the Maintenance of Social Security Rights Convention, remained unratified by ASEAN states.

The ASEAN Community's focus on prioritizing high-skilled migrants over low-skilled may seem to align with its aspirations for greater socio-economic progress but remains short-sighted as the region is likely to continue needing low- and medium-skilled workers due to economic disparities and projected labour shortages in some ASEAN states, such as Thailand (International Labour Organization [ILO] and Asian Development Bank [ADB] 2014). Moreover, a lack of focus on the development and training of low-skilled workers will likely result in industries that are heavily reliant on low-skilled labour to remain low-skilled and labour intensive. Technological advances and the expected increase in jobs that require technical knowledge and soft skills risk leaving many low-skilled workers behind and eventually out of jobs. ASEAN would also potentially be able to further reduce the level of irregular trans-border movement and the cost advantages that currently benefit companies who employ migrants illegally over those who do not if it were to give importance to the place of low-skilled migrants within the region (Martin and Abella 2014).

Wider discussion on issues surrounding forced migration within the region is needed as well as the inclusion of more specific categories of migrants beyond the legal/illegal binary within regional discourse and legislative documents. There is some indication that as ASEAN continues to commit to fulfilling the goals of the ASEAN Charter, it would continue to open up room for discussion on how to further elevate the lives of all people in the region. One of the items placed on the ASEAN Intergovernmental Commission on Human Rights' five-year work plan is a review of all human rights instruments and conventions that the member states have or have not acceded and ratified and to push for the ratification of more human rights instruments (AICHR 2015). However, only the Convention on the Rights of Persons with Disabilities was named specifically in that section of the work plan. Kneebone (2016) noted that a significant obstacle to the advancement of protection for forced migrants lays in the inconsistent approaches towards refugees between states and the commitment to individual state sovereignty. Malaysia, for example, views all refugees as "illegal immigrants" (Nah 2016; Don and Lee 2014), while Indonesia tolerates their existence and works with the UNHCR and the International Organization for Migration (IOM). Thailand allows the presence of the refugee's camps at the Thai-Burma border and registers all refugees through the Admission Boards (Petcharamesree 2016), while the Philippines has a long history of accepting and resettling refugees (Peñamante 2017). Non-interference and state sovereignty is mentioned in three of the six fundamental principles of ASEAN as agreed upon in the Treaty of Amity and Cooperation in Southeast Asia (TAC), 1976.

As ASEAN pushes forward in its bid to become a truly people-centred and integrated region, intra-ASEAN migration will continue to become a significant part of that development as states share resources and knowledge and increase multilateral sociopolitical partnerships. Migration should not be reduced to merely an abstract and impersonalized phenomenon as at its heart, it involves the people of ASEAN. Therefore, there is a greater need for ASEAN to include a more comprehensive discussion on who these people really are instead of reducing them to either "legal" or "illegal", so that their rights will continue to be upheld and their positive contributions to the region's growth will be acknowledged.

References

AICHR. 2015. *Five-Year Work Plan of the ASEAN Intergovernmental Commission on Human Rights (2016–2020).* ASEAN Intergovernmental Commission on Human Rights.

Andika Ab. Wahab. 2017. *The Future of Forced Migrants in ASEAN. In 50 Years of ASEAN—Still Waiting for Social and Ecological Justice.* Heinrich Böll Stiftung.

ASEAN. 2017. "ASEAN Leaders Commit to Safeguard the Rights of Migrant Workers." Accessed May 20, 2018. http://asean.org/asean-leaders-commit-safeguard-rights-migrant-workers/.

Association of Southeast Asian Nations (ASEAN). 2016. *ASEAN Economic Community at a Glance.*

Baker, Paul. 2006. *Using Corpora in Discourse Analysis.* London: Continuum.

Baker, Paul, Costas Gabrielatos, Majid KhosraviNik, Michal Krzyzanowski, Tony McEnery, and Ruth Wodak. 2008. "A Useful Methodological Synergy? Combining Critical Discourse Analysis and Corpus Linguistics to Examine Discourses of Refugees and Asylum Seekers in the UK Press." *Discourse Society* 19 (3): 273–306.

Baker, Paul, and Tony McEnery. 2005. "A Corpus-Based Approach to Discourses of Refugees and Asylum Seekers in UN and Newspaper Texts." *Journal of Language and Politics* 4 (2): 197–226.

Billig, M. 2008. "The Language of Critical Discourse Analysis: The Case of Nominalization." *Discourse & Society* 19 (6): 783–800.

Charteris-Black, Jonathan. 2006. "Britain as a Container: Immigration Metaphors in the 2005 Election Campaign." *Discourse & Society* 17 (5): 563–581.

Docquier, Frédéric, Giovanni Peri and Ilse Ruyssen. 2014. "The Cross-country Determinants of Potential and Actual Migration." *International Migration Review* 48: 37–99.

Don, Zuraidah Mohd, and Charity Lee. 2014. "Representing Immigrants as Illegals, Threats and Victims in Malaysia: Elite Voices in the Media." *Discourse & Society* 25 (6): 687–705.

Fairclough, Norman, and Ruth Wodak. 1997. "Critical Discourse Analysis." In *Discourse as Social Interaction (Discourse Studies: A Multidisciplinary Introduction: Vol. 2)*, edited by T. A. van Dijk, 258–284. London: Sage.

Fowler, R., B. Hodge, G. Kress, and T. Trew. 1979. *Language and Social Control*. London: Routledge.

Gabrielatos, Costas, and Paul Baker. 2008. "Fleeing, Sneaking, Flooding: A Corpus Analysis of Discursive Sonstructions of Refugees and Asylum Seekers in the UK Press, 1996–2005." *Journal of English Linguistics* 36 (1): 5–38.

Hart, Christopher. 2008. "Critical Discourse Analysis and Metaphor: Toward a Theoretical Framework." *Critical Discourse Studies* 5 (2): 91–106.

Hoewe, Jennifer. 2018. "Coverage of a Crisis: The Effects of International News Portrayals of Refugees and Misuse of the Term 'Immigrant'." *American Behavioral Scientist* 62 (4): 478–492.

Hunston, S. 2002. *Corpora in Applied Linguistics*. Cambridge: Cambridge University Press.

Ibrahim, Maggie. 2005. "The Securitization of Migration: A Racial Discourse." *International Migration* 43 (5): 163–187.

ILO. 2014. *Profits and Poverty: The Economics of Forced Labour*. Geneva: International Labour Organization.

ILO. 2015. "Analytical report on the international labour migration statistics database in ASEAN: Improving data collection for evidence-based policy-making." *Tripartite Action for the Protection and Promotion of the Rights of Migrants Workers in the ASEAN Region (ASEAN Triangle Project)*. Bangkok: ILO Regional Office for Asia and the Pacific.

ILO. 2018. *International Labour Migration Statistics Database in ASEAN*, edited by International Labour Organization (ILO).

International Labour Organization (ILO), and Asian Development Bank (ADB). 2014. *ASEAN Community 2015: Managing Integration for Better Jobs and Shared Prosperity*. Bangkok: International Labour Organization and Asian Development Bank.

IOM. n.d. "Key Migration Terms." http://www.iom.int/key-migration-terms.

Johnson, Heather L. 2011. "Click to Donate: Visual Images, Constructing Victims and Imagining the Female Refugee." *Third World Quarterly* 32 (6): 1015–1037. https://doi.org/10.1080/01436597.2011.586235.

Kaur, Amarjit. 2018. "Patterns and Governance of Labour Migration in ASEAN: Regional Policies and Migration Corridors." In *Handbook of Migration and Globalisation*, edited by Anna Triandafyllidou, 105–124. Cheltenham: Edward Elgar.

Kneebone, Susan. 2011. "ASEAN: Setting the Agenda for the Rights of Migrant Workers?" In *Human Rights in the Asia-Pacific Region: Towards Institution Building*, edited by Hitoshi Nasu and Ben Saul, 144–164. Hoboken: Routledge.

Kneebone, Susan. 2016. "Comparative Regional Protection Frameworks for Refugees: Norms and Norm Entrepreneurs." *The International Journal of Human Rights* 20 (2): 153–172. https://doi.org/10.1080/13642987.2016.1141499.

Koser, K. 2001. "The Smuggling of Asylum Seekers into Western Europe: Contradictions, Conundrums, and Dilemmas." In *Global Human Smuggling: Comparative Perspectives*, edited by D. Kyle and R. Koslowski, 58–73. Baltimore: John Hopkins University Press.

Malkki, Liisa H. 1996. "Speechless Emissaries: Refugees, Humanitarianism, and Dehistoricization." *Cultural Anthropology* 11 (3): 377–404.

Martin, Philip, and Manolo Abella. 2014. *Reaping the Economic and Social Benefits of Labour Mobility: ASEAN 2015*. Bangkok: ILO.

MOLES, and ILO. 2016. *Myanmar Labour Force, Child Labour and School to Work Transition Survey 2015*. Yangon: Central Statistical Organization and Ministry of Labour, Employment and Social Security.

MOM. 2016. *Labour Force in Singapore 2016*. Singapore: Ministry of Manpower.

Musarò, Pierluigi. 2011. "Living in Emergency: Humanitarian Images and the Inequality of Lives." *New Cultural Frontiers* 2: 13–43.

Nah, Alice M. 2016. "Networks and Norm Entrepreneurship Amongst Local Civil Society Actors: Advancing Refugee Protection in the Asia Pacific Region." *The International Journal of Human Rights* 20 (2): 223–240. https://doi.org/10.1080/13642987.2016.1139333.

Nieuwenhuys, Céline, and Antoine Pécoud. 2007. "Human Trafficking, Information Campaigns, and Strategies of Migration Control." *American Behavioral Scientist* 50 (12): 1674–1695.

Peñamante, Laurice. 2017. "Nine Waves of Refugees in the Philippines." Accessed May 28, 2018. http://www.unhcr.org/ph/11886–9wavesrefugees. html.

Petcharamesree, Sriprapha. 2016. "ASEAN and Its Approach to Forced Migration Issues." *The International Journal of Human Rights* 20 (2): 173–190. https://doi.org/10.1080/13642987.2015.1079021.

Pupavac, Vanessa. 2006. "Refugees in the 'Sick Role': Stereotyping Refugees and Eroding Refugee Rights." In *New Issues in Refugee Research*. Geneva: UNHCR.

Rajaram, Prem Kumar. 2002. "Humanitarianism and Representations of the Refugee." *Journal of Refugee Studies* 15 (3): 247–264. https://doi. org/10.1093/jrs/15.3.247.

Rathgeber, Theodor. 2014. "Human Rights and the Institutionalisation of ASEAN: An Ambiguous Relationship." *Journal of Current Southeast Asian Affairs* 33 (3): 131–165.

Sinclair, J. 1991. *Corpus, Concordance and Collocation*. Oxford: Oxford University Press.

Song, Jiyoung. 2015. "Introduction." In *Irregular Migration and Human Security in East Asia*, edited by Jiyoung Song and Alistair D. B. Cook, 1–19. London and New York: Routledge.

UN Population Division. 2017. "International Migrant Stock: The 2017 Revision." http://www.un.org/en/development/desa/population/migration/ data/estimates2/estimates17.shtml.

UNESCAP. 2017. *Trends and Drivers of International Migration in Asia and the Pacific*, edited by Economic and Social Commission for Asia and the Pacific. Bangkok: United Nations Economic and Social Council.

UNHCR. 2014. *South-East Asia Fact Sheet*.

UNHCR. n.a. "Asia and the Pacific." http://www.unhcr.org/en-my/asia-and-the-pacific.html.

van Leeuwen, Theo. 2008. "Representing Social Actors." In *Discourse and Practice: New Tools for Critical Discourse Analysis*, edited by Theo van Leeuwen, 23–54. Oxford: Oxford University Press.

Wongboonsin, Patcharawalai. 2006. "Asian Labour Migration and Regional Arrangements." In *Globalizing Migration Regimes: New Challenges to Transnational Cooperation*, edited by Kristof Tamas and Joakim Palme, 201–217. London and New York: Routledge.

8

Environmental Challenges Within ASEAN: Contemporary Legal Issues and Future Considerations

Sarah Yen Ling Tan and Hanim Kamaruddin

Introduction

The Association of Southeast Asian Nations (ASEAN) is a regional organization of ten-member states situated geographically within Southeast Asia. It was established in 1967 with the signing of the Bangkok Declaration[1] (also known as the ASEAN Declaration) and was intended primarily to promote and accelerate economic growth and social progress within the region.[2] The ASEAN Declaration was not anticipated to be absolute or unyielding in its influence; it was described at its inception as a simple document that "sought to set up a mechanism to foster mutual trust" (Woon 2012) while recognizing and maintaining the individual sovereignty of its member states.[3]

S. Y. L. Tan (✉)
Faculty of Law, University of Malaya, Kuala Lumpur, Malaysia
e-mail: sarahtan@um.edu.my

H. Kamaruddin
Faculty of Law, Universiti Kebangsaan Malaysia, Bangi, Malaysia
e-mail: hanim@ukm.edu.my

© The Author(s) 2019
A. Idris and N. Kamaruddin (eds.), *ASEAN Post-50*,
https://doi.org/10.1007/978-981-13-8043-3_8

Regardless, many efforts have since been made to build this community of states. Recognizing the existence of "mutual interests and common problems" (Preamble of the Bangkok Declaration 1967) this extended neighbourhood has in the past five decades worked towards joint efforts, regional solidarity and cooperation as a means to meeting and resolving these common interests and challenges. While this does not suggest a monolithic entity, the regional organization has made much effort in the past 52 years towards cohesive solidary.

One such common interest is founded on the fact that the region has been endowed with abundant and diverse natural resources. As a region, it "is a major contributor to global biodiversity, containing four of the world's 34 biodiversity hotspots and three mega-diverse nations" (SOER5 2017). Recent reports indicate that the region houses 20% of the world's plant and animal species, 35% of global mangrove forests and 30% of global coral reefs (Biodiversity and Wildlife in ASEAN 2018). Consequently, numerous challenges have arisen surrounding environmental conservation and sustainable development.

As an economy, ASEAN is one of the world's most dynamic regions, with growth rates of almost 5% in the past decade and energy consumption at approximately 7.5%, with both expected to continue to increase (Karki et al. 2005). It is also one of the world's largest markets and has a combined gross domestic product (GDP) of US$2.4 trillion. It is home to approximately 628 million people, with more than 75% of its population within urban areas (SOER5 2017). Within ASEAN, air pollution (and in particular haze or transboundary air pollution) are serious concerns when it is predicted that the Carbon Dioxide Emissions within ASEAN could rise by as much as 61% within the period of 2014–2025 (SOER5 2017); the decline of forest cover, the increase of commercial plantations and its effects on climate change, come alongside it. The economic growth of the region and the increasing demand for energy have also contributed to climate change concerns with CO_2 emissions rising rapidly within the region. Rising sea levels, induced by climate change is another key concern within the region given that Southeast Asia is home to many low-lying islands (Sovacool 2009). Resource degradation and extreme poverty within the region are similarly on the rise (ASEAN Socio-Cultural Community

Blueprint 2025). Lighting, droughts, cyclones, mudslides and landslides are some of the other natural disasters that have affected the economy, public health and the quality of life of the people in Southeast Asia (Lee et al. 2013).[4]

These factors pose a significant threat to the various natural resources and environmental systems in place. In particular concerns about the effects of climate change, the need to ensure sustainable use of energy and the challenges surrounding deforestation and forest degradation are key issues within ASEAN. It is the objective of this chapter to consider these key challenges and to lay down some ideas for policy consideration at the regional level, as ASEAN marches towards a united economic community. For a discussion on urban-level environmental challenges, please refer to Chapter 9.

This chapter has been divided into six sections. Section one introduces and outlines the chapter, while section two sketching out the history and the various efforts that have been undertaken by ASEAN towards dealing with existing environmental challenges. This will then be followed by section three, which will outline existing legal and policy considerations that ASEAN has taken in response to the three key environmental challenges identified, starting with the challenges surrounding energy. Section four will proceed to discuss the challenges surrounding deforestation while section five will expound on the effects of climate change. Finally, Section six will conclude with some possible consideration for the future.

ASEAN Environmental Cooperation

ASEAN is a region of great diversity—geographically, economically and politically—it has significant differences. From tiny island states to mountainous landscapes, from modern economies to middle-income developing nations, some with strong democracies while others (being newer democracies) are still grappling with this system of government. It includes those that boast of great civilizations and historic beginnings, to nations birthed as recent as the late nineteenth century. The region has also experienced colonization, war and considerable violence but more importantly, "…most of South-East Asia has enjoyed less than half a century of real, modern independence".[5]

Environmental concerns within the region also vary. For middle-income developing countries such as Thailand, Vietnam, Philippines and Indonesia, issues surrounding rapid development and urbanization such as water resources, infrastructure, urban environmental services and environmental migration are some of its key concerns.[6] The borders of Myanmar, Laos and Thailand house the Mekong River, and the key concerns of water resources, hydropower development, inland fisheries and agricultural lands.[7] While these similar issues do trouble Malaysia and Indonesia, deforestation, agriculture and plantation, and haze (regional air pollution) take a more prominent role. Singapore, on the other hand often called the "Garden city" share the concern for haze, and rising sea levels, land use planning and water sustainability.[8] Regardless of regional diversity, mutual interests and common concerns have brought this disparate group together.

When ASEAN was established, environmental challenges were not an express concern (Koh 1996); this stance has since positively taken an about turn with ASEAN recognizing the importance of sustainable development and regional cooperation. Today, ASEAN is guided by the ASEAN Socio-Cultural Community (ASCC) Blueprint 2025 as well as the ASEAN Strategic Plan on Environment (ASPEN). The latter was developed to "serve as a guiding reference for the ASEAN Senior Officials on Environment (ASOEN) and its subsidiary bodies" (ASPEN 2016). In addressing common environmental issues and challenges within ASEAN, ASPEN aims to chart out actions for ASEON and promote dialogue and cooperation among its member states as well as other non-ASEAN partners. ASPEN consists of action plans for seven strategic priorities that cover a wide environmental area. Each action plan contains specific programmes intended to build existing cooperation and to meet emerging needs. The ASCC, on the other hand, aims to realize (among others) a sustainable community that promotes environmental protection and a resilient one that is able to respond to environmental vulnerabilities such as climate change while sustaining its own identity (ASCC Blueprint 2025).

8 Environmental Challenges Within ASEAN ... 159

As an institutional framework, ASEAN cooperation began in 1978 with the creation of the ASEAN Expert Group on Environment (AEGE), a body that has since evolved into the present ASOEN. ASEON prepares for ASEAN's regional participation in international environmental governance deliberations, recommends policy guidelines pertaining to related environmental matters and monitors the state of ASEAN's natural resources and the quality of its environment while working towards harmonization of environmental standards throughout ASEAN member states (Koh and Robinson 2004). Below are 7 subsidiary bodies or working groups of ASEAN. These are the—

* ASEAN Working Group on Climate Change
* ASEAN Working Group on Chemicals and Waste,
* ASEAN Working Group on Coastal and Marine Environment,
* ASEAN Working Group on Environmental Education,
* ASEAN Working Group on Environmentally Sustainable Cities,
* ASEAN Working Group on Nature Conservation and Biodiversity, and
* ASEAN Working Group on Water Resources Management.

ASOEN and its subsidiary bodies meet once every year to ensure that the actions directed by ASPEN and the goals within ASCC Blueprint 2025 are implemented and put in place.

This institutional framework is headed by the ASEAN Ministerial Meeting on the Environment (AMME) that meets once every two years, to (among others) implement Summit decisions, to formulate and respond to environmental conventions and agreements. The ASEAN Summit decisions are ministerial-level meetings, held once every three years. It is ASEAN's highest decision-making body.

Sustainable Use of Energy

Approximately 90% of ASEAN's total commercial primary energy requirement is sustained by fossil fuel resources, such as coal, oil and gas; and the demand for primary energy is expected to grow "by an

160   S. Y. L. Tan and H. Kamaruddin

average of 4.7% per year from 2013 to... 2035" (Zamora 2015). These power-up oil refineries, agricultural-based industries (such as palm oil and rubber) and transportation while electrifying power generation plants (Karki et al. 2005; Sovacool 2009). Most of ASEAN's oil requirements are imported from non-ASEAN countries, and with levels of consumption expected to increase exponentially with development and economic growth when ASEAN imports about 60% of its oil requirements presently (Karki et al. 2005; Sovacool 2009), this inability to be self-sufficient has placed the region at risk. Oil dependency and the inability to meet increasing energy demands have contributed to growing concerns for regional energy security.

This lack of regional energy security drove ASEAN to form its first cooperative network after the oil crisis of 1973. The ASEAN Council on Petroleum (ASCOPE) was established in 1975 with the objective of establishing cooperation among member states (Karki et al. 2005; Nicolas 2009), and in 1986, the ASEAN Petroleum Security Agreement (APSA) was established to ensure that an emergency sharing scheme was put in place in the event of shortage or oversupply within the region.[9] Together with this, ASEAN also sought to cooperate on other fronts; in 1981, it established a task force, the Heads of ASEAN Public Utilities Authorities (HAPUA), as a platform to ensuring cooperation within the region on power grid connections. In 1986, the ASEAN Energy Co-operation Agreement was signed to expand this cooperation between member states to encompass a wider range of energy-related issues. Aspects such as conservation, energy development and supply, training, security and exchange of information form part of the cooperative activities within states.

In the 1997 Summit Declaration entitled "ASEAN Vision 2020", the importance of energy cooperation was reinforced by the ASEAN Heads of Government as they called for mutual collaboration to "establish interconnecting arrangements for electricity, natural gas and water within ASEAN through the ASEAN Power Grid (APG) and a Trans-ASEAN Gas Pipeline (TAGP) and promote cooperation in energy efficiency and conservation..." (ASEAN Vision 2020). This was subsequently translated into the Hanoi Plan of Action (HPA 1998). HPA was agreed to during the 1998 ASEAN Summit. As part of the Plan for the period 1999–2004, two main actions for energy cooperation were identified—the need to ensure the security and stability of energy supply, efficient utilization and rational management of energy in the region, and the need to create frameworks and implement modalities.

Reiterating ASEAN's commitment towards an integrated energy network, a series of action plans were formulated under the ASEAN Plan of Action for Energy Cooperation (APAEC).[10] The most recent two being the APAEC 2010–2015 and the present Plan implemented for the period 2016–2025.[11] Under the APAEC 2010–2015, targeted towards "enhancing energy security and sustainability for the ASEAN region including health, safety and the environment" (APAEC 2010–2015) a number of plans were put in place. These plans consist of seven components[12]—APG, the Trans-ASEAN Gas Pipeline (TAGP), Coal and Clean Coal Technology, Renewable Energy, Energy Efficiency and Conservation, Regional Energy Policy and Planning and Civilian Nuclear Energy. Enhancing these components further, APAEC 2016–2025 promoted a number of key initiatives that include a multilateral electricity trading system in order to expand and realize the full potential of the AGP, expanding the focus of the TAGP to promote Liquefied Natural Gas and to promote energy efficiency and renewable energy (APAEC 2015). These Plans fall within the energy component of the ASEAN Economic Community (AEC) Blueprint 2015.

Challenges for Sustainable Development

Given the objectives of APAEC 2016–2025, ASEAN member states have developed policies to ensure and establish sustainable energy supplies to accommodate different renewable energy targets, preferences, and have built capacity in order to meet 23% of its primary energy from modern and sustainable renewable sources by 2025 (IRENA 2018).

Research indicates that there is a diversity of energy use among the ASEAN states. For example, Brunei and Singapore's primary energy mix[13] is crude oil and natural gas concentrates, whereas Cambodia and Myanmar primarily focus on renewable energy resources (Kanchana and

Unesaki 2014), while Indonesia and the Philippines rely on geothermal energy (Lidula et al. 2007). While each country has its own priorities and capacities, different forms of instruments and supporting mechanisms have been put in place to achieve the energy targets of ASEAN member states. For example, individual countries such as Malaysia, Indonesia, Myanmar, Philippines and Vietnam have completed guidelines for various forms of renewable energy ranging from biomass, biogas and hydropower to solar power. While Singapore does not have specific policies or mandates for production of renewable energy, it has focused on energy efficiency and the use of renewable energy to reduce pollution and greenhouse gas (GHGs) as laid down in Singapore's Climate Action Plan 2016.

Despite the potentials generated from appropriate regional or national policies to deploy renewable energy, there remain challenges in achieving common objectives within ASEAN, objectives that require coordination and harmonization from all member states. In terms of CO_2 emissions per capita, Brunei has the highest of ASEAN member states, with overall trends of CO_2 similarly on an upward trend for other member states, except for Singapore and the Philippines (Kanchana and Unesaki 2014). While there is an abundance of sources of renewable energy in ASEAN—solar, wind power, hydropower and biomass—yet most of these are underutilized with states relying primarily on conventional sources for energy (Kanchana and Unesaki 2014). It has been suggested that there are a number of barriers to renewable energy, some are common to most states within ASEAN such as the "lack of funding, lack of experience and knowledge and limited policy frameworks" (Lidula et al. 2007). In the latter, the lack of or insufficient regulatory framework or policies, in relation to land use and the environmental impact of renewable energy technology to regulate renewable energy development is outlined in Table 8.1. Interestingly, Brunei does not have a clear and dedicated policy framework for the development of renewable energy.

Some of the other major factors that may impede the development of renewable energy can be summarized below:

8 Environmental Challenges Within ASEAN ...   163

Table 8.1 Relevant framework on renewable and sustainable energy development in ASEAN

ASEAN countries	Framework
Brunei	–
Cambodia	National Policy on Rural Electrification by Renewable Energy 2006, National Strategic Development Plan 2014–2018, Power Sector Strategy 1999–2016
Indonesia	National Energy Policy (Government Regulation No.79/2014), Regulation Number 22 of 2017 on the General Planning for National Energy (RUEN), Law No. 30/2007 on Energy, National Electricity Plan (RUKN) (2015–2034) and Electricity Supply Business Plan (Rencana Umum Penyediaan Tenaga Listrik – "RUPTL") 2016–2025.
Laos	Renewable Energy Strategy Development 2011–2025
Malaysia	National Renewable Energy Policy and Action Plan 2009
Myanmar	Myanmar Energy Master Plan 2016
Philippines	Biofuels Act 2006, Renewable Energy Act 2008
Singapore	Does not have one specifically but focuses on energy efficiency and becoming a hub for research and development (RND) in alternative energy solutions
Thailand	Alternative Energy Development Plan (AEDP) 2015–2036, Renewable Energy Development Plan (REDP) 2008–2022
Vietnam	Vietnam Renewable Energy development Strategy 2016–2030, National Power Development Plan 2011–2030

* The lack of coordination among government agencies and private sectors in managing incentives associated with renewable energy development, tax exemption and subsidy.
* The monopolization and domination of electricity generation by a sole company in a country create an impediment to potential investors to invest in ASEAN.
* Complex bureaucracy, top-down policy planning and lack of clear mechanisms to meet specified targets prevent positive feedbacks and involvement from main stakeholders.
* The high costs in capital intensive renewable energy projects and lack of adequate financial access.
* There is a lack of experience and expertise in ASEAN countries to evaluate risks of renewable energy investment.
* Geographical limitations and technical conditions including limited infrastructure capacity to build energy plants.

164   S. Y. L. Tan and H. Kamaruddin

* The implementation of import tariffs for renewable energy technologies by some ASEAN countries will increase the cost of energy projects.
* Lack of public awareness and support concerning values of renewable energy usage and its potential to protect the environment.

Challenges Surrounding Deforestation and Mitigation Responses

Within ASEAN deforestation stands out as a challenge. The high rates of forest loss or deforestation, in particular Indonesia and Malaysia, have raised concerns about future expansions of oil palm plantations. Forest loss as a result of land clearing for plantations or industrial agriculture and commercial or illegal logging is on the increase when the estimated rate of deforestation is 1.8% per year, compared to 1.4% in the 1980s (Elliot 2003). From 1989 to 2013, data showed (Table 8.2) large increases from the earlier period of 1989–2013, in areas planted for oil palm in these two countries where deforestation is intrinsically linked with increases in planted areas (Vijay et al. 2016). The depletion of forests has impacted tremendously on the loss of biodiversity, threatening large numbers of species of wildlife within Southeast Asia (Rao 2018). Changing land-use and degradation has also resulted in increasingly unsustainable agricultural or commercial practices, threatening existing water

Table 8.2 Per cent increase in FAO total oil palm planted area from 1989 to 2013 in selected ASEAN countries and estimated per cent of oil palm planted areas from deforestation since 1989

Producer country	Per cent increased in planted area	Per cent of area in deforestation
Indonesia	91.7	53.8
Philippines	72.1	0
Thailand	85.5	0
Malaysia	63.3	39.6

Source Vijay et al. (2016)

resources, increasing soil and river pollution, while destabilizing natural biological life cycles with the increased use of fertilizers, chemicals and pesticides (Elliot 2003).

The environmental evidence has strengthened ASEAN's commitments towards achieving "a sustainable environment in the face of social changes and economic development" (ASEAN Socio-Cultural Community Blueprint 2025). As part of its strategic measures, reducing carbon emissions from deforestation and agricultural activities and the effective implementation of climate change adaptation programmes by enhancing regional integration was identified.[14]

Over the past decades, it has become increasingly apparent that ASEAN is pointing towards a positive trend in addressing current and future mitigation commitments among the member states in the area of agriculture, forestry and carbon trading. Therefore, there is a need for ASEAN member states to sustain such a momentum to ensure regional and national challenges are dealt with on a timely basis.

Other key issues plaguing ASEAN's pledge to reducing emissions from deforestation and forest degradation should also be addressed. Although not exhaustive, these include:

- The enforcement of domestic laws and punishment on forest degradation arising from foreign business activities (Jayakumar 2015).
- Continuous monitoring and assessment by relevant government agencies is a major challenge. The political system must ensure that regional governments and the bureaucracy at all levels have the motivation to state that targets are being met.
- Decision-making in the interests of long-term sustainability are made more difficult by logging and palm oil companies, both domestically and foreign-owned, who use their influence over regional economies to extract favourable treatment from politicians (Howes and Wyrwoll 2012).
- Strengthening funding facilities for adaptation planning, establish monitoring and evaluating systems, sharing of expertise to achieve coherent national adaptation strategies.

- Corporate social responsibility initiatives, such as policy frameworks to attach companies to be environmentally aware of the impacts their activities have on the environment and society, are found to be piecemeal and voluntary limiting to tax incentives/benefits (Kamaruddin 2016).
- The minimal cooperative management between government departments/agencies and knowledge providers and users that is critical to achieving shared benefits and outcomes from mitigation programmes.

Climate Change Implications

The multifaceted impacts of climate change experienced by ASEAN member states range from climate-related interstate issues associated with human migration, extreme weather events, food security risks, altered river flow, transboundary air pollution (or more commonly known as haze) to reducing GHGs emissions from national activities. These have individually and collectively encouraged member states to strengthen their rapid response capacities in climate change adaptation through the ASEAN Agreement on Disaster Management and Emergency Response (AADMER).[15]

Furthermore, socio-economic impacts from human activities namely agricultural, forestry activities and climatic changes are perceived as central elements to whether ASEAN can maintain or provide a sound

Table 8.3 Ranking climate risk of ASEAN countries

1	Myanmar
2	Philippines
3	Vietnam
4	Thailand
5	Cambodia
6	Indonesia
7	Laos
8	Malaysia
9	Brunei Darussalam
10	Singapore

Source Kreft et al. (2016)

quality of life. Hence, the complex relationship between climate change with economic development and poverty has never been more evident (Guemide 2017). According to the Global Climate Risk Index, four of the ten ASEAN countries most affected by climate change are Myanmar, the Philippines, Thailand and Vietnam (Table 8.3).

The efforts to enhance and support on-going efforts to mitigate the implications of climate change on human survival and development undoubtedly requires multilateral international cooperation among the ASEAN member states. Such a commitment is vital towards addressing climate change impacts; this commitment was reflected in the ratification of the Kyoto Protocol by all ASEAN member states. Further, all states except Myanmar have signed the Paris Agreement to reaffirm their shared responsibility on climate change issues.[16] The US withdrawal from the Paris Agreement seemed to have far-reaching consequences towards regional cooperation in the Asia Pacific and within ASEAN in tackling climate change (Table 8.4). A recent study had found that "despite their positive stances on climate change, most ASEAN countries have not taken on prominent roles in international climate policy and as a result, they remain takers rather than makers in international climate politics. ASEAN as an organization stands to gain or lose status by following up or not following up its member states on climate issues, and by member states succeeding or failing to meet their NDCs" (Øverland et al. 2017).

There is an invariable call to ASEAN for continuous and effective efforts based on coordinated approaches in various memorandums and agreements to tackle issues on climate change.[17] While this issue has gained much publicity and regional initiatives have begun, these have been hampered by the different levels of national development within individual ASEAN member states or insufficient or lack of regional and/or national coordination in climate change reduction strategies. Given that ASEAN embraces the idea of common but differentiated responsibilities, member states can decide how much to implement and how best to achieve regional-level goals, at national levels. On a more positive note, the adaptation policies or frameworks established in each ASEAN member countries are relatively new and adaptation efforts are seemingly on the right path (Pulawska 2016).

168   S. Y. L. Tan and H. Kamaruddin

Table 8.4 ASEAN's reaction to the United States withdrawal from Paris Agreement

Indonesia	Withdrawal is not in line with a commitment to international cooperation. No country can face climate change alone, international cooperation is needed (Arisandi 2017)
Malaysia	"Profound regret and deep concern". "Retrogressive". As the world's second-largest emitter of greenhouse gases, and with a per capita emissions level that far exceeds the global average, the United States has a "moral obligation" to continue to champion environmental issues. However, with the drive and dedication shown by other countries to battle the issue of global warming, coupled with great powers such as China and the European Union assuming leading roles, the Paris Agreement will continue to be a success despite the US withdrawal (Wan Junaidi Tuanku Jaafar 2017)
Philippines	"The Philippines is deeply troubled by the decision of the US to with-draw from the Paris Agreement and appeals that they reconsider their position. The United States, as the second-largest emitter of greenhouse gases, and more importantly, one of the world leaders, would have played a key role in creating the much-needed global paradigm shift towards a more climate-resilient and climate-smart future" (Climate Change Commission under the Office of the President 2017)
Singapore	"Disappointed" at the decision and called for a continued push in global support for the Paris Agreement. "A great pity". Climate change is a "clear and present danger", the resolution of which requires a concerted global effort (Zulkifli Masagos 2017)
Thailand	Reiterated Thailand's commitment and the importance of the Paris Agreement (ONEP Thailand 2017)

Source Øverland et al. (2017)

Other critical challenges that ASEAN member states may face in relation to mitigation and adaptation to climate change includes (but is not limited to) the following:

* Insufficiency in building competence, visibility and awareness in ASEAN's initiatives and commitments in climate change and reduction of GHG's.

8 Environmental Challenges Within ASEAN ... 169

* Absence or lack of publishing and sharing of comprehensive data and up-to-date analysis to highlight the vulnerability of Southeast Asia countries to climate change.
* There is no compliance mechanism to monitor and comment on the implementation of nationally determined contributions (NDCs) by the ASEAN member states at any interval.
* Technology transfer or access to cost-effective technology to reduce carbon that promotes best practices and technology-related investments in clean energy is lacking.
* To continuously enhance regional cooperation on transboundary haze, explore the adoption of transboundary mitigation strategies or water resources management, extreme weather conditions, climate-induced migration, coastal and marine ecosystems protection and outbreaks of heat-related illnesses.
* There is no regional benchmark for clean energy good practices and strategies.
* Lack of expertise in climate change or climate policy for international affairs in Southeast Asia attributing to human and technological capacity constraints.
* Different responses to climate change in each individual ASEAN member states based on vulnerability/capacity of each individual state resulting in different achievements by each country leading to incoherence/non-harmonization in strategies and mechanisms.
* ASEAN agreements are difficult to regulate directly by international law especially in transboundary pollution caused by corporate and non-state activities that pose compliance challenges. Since the corporate entities are not treaty parties, individual national laws must be enforced to regulate activities by non-state actors. On this note, Singapore has paved the way for international law on extra-territoriality to be enforced in transboundary haze pollution problems in its own domestic law to prevent future emissions of air pollution.[18]

Climate-related mechanisms will need to consider the "ASEAN way" of resolving regional matters, with its emphasis on national sovereignty, non-interference and consensus in decision-making. Furthermore, as an example, the United Nations Framework Convention on Climate Change (UNFCCC) has provided common but differentiated capabilities and responsibilities, reaffirmed in the Paris Agreement's concept of NDCs. This approach is seen to be amply compatible with the traditional "ASEAN way" to regional cooperation on any commonly shared concerns in Southeast Asia. ASEAN should further strengthen advocacy on the implementation of various mitigation and adaptation programmes based on the underlying policy framework, cooperation and identification of common and shared solutions to mitigate the climatic change in the region.

Some Considerations

Among the many environmental challenges that presently affect ASEAN member states, three significant issues were outlined—firstly, concerns about the effects of climate change, followed by the need to ensure sustainable use of energy and finally, the challenges surrounding deforestation and forest degradation. A number of weaknesses were identified as issues to be addressed in order to ensure the successful implementation of the goals that ASEAN had set out under ASPEN and the ASCC Blueprint 2025. Yet, apart from these efforts, a number of other broader prospects could also be taken into consideration.

The AEC was a major milestone towards regional economic integration. The ideals of the AEC were adopted by ASEAN leaders in November 2015 in Kuala Lumpur. AEC's vision is to have an ASEAN that is "highly integrated and cohesive; competitive, innovative and dynamic; with enhanced connectivity and sectoral cooperation; and a more resilient, inclusive, and people-oriented, people-centred community, integrated with the global economy"[19] by 2025. This agenda, should it be realized, requires a paradigm shift from the old modus operandi to a completely new one. The traditional means preferred non-interference, it emphasized and favoured cooperation and consensus over clear resolutions, soft law formulations over concrete legally binding instruments and national-level attempts subject to differentiated capacities over the clear assignment of responsibilities. While this may have been the necessary approach at the inception of ASEAN in 1967, much has changed. The democratization of many ASEAN member states since then have given impetus to principles of transparency and accountability, particularly in the light of existing environmental degradation this has become pertinent.

The key to ensuring sustainable development, to remaining competitive in the global market and to safeguarding and managing the region's environmental challenges may be to move towards an environmental governance system. A system that is based on binding legal instruments, one that builds capacity and supports existing legal systems via institutions with jurisdiction to enforce its decisions. One such consideration is a regional dispute settlement body. While conciliation and negotiations are priorities in any ASEAN disputes, when these are not achievable the principle of non-interference with national policies of member states and the "ASEAN way" becomes a significant challenge. Presently, there is no transparent established system of resolution in environmental related matters, although few territorial disputes within ASEAN have ever been referred to international bodies and arbitrators.[20] Having an established dispute resolution mechanism will add weight to and encourage compliance of its environmental objectives regardless of the challenges.

Concluding Remarks

The key question for policymakers in the subject of a new environmental paradigm shift will circle around the key question of obtaining requisite political will from all ASEAN member states to reassess its common identity. Beyond this, questions of funding and the capacity of member states to translate regional ideals into national plans are potential challenges that seemed even more daunting.

Environmental challenges are only one subcategory in the greater scheme but with any success that could result from thoughtful assessment to recreate a new regional identity may result into other subcategories (such as the economy, trade, energy, etc.) that are reliant on environmental protectionism. Thus, environmental protection and related concerns should be seen as a common priority, leading to regional shared benefit and liability alike. The IPCC Report released in October 2018 that called for an urgent cut in carbon emissions by half within the next ten years only proves that environmental challenges are no longer ancillary developmental challenges but significant challenges that will determine the fate of the next generation and the planet as a whole.[21] Given such importance and urgency, can ASEAN afford not to act?

Notes

1. ASEAN began with the original group of 5 nations, namely Indonesia, Malaysia, Philippines, Singapore and Thailand. It since grew to include Brunei Darussalam in 1984, Vietnam in 1995, Laos and Myanmar in 1997 and Cambodia in 1999.
2. Among other aims—such as the need for regional stability—see the Bangkok Declaration, available at: http://asean.org/the-asean-declaration-bangkok-declaration-bangkok-8-august-1967/.
3. Given the political turmoil within the region at this period, states jealously guarded its sovereignty and upheld the notions of non-interference. See Woon (2012, 2–6) for short history. Similarly during ASEAN's first few years "the National ASEAN Secretariats carried out projects without a formal treaty system" suggesting that it was a loose arrangement that has since grown more and more sophisticated methods of cooperation. See Koh, K. L. and Robinson, N. A., "Regional Environmental Governance: Examining the Association of Southeast Asian Nations (ASEAN) Model".
4. It was also reported that in 2011 Thailand suffered losses of approximately US$45 billion as a result of the nationwide flood. See Fifth ASEAN State of the Environment Report (SOER5).
5. Harold Brookfield and Yvonne Byron, "South-East Asia's Environmental Future: The Search for Sustainability", United Nations University Press and Oxford University Press, Singapore, 1993, p. ix.

6. See generally Edsel E. Sajor, "Peri-Urbanization and Environmental Issues in mega- urban Regions", Philip Hersch (Ed.), Routledge Handbook of the Environment in Southeast Asia, Routledge, 2017, p. 264.
7. Jeremy Carew-Reid, "The Mekong: Strategic Environmental Assessment of Mainstream Hydropower Development in an International River Basin", Philip Hersch (Ed.), Routledge Handbook, see Footnote 16 above, p. 334.
8. See Carl Grundy-Warr and Victor Savage, "Singapore: Sustaining a Global City-State and the Challenges of Environmental Governance in the Twenty-Fist Century", Chapter 27, Philip Hersch (Ed.), Routledge Handbook, see Footnote 16 above, p. 448.
9. APSA established the ASEAN Emergency Petroleum Sharing Scheme that committed ASEAN member states to meeting the oil needs for its members.
10. The ASEAN Plan of Action on Energy Cooperation (APAEC) began in 1999–2004 and was formulated in Jakarta, Indonesia. This expanded to APAEC 2004–2009 adopted at the 22nd AMEM in Manila on 9 June 2004, to APAEC 2010–2015 and the present from 2016 to 2025.
11. It is themed "Enhancing Energy Connectivity and Market Integration in ASEAN to Achieve Energy Security, Accessibility, Affordability and Sustainability for All". The initiatives under APAEC 2016–2025 will be implemented in two phases covering specific measures towards cooperation and connectivity. Phase 1 will be for the period 2016–2020 and Phase 2 during 2021–2025.
12. Though not limited to these seven.
13. Primary Energy Mix is defined as primary energy sources that refer to coal, crude oil, natural gas and renewables.
14. See the ASEAN Socio-Cultural Community Blueprint 2025, under the strategic measure C1–C3.
15. See http://agreement.asean.org/media/download/20140119170000.pdf.
16. Refer to http://asean.org/storage/2017/08/Final-ASEAN-EU-Statement-on-the-Paris-Agreement.pdf, for ASEAN-EU Statement on the Paris Agreement: Reaffirming Commitment to Cooperation to Address the Shared Challenge of Climate Change.
17. Refer to memorandum developed by the ASEAN Institutes of Strategic and International Studies (ASEAN ISIS) on 15 February 2017 titled *The Future of ASEAN: Meeting the Challenges of a Changing Global and Regional Landscape* (ASEAN ISIS 2017) and ASEAN Joint Statement

on Climate Change issued Declarations/Statements related to climate change in 2007, 2009, 2010, 2011 and 2014.

18. See Transboundary Haze Pollution Act 2014 (No. 24 of 2014) which imposes criminal or civil liability for "…any conduct or thing outside Singapore which causes or contributes to any haze pollution in Singapore".

19. See http://asean.org/asean-economic-community/.

20. See the cases of Sipadan and Ligitan between Malaysia and the Philippines, and the case of Batu Putih between Malaysia and Singapore.

21. See "Summary for Policymakers of IPCC Special Report on Global Warming of 1.5 °C Approved by Governments", https://www.ipcc.ch/2018/10/08/summary-for-policymakers-of-ipcc-special-report-on-global-warming-of-1-5c-approved-by-governments/ (last accessed on 22 January 2019).

References

ASEAN. "Strategic Plan on Environment (ASPEN) 2016–2025." Available from: http://division.dwr.go.th/bic/?p=3208.

ASEAN. 1967. "Bangkok Declaration 1967." Available from: https://asean.org/the-asean-declaration-bangkok-declaration-bangkok-8-august-1967/.

ASEAN. 2018. "Biodiversity and Wildlife in ASEAN." *ASEAN Focus* 1(6): 6–7. Accessed May 15, 2018. https://think-asia.org/handle/11540/8045.

Elliott, Lorraine. 2003. "ASEAN and Environmental Cooperation: Norms, Interests and Identity." *The Pacific Review* 16 (1): 29–52, p. 34.

Guemide, Boutkhil. 2017. "The Effects of Climate Change on the Economic Growth of ASEAN Countries." Accessed May 10, 2018. http://web.isanet.org/Web/Conferences/HKU2017-s/Archive/05d22192-b7f5-43cc-af17-6d2e1760b191.pdf.

Howes, Stephen, and Paul Wyrwoll. 2012. *Asia's Wicked Environmental Problems*. ADBI Working Paper Series, No. 348. https://www.adb.org/sites/default/files/publication/156203/adbi-wp348.pdf.

IRENA. 2018. "Higher Shares of Renewable Energy Central to Sustainable Development Across Southeast Asia." Accessed February 21. http://www.irena.org/newsroom/pressreleases/2018/Feb/Higher-Shares-of-Renewable-Energy-Central-to-Sustainable-Development-Across-Southeast-Asia.

Jayakumar, S., Tommy Koh, Robert Beckman, and Hao Duy Phan, ed. 2015. *Transboundary Pollution Evolving Issues of International Law and Policy*, 344. Cheltenham, UK: Edward Elgar Publishing.

Kamaruddin, Hanim, Rasyikah Md Khalid, Dina Imam Supaat, Syahirah Abdul Shukor, and Normawati Hashim. 2016. "Deforestation and Haze in Malaysia: Status of Corporate Responsibility and Law Governance." European Proceedings of Social and Behavioural Sciences (EpSBS), 2016 BE-ci International Conference on Business & Economics. Future Academy, UK. https://www.researchgate.net/publication/311254323_Deforestation_and_Haze_in_Malaysia_Status_of_Corporate_Responsibility_and_Law_Governance.

Kanchana, Kamonphorn, and Hironobu Unesaki. 2014. "ASEAN Energy Security: An Indicator-Based Assessment." *Energy Procedia* 56: 163–171.

Karki, Shankar K., Michael D. Mann, and Hossein Salehfar. 2005. "Energy and Environment in the ASEAN: Challenges and Opportunities." *Energy Policy* 33: 499–509.

Koh, Kheng Lian. 1996. *ASEAN Environmental Law, Policy and Governance: Selected Documents*, Vol. 1. Singapore: World Scientific.

Koh, Kheng Lian, and Nicholas A. Robinson. 2004. "Regional Environmental Governance: Examining the Association of Southeast Asian Nations (ASEAN) Model." In *Global Environmental Governance: Options and Opportunities*, edited by Daniel C. Esty and Maria H. Ivanova, 101–120. Yale, CA, USA: Yale School of Forestry & Environmental Studies.

Kreft, Sönke, David Eckstein, and Inga Melchior. 2016. "Global Climate Risk Index 2017: Who Suffers Most from Extreme Weather Events? Weather-Related Loss Events in 2015 and 1996 to 2015." Germanwatch Nord-Süd Initiative eV, 2016. Accessed May 15, 2018. https://www.researchgate.net/deref/https%3A%2F%2Fgermanwatch.org%2Fde%2F-download%2F16411.pdf.

Lee, Zhi Hua, Sumathi Sethupathi, Keat Teong Lee, Subhash Bhatia, and Abdul Rahman Mohamed. 2013. "An Overview on Global Warming in Southeast Asia: CO_2 emission status, efforts done, and barriers." *Renewable and Sustainable Energy Reviews* 28: 71–81.

Lidula, N. W. A., N. Mithulanathan, W. Ongsakul, C. Widjaya, and R. Henso. 2007. "ASEAN Towards Clean and Sustainable Energy: Potentials, Utilization and Barriers." *Renewable Energy* 32: 1441–1452.

Nicolas, Francoise. 2009. "ASEAN Energy Cooperation: An Increasingly Daunting Challenge." *Institut Francais des Relations Internationles (IFRI)*. http://www.nst.or.th/n-power/Asean-energy-IFRI_fnicolas.pdf.

Øverland, Indra, and Roman Vakulchuk. 2017. "Impact of Climate Change on ASEAN International Affairs: Risk and Opportunity Multiplier." *NUPI Report.* https://www.researchgate.net/publication/320622312_Impact_of_Climate_Change_on_ASEAN_International_Affairs_Risk_and_Opportunity_Multiplier.

Pulawska, Grazyna, ed. 2016. *Handbook for ASEAN Government Official on Climate Change and SDGs.* Singapore: AIS—Europe Environmental Forum.

Rao, Madhu. 2018. "ASEAN's Biodiversity on the Brink." *ASEAN Focus.* 1: 2. https://www.iseas.edu.sg/images/pdf/ASEANFocusIssue12018.pdf.

Sovacool, Benjamin K. 2009. "Energy Policy and Cooperation in Southeast Asia: The History, Challenges, and Implications of the Trans-ASEAN Gas Pipeline (TAGP) Network." *Energy Policy* 37 (6): 2356–2367.

Vijay, Varsha, Stuart L. Pimm, Clinton N. Jenkins, and Sharon J. Smith. 2016. "The Impacts of Oil Palm on Recent Deforestation and Biodiversity Loss." *PLOS One* 11 (7). https://doi.org/10.1371/journal.pone.0159668.

Woon, Walter. 2012. "Dispute Settlement the ASEAN Way." Available from: https://cil.nus.edu.sg/wp-content/uploads/2010/01/WalterWoon-Dispute-Settlement-the-ASEAN-Way-2012.pdf.

Zamora, Christopher G., ed. 2015. "ASEAN Plan of Action for Energy Cooperation (APAEC) 2016–2025." ASEAN Centre for Energy, 1–51.

International Treaties/Documents

ASEAN Socio-Cultural Community Blueprint. 2025. Available from: http://asean.org/storage/2016/01/ASCC-Blueprint-2025.pdf.

ASEAN Vision. 2020. Available from: http://asean.org/?static_post=asean-vision-2020.

Executive Summary of the APAEC. 2010–2015. Available from: http://www.wise.co.th/wise/References/Energy_Management/ASEAN_Energy_Cooperation_2010_2015.pdf.

Fifth ASEAN State of the Environment Report (SOER5), launched 12 September 2017. Available from: https://environment.asean.org/soer5/.

Hanoi Plan of Action. 1998. Available from: http://asean.org/?static_post=hanoi-plan-of-action.

9

Environmental Threats to the Performance of Urban Areas in ASEAN Integration

Zakaria Alcheikh Mahmoud, Yahaya
Ahmad, Melasutra Md. Dali
and Nikmatul Adha Nordin

Introduction: Urban Areas of ASEAN and the Regional Integration

Since the existence of ASEAN, the rate of the region's urban population has been increasing. It is expected that the growth of ASEAN urban population will continue in the coming decades. 24.3% of ASEAN

Z. Alcheikh Mahmoud (✉) · M. Md. Dali · N. A. Nordin
Centre for Sustainable Urban Planning & Real Estate (SUPRE),
University of Malaya, Kuala Lumpur, Malaysia
e-mail: zakaria2009@um.edu.my

M. Md. Dali
e-mail: melasutr@um.edu.my

N. A. Nordin
e-mail: nikmatul@um.edu.my

Y. Ahmad
Centre for Building Construction and Tropical Architecture (BUCTA),
University of Malaya, Kuala Lumpur, Malaysia
e-mail: yahaya@um.edu.my

© The Author(s) 2019
A. Idris and N. Kamaruddin (eds.), *ASEAN Post-50*,
https://doi.org/10.1007/978-981-13-8043-3_9

population was living in urban areas in 1980. The rate of urban population increased to 47% in 2015 (The ASEAN Secretariat 2003). It is expected that in 2050, ASEAN population will reach 785 million, out of which 63% will be urban. The rate of urban population at the country level, however, varies significantly. Table 9.1 shows the urban population share of ASEAN countries and the degree of urbanization.[1] As seen in the table, in 2016, 100% of the Singaporean population, 78% of the population of Brunei Darussalam, 75% of Malaysians and 54% of the Indonesian population lived in urban areas. The rate was lower in other countries with the lowest in Cambodia (21%) (The ASEAN Secretariat 2017a). The urban population of ASEAN live in cities[2] and towns of various sizes ranging from megacities, each is with a population of more than 10 million, to small cities where each city has a population of 500,000 to one million.[3]

Most of the urban population is still living in small cities (62% in 2015). (ASEAN UP 2017; Economist Intelligence Unit 2016) The urban areas of ASEAN, particularly the large ones, have been the generators of development at the respective country level as well as the regional integration level. In 2015, the urban areas produced 80% of the gross domestic products (GDP) of ASEAN. The role of generating development has been enhanced by the improvement of infrastructure and

Table 9.1 Rate of Urban population share in ASEAN Countries—1975–2050

ASEAN Countries	% share of urban population				
	1975	2000	2016	2025	2050
Brunei	26.8	71.1	78	80.9	87.2
Cambodia	10.2	16.9	21	26.3	43.8
Indonesia	12.4	42	54	50.7	65.9
Laos	7.2	22	40	49	68
Malaysia	20.4	62	75	80.5	87.9
Myanmar	16.2	27.8	35	44.4	62.9
Philippines	27.1	35.6	44	55.4	69.4
Singapore	99.4	100	10	100	100
Thailand	16.5	31.1	52	42.2	60
Vietnam	9.9	24.3	34	36.4	54.9

Source The ASEAN Secretariat 2003; Asia Research Institute 2013; The ASEAN Secretariat 2017a

9 Environmental Threats to the Performance of Urban Areas ... 179

the competition between urban centres (Dahiya 2015). Smaller urban settlements, particularly those located along regional transport network, will gain more importance and grow faster with the implementation of the three pillars ASEAN community started in 2015 (political and security community, economic community and socio-cultural community) and the adoption of the ASEAN Vision 2025 (Thant 2012).

The urban areas of ASEAN will contribute significantly to the economic community and to the socio-cultural community. In the urban areas, the main objectives of the two communities can be met. The economic integration among the member states and between ASEAN and the global economy will take place through the economic centres which are concentrated in the region's urban areas. The proper performance of cities and towns of each ASEAN country will facilitate the fair distribution of developmental benefits to all population groups leading to equitable and inclusive development. The proper performance will also facilitate and sustain the growth of the middle-income class which emerged and expand in ASEAN cities with the recent decades' economic development. This narrows socio-economic gaps in society (Economist Intelligence Unit 2016). The main role of the urban areas of ASEAN in reaching the objectives of ASEAN socio-cultural community (ASCC) is in contributing to sustainable development and in environmental protection. The best performance of this role is in making economic development in balance with the environment and society to reserve the ability to meet the coming generations' needs as well as the needs of the present ones. This can be reached through the best utilization of resources along with minimum impacts of the economic activities on society and nature[4] (Fig. 9.1).

Since the early years of existence, ASEAN recognized the importance of a healthy environment, in and outside urban areas, for their regional integration. The member states have, since 1977, closely cooperated in promoting environmental cooperation in line with the international environmental concern. The environmental cooperation was enhanced with the adoption of the concept of sustainable development and the incorporation of the Millennium Developmental Goals (MDG) of the year 2000 into the main strategies for ASEAN regional integration.

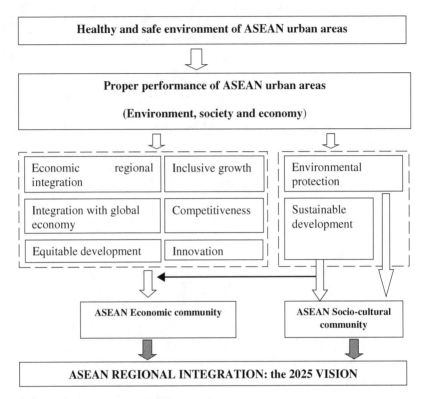

Fig. 9.1 Contribution of healthy performance of urban areas to regional integration of ASEAN 2025 vision (*Source* Conceptualized by authors)

In 2016, ASEAN followed the international community in adopting the Sustainable Development Goals (SDG) for guiding the development up to 2030. Since then, ASEAN has been working on adapting the goals into their regional as well as national contexts. ASEAN policies and cooperation on the environment are currently guided by the ASEAN Socio-Cultural Blueprint 2025 which calls for promoting and ensuring balance and sustainability in social development and environment to meet the needs of the people at present and in the future. The sociocultural blueprint aims to reach an inclusive ASEAN community with equitable access to a sustainable environment for its entire people (The ASEAN Secretariat 2017b). Making the environmental concern as a part of the sociocultural pillar, however, has led to a lack of integration

9 Environmental Threats to the Performance of Urban Areas ... 181

between this pillar and the other two pillars of safety and political and economic communities.

The up to date evidence shows that the progress in ASEAN countries focused on economic development at the cost of environment. This has led to the emergence and development of environmental issues such as air and water pollution. These issues, along with some external issues such as the climate change and the sea-level rise, constitute, in the coming years, a threat to the urban areas' performance, particularly the large ones and consequently to the process of ASEAN regional integration (Institute of Southeast Asian Studies 2010; Kio and Thuzar 2012; Economist Intelligence Unit 2016). These threats are discussed in the following sections.

Air Pollution in ASEAN Urban Areas

Evolution and Trends

Air pollution is a widespread phenomenon in the urban as well as rural areas of ASEAN. The annual mean level of air pollution in the urban areas is often more than 5–10 times the World Health Organization (WHO) limits. There are two major sets of pollutants in the ASEAN atmosphere, "Particular Matters" (PM) and greenhouse gases (GHG). The "Particular Maters" is a mixture of tiny particles of solid or liquid suspended in the air. They are of two types: the particles with 10 micrometres and smaller (Known as PM10) and those with 2.5 micrometres and less[5] (Known as PM2.5) (World Health Organization, n.d.). A measurement of PM2.5 that was carried out in 2018 in ASEAN cities revealed a wide range of air quality in terms of PM2.5 presence in the atmosphere of the city (Table 9.2). The table shows that while the presence of PM2.5 has reached very critical levels (256) in Hanoi, Vietnam, the level of this particular matter is still good to the citizens' health at the level of 36 in Kuala Lumpur, Malaysia.

The critical level of PM2.5, according to the WHO, is 150 (Living ASEAN 2018). The GHGs are a set of pollutants that are usually produced by the combustion of fossil fuels such as petroleum and coal.

182 Z. Alcheikh Mahmoud et al.

Table 9.2 PM2.5 level in some ASEAN cities*

Hanoi (Vietnam)	Bangkok (Thailand)	Chiang Mai (Thailand)	Ho Chi Minh (Vietnam)	Jakarta	Manila	Singapore	Kuala Lumpur (Malaysia)
256	186	169	169	165	91	91	36

Source Constructed by authors based on information from (Air Pollution in the World 2018)
*The level of PM2.5 is considered good when it is 0–50, moderate when it is 51–100, unhealthy for sensitive group when it is 100–150, unhealthy for sensitive group when it is 100–150, unhealthy for everyone when it is 151–200, very unhealthy when it is 201–300, and hazardous when it is 300+

9 Environmental Threats to the Performance of Urban Areas ... 183

The GHGs are the main cause of global warming and climate change. The main components of GHGS include "carbon dioxide (CO_2), methane (CH_4), nitrous oxide (N_2O), ozone (O_3), water vapour (H_2O), chlorofluorocarbons (CFCs), and hydrofluorocarbons (HFCs)" (The ASEAN Secretariat 2017b, 57). The overall GHG emission level in ASEAN made a little decrease of 4.66% between 2009 and 2013. There is still, however, a significant increase in the emission in some of the countries of the region. The GHG emission level increased during the same period of 2009–2013, by (19.7%), (15.5%), (12.2%) and (12.1%) in Thailand, Singapore, Myanmar and Lao PDR, respectively (World Resources Institute 2017). Urban areas usually consume the largest part of the fossil fuels in the sectors of industry, construction and transport and for generating electricity.

Source of Air Pollution

Energy production and consumption are the main sources of air pollution in ASEAN urban areas. The demand for energy increased in the last decades and is expected to further increase in the coming years. Energy is demanded by the expanding sectors of industry, transportation and construction to accommodate the expansion of ASEAN urban areas and socio-economic development. Energy sector still depends heavily on the combustion of fossil fuel such as petroleum and coal which are the main sources of PMs and GHGs. The World Bank indicators show that the per capita kilograms of oil equivalent[6] increased significantly in most ASEAN states between 2010 and 2014.

For instance, in Thailand, it increased from 1699 in 2009 to 1990 in 2014 while it increased from 2558 to 3000 in Malaysia in the same period. The demand for fossil fuel is expected to grow by 61% between 2014 and 2025 in ASEAN for economic activities, transportation and other uses (The ASEAN Secretariat 2017b). A study by GFEI (Global Fuel Economy Initiative) expected that the number of vehicles per 1000 citizens of ASEAN will increase from 150 in 2010 to 327 in 2025

(GFEI 2010). The largest number of vehicles usually runs on the roads of urban areas.

There are some additional factors contributing to air pollution. These factors are related to the quality of the consumed fuel, burning on the land surface and converting forests and peatlands into other uses for commercial purposes. According to UNEP (2016), ASEAN countries adopt various fuel qualities and standards much lower than other parts of the world. A largest part of the fuel is consumed in urban areas producing air pollutants, as mentioned earlier in this chapter. The ASEAN Secretariat (2017b) reported that peat fires to prepare the land for rubber and oil palm plantation are responsible for up to 90% of trans-boundary smoke haze in ASEAN.

Responses to Air Pollution

ASEAN member states have made several initiatives at global, ASEAN group, country and city level to deal with air pollution. However, the present levels of air pollution in ASEAN countries in general and in particular in the region's urban areas indicate an outcome less than expected. At the international level, all ASEAN countries expressed their commitment towards reducing GHG by submitting the Intended Nationally Determined Contributions (INDCs) and targets under the 2015 Paris Agreement (Priebe and Ateinle 2013; The ASEAN Secretariat 2017b). Instances for regional efforts to reduce air pollution are the adoption of the Trans-boundary Haze Pollution (AATHP) agreement in 2013 and the Roadmap on ASEAN Cooperation towards Trans-boundary Haze Pollution Control with effect in 2016. At the country level, programmes directed to air pollution from transport, industry, energy sectors and urban centres were put for implementation. Other programmes for dealing with air quality monitoring were established.

Along the programmes, national level policies and action plans were developed with the aim of reducing air pollution. The 2011 National Environmentally Sustainable Transport (EST) Strategy of the Philippines and the Malaysia National Electric Mobility Blueprint

9 Environmental Threats to the Performance of Urban Areas ...

2011 are some examples. For further details, refer to Chapter 8. As for the city level, the main initiatives have been geared towards creating citizens' awareness and making information on air pollution accessible to the public as well as the concerned government officials. Air quality monitoring information will be made available in Hanoi and other 18 Vietnamese cities under the National Action Plan for Air Quality Management which has been launched in September 2016 and covers up to 2020. In addition, the central government of Vietnam has planned to increase the number of stations that monitor air quality in Hanoi and the other 18 cities (Filek-Gibson 2017). In Kuala Lumpur, which recorded the best air quality (as mentioned above), the city efforts concentrate on dealing with the heavy dependency on private cars as a main source of pollution.

The concerned authorities of Kuala Lumpur are working on creating public awareness, enhancing the existing public transport system and encouraging sustainable transport modes such as walking and cycling. The citizens of Kuala Lumpur and the city officials will be able to access the data on air quality through a network for monitoring air quality. The network was enhanced in February 2018 by local and international agencies such as the United Nations Urban Development Programme (UNUDP) and Clarity Movement Co. Further, a living lab was set up in Kuala Lumpur with the support of UN-Habitat, Clarity and some local private partners to enhance public awareness on environmental and social benefits of active transport.

The lab is intended also to support the efforts of Kuala Lumpur's authorities in promoting cycling and walking as sustainable forms of transportation. In addition to creating awareness, in 2013 local authorities initiated Kuala Lumpur's Car-Free Morning. On the first and third Sunday of each month, car access is restricted on selected routes to encourage green transportation alternatives such as cycling, walking and skating (Clarity Team 2018). Further, large-scale Mass Transit System Projects and Light Rapid Transit System are being constructed in Kuala Lumpur to connect more parts of the city and more suburban areas. This is expected to enhance the efficiency of the existing public transport system.

The implementation of the national and regional initiatives, however, has in general, hardly been realized. The member states focused on making progress in economic development with no serious measures to restrict pollution emission. ASEAN countries lack enforcement measures for the implementation of the agreement. This made the implementation of the agreements and programmes as a matter of diplomacy. For further details refer to Chapter 8. The efforts at the level of the urban area are either still in the initial stage or need evaluation (Priebe and Ateinle 2013).

Urban Areas Air Pollution Impacts: Issues and Challenges

The unhealthy air quality particularly in urban ASEAN areas has had long-term and wide-ranging consequences relating to health and local, national and regional economy. Air pollution is responsible for a significant number of deaths and diseases. On the other hand, the cost of pollution is a heavy economic burden for the member states of ASEAN. According to WHO (2016), the number of deaths attributed to ambient air pollution in ASEAN was 175,004 in 2012. The death toll by air pollution will more than triple by 2035 if no proper measures are made (Filek-Gibson 2017). Air pollution causes critical ills for various age groups such as asthma, bronchitis, cough rhinitis lung cancer, cardiovascular and other diseases. For instance, in the case of sick people aged 25 and more in ASEAN, air pollution is responsible for 32.5, 19 and 19% out of the total affected people by Lung Cancer, Stroke and Ischemic Heart Diseases, respectively (World Health Organization 2016).

Thus, air pollution health-related consequences increase the pressure on relevant urban health care facilities in terms of their capacity and expenses. More money is needed to increase the capacity of the healthcare facilities and to enhance their services quality. This increases the economic burden, caused by air pollution, in ASEAN countries. The ASEAN Secretariat (2017b) found that the total cost of outdoor air pollution in ASEAN reached as high as US$280 billion in 2012. In the same year, Singapore, Indonesia, Thailand and Vietnam spent US$280 billion, US$160 billion,

9 Environmental Threats to the Performance of Urban Areas ... 187

US$50 billion, US$27 billion and US$20 billion, respectively, to handle air pollution and its consequences. The huge amount of money that was lost because of air pollution could be otherwise spent on various types of social, cultural and economic development. Further, air pollution is a major contributor to climate change and its results. The disasters caused by climate change are increasing in number in ASEAN. Climate change is discussed later in this chapter.

In the coming decades, ASEAN will be more urbanized with more industrial and other economic activities. Transportation sector and supportive infrastructure will expand. More energy is needed in terms of production and consumption. More peat and forest land will probably be converted to other commercial uses. These processes are needed for national development and regional integration. But, they are the main sources of air pollution. Therefore, the major challenge faces ASEAN at the country and the regional level is how to keep these processes active and efficient with less or no harmful pollution. Some directions seem relevant and important for ASEAN to follow. They are:

- Sustainable urbanization and urban planning (Economist Intelligence Unit 2016);
- Long-term policies on sustainable transport for a hygienic environment and economic prosperity which are the basic requirement for a healthy population and prosperous economies (UNESCAPE 2013; cited in Kaffashi et al. 2016);
- Low-carbon economy and infrastructure;
- Efficient land management; and
- Controls on the land conversion into commercial plantations.

However, a significant number of measures, relevant to these directions, are in place. ASEAN needs to work out the right implementation tools locally and regionally (The ASEAN Secretariat 2017b). Will ASEAN be able to successfully make it? This is a key challenge.

At the city level, the authorities face some interlinked and critical challenges: convincing the city people to reduce their heavy dependence on private cars, increasing the people's confidence on public transport and encouraging them to go for other transport modes such as walking and cycling. At present, there are some initiatives to deal with these challenges, but they are either undergoing or they need evaluation. In addition to recommending the enhancement and evaluation of the existing initiatives, some more recommendations can be made as in the following.

Long-term awareness programme starting from primary education on air pollution consequences and proper measures to deal with them;

* Implementing long-term programmes to reduce urban citizen's dependency on private cars and vehicles for their journeys.. Owning and using a car has become a part of local culture in ASEAN countries. Influencing or changing this culture requires a long time;
* Electrical vehicles provide a good opportunity to reduce harmful emission in urban areas. The challenge is, however, how to make this type of vehicles affordable and how to prepare the cities to accommodate them.
* Efforts are needed to develop and improve the citizens' trust and confidence in public transport. This can be mainly reached by improving the efficiency of transport.
* Enhancement of traffic management measures such as inspection and maintenance programmes. Cars of better conditions emit less harmful charges.
* Sharing experience among ASEAN cities is important to all of the above recommendations.

Climate Change

Current Situation and Future Risk

Current global warming (climate change) started in the mid of the twentieth century. The main reason for this warming is the increased concentration of GHGs in the atmosphere of the earth. In addition to the higher temperature of the atmosphere, the concentration of GHGs leads to ocean acidification. These two impacts result in warmer land

9 Environmental Threats to the Performance of Urban Areas ... 189

surface and oceans, more frequent extreme weather events (heavy rainfall with floods), droughts and heat waves, sea-level rise and coral bleaching. Many of these effects will continue for many years to come, because the GHGs will remain in the atmosphere for a very long time (IPPC 2014). ASEAN is one of the most vulnerable regions to the consequences of climate change. In the last five decades, the surface temperature in ASEAN increased between 0.5 and 1.5C. This increase is expected to reach 2–4C by the end of the present century with the highest increase in Thailand, Indonesia and Vietnam (USAID 2010).

Influenced by climate change, hydrological, meteorological and climatological disasters have been taking place more intensively and frequently over the last 50 years in ASEAN countries particularly in the Philippines, Indonesia, Vietnam and Thailand. The most common disasters are tropical storms, heat waves (meteorological hazards), floods (hydrological hazard type) and droughts (climatological hazards) (IPPC 2014). The disasters affect a large number of urban population. According to UNESCAPE (2015) cited in the ASEAN Secretariat (2017), the population of 17 cities of ASEAN, estimated at 46 million people, are threatened by extreme multi-hazard risk. The number of urban population, who will be exposed to the multi-hazard risk in 2030, is expected to reach 66 million.

The long-term sea-level rise will exacerbate the meteorological, hydrological and climatological hazards in the coastal cities of ASEAN where 36% of ASEAN urban population lives (IPCC 2014). Under 4°C world warming, the sea level in ASEAN is expected to rise, more than 15 cm above the present level by 2030 and more than 50 cm above the present level by 2060. The projected rise in sea level for 2050 will constitute a critical threat to a huge number of ASEAN people, 20 million in Indonesia, 15 million in the Philippines and 10 million Vietnam, and to a lesser extent, Thailand, Malaysia and Myanmar. Bangkok (Thailand) and Manila (the Philippines) will probably be the most affected places. Each of the two cities is the major urban centre of its country. Each of the two cities houses a significant portion of its country urban population and economic activities (USAID 2010; UNEP 2014 cited in ASEAN Secretariat 2017b).

Contributing Factors to Climate Change

As mentioned earlier in this chapter, GHGs such as CO_2 and PM such as PM2.5 are main contributors to climate change. The gases and particles trap, in the atmosphere, the heat from the sun that is reflected by the earth and consequently causing an increase in the earth surface and oceans temperature. In addition to GHGs and PMs, there are two more contributors to climate change, heat island effect and forest land conversion. City development in ASEAN tends to focus on producing high-quality physical appearance with little concern for the urban environment. This type of urban development enhances the phenomenon of heat island and its consequences (Institute of Southeast Asian Studies 2010). On the other hand, forest's cover in most ASEAN member states has been declining, particularly between 1990 and 2012. This mainly happened because of replacing the existing plants with other types of trees, particularly rubber and oil palm, for commercial purposes. Removing the forest cover decreases the natural process of Carbon sequestration and consequently increasing the density of Carbon in the atmosphere (The ASEAN Secretariat 2017b).

ASEAN Responses to Climate Change

ASEAN efforts to tackle climate change contain two sets of actions, one is to handle the contributing factors and the other one is to mitigate the impacts of the change. Only the first set will be discussed in this section. ASEAN has made climate change and its consequences as a major concern and started working closely with the international community since the 2007 ASEAN Summit in Singapore. Apart from Myanmar, the other members of ASEAN have ratified the Paris Agreement through which ASEAN will work with other parts of the world to combat climate change and adapt to its effects (Wijaya and Idris 2017). At the regional level, climate change issues are addressed in the ASCC Blueprint 2009–2015 and ASEAN Vision 2015, under the section of "Ensuring Environmental Sustainability" (The ASEAN Secretariat

9 Environmental Threats to the Performance of Urban Areas … 191

2017b). Along with this step, many measures have been designed to tackle the contributing factors to climate change such as the emission of GHGs and PMs. The implementation of these measures, as discussed earlier, has been stumbling (refer to 2–3 and 2–4).

Impacts of Climate Change: Urban Issues and Challenges

Climate change and its consequences have, particularly in the recent decades, brought about significant harms to the economy, well-being, ecosystem, livelihoods, services and infrastructure, property and culture in ASEAN (IPPC 2014). The harms were more severe in urban areas because of the high concentration of population and activities. (Astriana 2014). In 2004, about 175,000 people lost their lives in Indonesia, Thailand, Malaysia and Myanmar, because of the Indian Ocean Tsunami. In 2011, Bangkok metropolitan area and central area of Thailand suffered damages worth over US$45 billion because of the floods. In 2013, Typhoon Haiyan hit the Philippines and left behind an economic loss and damages worth US$10 Billion (The World Bank 2013).

The impacts of climate change and its resultant disasters are major challenges to ASEAN. Even with no more contributing emissions to global warming, the effects of the existing levels of GHGs and PMs are expected to remain for a long time. Thus, ASEAN countries need to work on the immediate and serious cut of GHGS and MPs emissions, and at the same time, they need to adapt to the existing climate change conditions. The challenge is how to cut down the emissions and at the same time maintain socio-economic development? As mentioned earlier, the economic development of ASEAN countries depends heavily on fossil fuel which is the main source of GHGs and PMs Emissions. On the other hand, to reach influential cut down of the emissions, there is a need for effective cooperation among ASEAN countries and between ASEAN and the rest of the world. This cooperation is another challenge (Wijaya and Idris 2017).

If no sufficient and timely progress in tackling climate change is made, ASEAN member states will face critical threats to their urban and rural areas and consequently to their region's integration process.

It is expected, with the continuity of the climate change, that extreme weather events will strike ASEAN more widely causing huge losses. In addition, if the sea level continues at the same pace, it will be a critical threat to the coastal cities of ASEAN where a significant portion of the urban population and economic activities exist. Further, the sea-level rise and the intensive tropical cyclones will badly affect the beautiful beaches and coral reefs which are interesting tourist attractions. This constitutes a critical threat to the tourist industry in ASEAN (The World Bank 2013). All these conditions can force people in the coastal cities as well as in rural areas to move to other places. Earlier experience shows that people prefer to move towards large urban centres (Wijaya and Idris 2017). This increases the pressure on various urban sectors and consequently affecting the performance of main urban areas which are the main pillars of the regional integration of ASEAN.

Water Pollution

Fresh Water and Its Availability in ASEAN

Clean and fresh water is essential for urban as well as rural development and thus, it is important for the regional integration process of ASEAN. The demand for fresh water increased significantly in the last decades by ASEAN countries to meet the needs of the fast-growing urban areas and economic activities, particularly industry (ASEAN Secretariat 2017b). Industrial consumption of water constitutes 40% of the total water consumption in Brunei Darussalam, Malaysia and Singapore, and about 10% of the total water consumption in each of the remaining seven ASEAN countries. Most of the industrial activities of ASEAN countries are located in and around the major urban centres.

ASEAN problem is not with the availability of water. The region has 27% of the world water resources (FAO 2017). The problem is the growing pollution of both surface and groundwater. In Thailand, 15% of the rivers had deteriorated water quality in 2011. This rate increased to 23% in 2015. The main Thai urban centres are located along the rivers. 62% of water in Indonesia was heavily polluted in 2009. This rate increased to 80% in 2013 (WHO and UNICEF 2014). The Indonesian Citarum River which supplies water for 25 million people in both the city of Bandung and the greater Jakarta region and feeds more than 2000 factories on its banks, has not met Indonesian water quality standards since its existence in 2008 (Jack Hewson 2013). The rivers' water of Metro Manila is unsuitable for aquatic life. Various types of pollutants are found in the water of ASEAN. Some drinking water sources are contaminated with pathogenic microorganisms. In some countries, pollution is with chemical materials such as arsenic and fluoride (Hershberger 2014).

Contributing Factors to Water Pollution in ASEAN

The main source of water pollution in ASEAN is the wastewater from residential, industrial and commercial urban areas and from agriculture. Urban sanitation facilities have been significantly improved in this region to cover more than 71% of the entire ASEAN population (ASEAN Secretariat 2017b) and more than 96% of the population of some countries such as Myanmar, Thailand and Vietnam (Koottatep et al. 2018). However, wastewater, which is usually discharged into natural water bodies, mostly reaches these destinations untreated (ASEAN Secretariat 2017b). A study by the Asian Development Bank in 2014, cited in McIntosh (2014), covered 12 cities of ASEAN found that in some of the cities only small portion of wastewater is treated before disposing of it. In Bangkok, only 25% of the wastewater is treated. Treated wastewater constitutes 12 and 10% of the disposed of wastewater in the Vietnamese city of Ho Chi and the Philippines capital city of Manila, respectively.

Flood water contributes to water pollution when it carries polluting materials and is disposed to the sewer system. The discharge of untreated or partly treated wastewater happens in spite of the existence of concerned institutions, laws and regulations which require processing the wastewater to certain quality before dumping it (McIntosh 2014). The implementation of the laws and regulations at the country level is poor. The institutions lack proper management, coordination and sufficient trained staff (The ASEAN Secretariat 2017b).

The Responses of ASEAN to Water Pollution

Since 2005, the Integrated Water Resource Management (IWRM) approach has been adopted by some ASEAN states and recommended for the other member states to deal with various water resources issues. Based on the approach, initiatives were made at the regional level and at the individual country level. At the regional level, ASEAN Strategic Plan of Action on Water Resources Management (ASPA-WRM) was adopted. The plan emphasized on supply, demand, allocation, water quality and sanitation, climate change and extreme events, governance and capacity.

This has been followed by more initiatives in the next years such as establishing ASEAN Water Data Management and Reporting System and developing and adopting key performance indicators in 2015 for water resource management in each state of ASEAN. At the country level, most of the member states developed relevant policies, programmes, strategies and plans (ASEAN Secretariat 2017b). Malaysia, for instance, prepared the National Water Resource Policy in 2012 (MNRE 2012) and Thailand put into implementation the Master Plan on Water Resource Management as a response to the 2011 destructive floods (ADB 2012).

After all these efforts, water quality is deteriorating in most of ASEAN member states. This situation can be attributed to lack of institutional coordination, poor management, uncontrolled urban development and inefficient spatial planning. For the coming years, water issues are covered by the ASCC 2025 which emphasized on sustainable development for water resources in terms of quality and quantity for present and future (The ASEAN Secretariat 2017b).

At the city level, efforts have been made in some ASEAN cities such as Kuala Lumpur and Jakarta to clean up the riverbed. In 2008, depending on foreign financial assistance, a wide-ranging cleanup and rehabilitation plan started for the Citarum River basin. After 7 years of the cleanup operation, there was a long way to go (Asian Development Bank 2014). In 2012, the government of Kuala Lumpur launched the River of Life Project to clean Kang Riverbed and to develop its waterfront through about 10.7 KM stretch. The multistage project which is planned to end by 2020 includes three main components—river cleaning, river master-planning and beautification. The first phase of the project was completed and put into use at the end of 2017 (AECOM 2018). The project needs more time before the impact can be analysed.

Urban Issues and Challenges of Water Pollution in ASEAN

While the present water issues in ASEAN member states are related to the quality, in the coming decades, quality as well as quantity water issues will face ASEAN, if no proper actions are made in time. Current ground and surface water pollution constitute indirect major threat to the residents and direct threat to the natural environment and economic development in urban and rural areas. The vast majority of the urban residents, according to the ASEAN Secretariat (2017b), consume agricultural products which are irrigated with water that is polluted with industrial as well as domestic untreated or improperly treated discharges (Koottatep et al. 2018). This is a threat to urban public health (UNEP 2016). On the other hand, polluted water causes serious damage to the ecosystem inside and outside urban areas. It kills aquatic living creatures, such as fish, which result in economic loss. In addition to the negative consequences on public health and environment, water pollution has negative impacts on economic development (ADB 2012). The degradation of water quality can have a critical impact on various economic activities such as industry, tourism, agriculture and fisheries (The World Bank 2008). According to the Asian Development Bank (2012), Cambodia, Vietnam, Lao PDR, Indonesia and the Philippines, suffer from more than US$9.2 billion a year because of poor water quality.

Restoring the quality of polluted water resources and eliminating water pollution are big challenges to ASEAN. In addition, ASEAN needs to meet the increasing demand for fresh water. The first two challenges require sophisticated treatment process which usually needs huge cost. A study by Sacha (2012) estimated that, up to 2050, ASEAN needs to spend more than US$383 billion for basic coverage of water, sewerage and sewage treatment. In addition to the heavy cost, ASEAN countries need to revise their current practices of economic development which has been on the cost of the environment. All these required steps are serious challenges to economic development which is mainly concentrated in urban areas. Working on the challenges related to pollution will contribute to dealing with the third water-related challenge namely meeting the increasing demand for fresh water. However, the increasing demand for water in ASEAN is accompanied by declining in its resources. The demand for water is expected to grow by about 33% up to 2025 and by 100% between 2050 and 2100. The demand will increase while the renewable internal freshwater resource in the ASEAN region has been declining during the last two decades (The ASEAN Secretariat 2017b).

Summary

The rate of urban population has been increasing in ASEAN. It is expected that the rate will increase in the coming decades. At present, the size of the population and the scale of activities in large urban areas have a significant contribution to the integration process of ASEAN. In the coming decades, the small urban centres will gain more importance at the national and regional level. The environmental threats of air and water pollution along with climate change have created serious economic and social problems in ASEAN countries in general and in urban areas in particular. ASEAN countries have made appreciable efforts at various local, national and regional levels to deal with the environmental issues of air pollution, water pollution and climate change.

The efforts at the regional and national levels suffer from a lack of institutional and administrative issues. The initiatives at urban areas level are promising, but mostly either in progress or need evaluation. The awareness programmes in Hanoi and Kuala Lumpur are vital to getting the public involved in handling air pollution. There is a need to initiate similar programmes on climate change and water pollution. Public involvement is essential to make a good move towards cutting down the pollution and adjusting to climate change. If extended and successfully implemented, Kuala Lumpur programme to encourage more sustainable transport and reduce the dependency on private cars can well contribute to cutting down the harmful emissions to the city environment. This programme can be imitated in other ASEAN cities.

Lessons from Kuala Lumpur experience should be shared with other cities in the region. On the other hand, technology can provide important opportunities for new directions. For instance, cars run with electricity constitute an environmentally friendly transport mode. City authorities need to plan for accommodating electrical cars as there is a great potential for making this type of transport mode affordable. ASEAN countries need to seriously consider the urban environmental challenges and their impacts on group integration if they want to successfully reach the objectives of the integration.

Notes

1. Degree of urbanization is defined as the share of urban population in the total population.
2. In this chapter, the city refers to the city metropolitan area rather than the city administrative boundaries.
3. Megacities (more than 10 million, such as Jakarta), large cities (5–10 million such as Kuala Lumpur), medium-sized cities (1–5 million such as Yangon) and small cities with populations ranging between 500,000 and 1 million (such as Vientiane). ASEAN contains five megacities, four large cities, 20 medium-sized and 21 small cities.
4. See https://www.giz.de/en/worldwide/14509.html.
5. This "particular matter" is the most injurious to human health.
6. A normalized unit of energy. It is the equivalent to the approximate amount of energy that can be extracted from one Kilogram of crude oil (41,868 Kilojoules).

References

AECOM. 2018. *River of Life, Klang Valley.* Kuala Lumpur, Malaysia. https://www.aecom.com/projects/river-life-klang-river-malaysia/.

Air Pollution in the World. 2018. *Real Time Air Quality Index (AQI).* Accessed February 1, 2018. http://aqicn.org/city/all/.

ASEAN UP. 2017. "Info Graphic: Top Cities and Urbanization in ASEAN." Accessed January 2, 2018. https://aseanup.com/infographic-top-cities-urbanization-asean/.

Asia Research Institute. 2013. "The Population of Southeast Asia." http://www.ari.nus.edu.sg/wps/wps13_196.pdf.

Asian Development Bank (ADB). 2012. "Wastewater Management and Sanitation in Asia." https://www.adb.org/features/wastewater-management-and-sanitation-numbers.

Asian Development Bank. 2014. "Cleaning Up Indonesia's Citarum Basin." https://www.adb.org/features/cleaning-indonesias-citarum-basin.

Astriana, Fina. 2014. "ASEAN's Responses to Climate Change. Asean Studies Programme." Accessed January 1, 2018. http://thcasean.org/read/blog/118/ASEANs-Response-to-Climate-Change.

Clarity Team. 2018. "Kuala Lumpur Deploys Hyper Local Air Quality Monitoring Network at WUF9." *Clarity Movement.* Accessed January 26, 2018. https://medium.com/clarity-movement/kuala-lumpur-deploys-hyperlocal-air-quality-monitoring-network-at-wuf9-d85dcd1e037e.

Dahiya, Bharat. 2015. "ASEAN Economic Integration and Sustainable Urbanisation." *Heinrich Böll Foundation.* Accessed January 17, 2018. https://www.boell.de/en/2015/10/28/asean-economic-integration-and-sustainable-urbanisation.

Economist Intelligence Unit. 2016. *ASEAN Cities Stirring the Melting pot.* 1st ed. [pdf]. Hong Kong: The Economist Intelligence Unit. Accessed January 2, 2018. http://www.urbangateway.org/system/files/documents/urbangateway/asean-cities-2016.pdf.

Filek-Gibson, Dana. 2017. "Southeast Asia's Air Pollution Deaths Could Triple by 2030." *Saigoneer.* Accessed February 1, 2018. https://saigoneer.com/asia-news/9175-southeast-asia-s-air-pollution-could-triple-by-2030.

Food and Agriculture Organization of the United Nations (FAO). 2017. "AQUASTAT." Accessed December 12, 2017. http://www.fao.org/nr/water/aquastat/water_res/index.stm.

GFEI. 2010. "Improving Vehicle Fuel Economy in the ASEAN Region." Accessed January 29, 2019. https://www.globalfueleconomy.org/media/44070/wp1-asean-fuel-economy.pdf.

Hershberger, Matt. 2014. "6 Environmental Challenges Facing Southeast Asia (And What You Can Do to Help)." *MATADOR Network.* Accessed February 2, 2019. https://matadornetwork.com/change/6-environmental-challenges-facing-southeast/.

9 Environmental Threats to the Performance of Urban Areas ... 199

Institute of Southeast Asian Studies. 2010. *Urbanisation in Southeast Asian Countries*. 1st ed. Singapore: ASEAN Studies Centre. Accessed October 2, 2017. https://www.iseas.edu.sg/images/centres/asc/pdf/UrbanSEAsia-prelimasof13Jul10.pdf.

IPPC. 2014. *Climate Change 2014: Synthesis Report*. Geneva: Intergovernmental Panel on Climate Change, 40–54. Accessed December 2, 2017. https://www.ipcc.ch/pdf/assessmentreport/ar5/syr/AR5_SYR_FINAL_All_Topics.pdf.

Jack, Hewson. 2013. "Pollution Flows Freely in Indonesia's Rivers." *Aljazeera*. https://www.aljazeera.com/indepth/features/2013/11/pollution-flows-freely-indonesia-rivers-2013112013166643513.html.

Kaffashi, Sara, Mad Nasir Shamsudin, Maynard S. Clark, and Shaufique Sidique. 2016. "Road Transport System in Southeast Asia: Problems and Economic Solutions." *Current World Environment* 11 (1): 10–19. http://www.cwejournal.org/pdf/vol11no1/Vol11_No1_p_10-19.pdf.

Kio, Sheng Yap, and Thuzar Mae. 2012. "Urban Challenges in South-East Asia." In *Urbanisation in Southeast Asia, Issues and impacts*, edited by Kio Yap and Thuzar Mae. 1st ed., 145–162. Singapore: Institute of Southeast Asian Studies.

Koottatep, Thammarat, Saroj Kumar Chapagain, Chongrak Polprasert, Atitaya Panuvatvanich, and Kyu-Hong Ahn. 2018. "Sanitation Situations in Selected Southeast Asian Countries and Application of Innovative Technologies." *Environment, Development and Sustainability* 20 (1): 495–506.

Living ASEAN. 2018. *Air Quality Around the ASEAN*. Accessed February 1, 2018. http://livingasean.com/explore/air-quality-asean-air-pollution-bangkok-hanoi-jakarta/.

McIntosh, Arthur C. 2014. *Urban Water Supply and Sanitation in Southeast Asia a Guide to Good Practice*. Manila, the Philippines: Asian Development Bank. Accessed January 2, 2018. http://admin.indiaenvironmentportal.org.in/files/file/urban-water-supply-sanitation-southeast-asia.pdf.

Ministry of Natural Resources and Environment Malaysia (MNRE). 2012. *National Water Resource Policy*. Second Printing. Kuala Lumpur: Ministry of Natural Resources and Environment Malaysia. Accessed December 12, 2017. http://www.nre.gov.my/ms-my/PustakaMedia/Penerbitan/Dasar%20Sumber%20Air%20Negara.pdf.

Passi, Sacha. 2012. *Stagnant Systems: Sanitation in Cambodia. Southeast Asia Globe*. Accessed December 3, 2017. http://sea-globe.com/.

Priebe, Max, and Ateinle Flix. 2013. "Environmental Issues in South East Asia." *Fair Observer*. Accessed March 23, 2018. https://www.fairobserver.com/region/central_south_asia/environmental-issues-southeast-asia/.

Thant, Meyo. 2012. "Regional Cooperation and the Changing Urban Landscape of Southeast Asia." In *Urbanisation in Southeast Asia, Issues and impacts*, edited by Kio Yap and Thuzar Mae. 1st ed., 154–172. Singapore: Institute of Southeast Asian Studies.

The ASEAN Secretariat. 2003. *ASEAN Statistical Year Book 2003*. Jakarta: ASEAN Secretariat. Accessed December 1, 2017. http://www.aseanstats.org/wpcontent/uploads/2016/10/ASEAN_Statistical_YearBook_2003.pdf.

The ASEAN Secretariat. 2017a. *ASEAN Statistical Year Book 2016/2017*. Accessed February 1, 2018. Bangkok: ASEAN Secretariat. Available at: https://www.aseanstats.org/wp-content/uploads/2018/01/ASYB_2017-rev.pdf.

The ASEAN Secretariat. 2017b. *Fifth ASEAN State of the Environment Report*. 1st ed. Accessed February 2, 2018. Jakarta: The ASEAN Secretariat. http://environment.asean.org/wp-content/uploads/2018/01/SOER5.pdf.

The World Bank. 2008. *Economic Impacts of Sanitation in Southeast Asia; A Four-Country Study Conducted in Cambodia, Indonesia, the Philippines and Viet Nam Under the Economics of Sanitation Initiative (ESI)*. 1st ed. Jakarta: Water and Sanitation Programme. Accessed February 22, 2018. http://documents.worldbank.org/curated/pt/246121468231556842/pdf/463510WSP-0Box31n1Impact1Synthesis12.pdf.

The World Bank. 2013. "Turn Down the Heat, Climate Extremes, Regional Impacts, and the Case for Resilience," 66–95. Washington: The World Bank. Accessed December 20, 2017. https://unfccc.int/sites/default/files/resource/World%20Bank_Turn%20Down%20the%20Heat.pdf.

UNEP. 2016. *GEO-6 Regional Assessment for Asia and the Pacific*, 44–55. Nairobi, Kenya: United Nations Environment Programme. Accessed January 25, 2018. https://uneplive.unep.org/media/docs/assessments/GEO_ASSESSMENT_REPORT_ASIA_Wam.pdf.

USAID. 2010. "Final Report: Findings and Recommendations." *Asia-Pacific Regional Climate Change Adaptation Assessment*, 11–27. Accessed December 22, 2017. Washington, DC: United States Agency for International Development. https://pdf.usaid.gov/pdf_docs/PNADS197.pdf.

WHO, and UNICEF. 2014. "Progress on Sanitation and Drinking-Water—2014 Update, 1st ed." Geneva: World Health Organisation and UNICEF. Accessed February 3, 2018. https://www.unicef.org/gambia/Progress_on_drinking_water_and_sanitation_2014_update.pdf.

Wijaya, Arief, and Idris Shira. 2017. "ASEAN Countries Must Act Together to Confront Climate Change." World Resource Institute. Accessed January 20, 2018. http://www.wri.org/blog/2017/11/asean-countries-must-act-together-confront-climate-change.

World Health Organisation (WHO). 2016. *Ambient Air Pollution: A Global Assessment of Exposure and Burden of Disease.* 1st ed. Geneva: World Health Organisation. Accessed February 1, 2018. http://apps.who.int/iris/bitstream/handle/10665/250141/9789241511353eng.pdf?sequence=1.

World Health Organization. (n.d.). "Fact Sheet 1." *New Delhi: Regional Office for Southeast Asia.* Accessed February 1, 2018. http://www.searo.who.int/topics/air_pollution/what-is-air-pollution.pdf?ua=1.

World Resources Institute. 2017. *CAIT Climate Data Explorer.* Accessed February 1, 2018. http://cait.wri.org.

10

Regulatory Incoherence in Nutrition Labelling of Pre-packaged Food in ASEAN: What Next?

Evelyn S. Devadason and VGR Chandran Govindaraju

Regulatory heterogeneity (Pettman 2013; USAID 2013; Othman 2014, 83–92) is identified as a challenge for increasing trade, harmonizing standards, and ultimately creating a single integrated Association of Southeast Asian Nations (ASEAN) market, which was a major objective in the formation of the ASEAN Economic Community (AEC) in 2015. One diverse technical regulation that governs the pre-packaged food and beverage (PPF) industry is nutrition labelling. The labelling regulations across the AMS rest on the different International Guidelines followed by member countries when preparing national regulations. Kasapila and Shaarani (2011) point out that for nutrition labelling, Singapore, Malaysia, Brunei, Laos, Vietnam and Cambodia have followed the Codex[1] guidelines in preparing their regulations.

E. S. Devadason (✉) · V. C. Govindaraju
Faculty of Economics and Administration, University of Malaya,
Kuala Lumpur, Malaysia
e-mail: evelyns@um.edu.my

V. C. Govindaraju
e-mail: vgrchandran@um.edu.my

© The Author(s) 2019
A. Idris and N. Kamaruddin (eds.), *ASEAN Post-50*,
https://doi.org/10.1007/978-981-13-8043-3_10

203

Conversely, Thailand and the Philippines, to some extent have adopted the United States (US) nutrition labelling guidelines. Even within those member countries that adopt Codex, there are differences in the regulatory regime. Malaysia made nutrition labelling mandatory for energy, protein, carbohydrate, fat and total sugars for foods that are commonly consumed, and for various types of beverages in 2005 (AFBA 2014; Kasapila and Shaarani 2011, 1–8; see also Pettman 2013). Nutrition labelling is also mandatory in the Philippines and Thailand, for certain food items. For other ASEAN countries that follow the Codex guidelines, nutrition labelling is voluntary; if nutrition and/or health claims are made on food packaging or if the food is for a special purpose (diabetic and fortified foods), nutrition labelling would then be mandatory.

Inter-country differences in nutrition labelling create budget issues for companies (AFBA 2014; Gautier 2010; OECD 2003), as they have to conform to labelling requirements that differ across national markets; exporters have to produce and pay for different labels and compliance procedures. These additional costs can be so considerable (Bode 2017) that they prevent some exporters from competing in the market and reduce trade. It is also noted that nutrition labelling, which is mainly for consumer information, may have more impact on trade then quality labelling, due to information overload on nutrition (Miller and Cassady 2015, 207–216; OECD 2003). Hence, nutrition labelling may constitute potential non-tariff barriers (NTBs) (Rimpeekool et al. 2015, 59–66; ILSI 2014).

In this respect, harmonization (at least at the regional level and at the minimum, see Corazon and Cabrera 2008) is necessary to preclude multiple compliance costs and arrest discriminatory/protective regulations. The AMS has therefore begun to recognize the desirability of having common measures (see also Devadason 2016; Alemanno 2015, 9–43; RSIS 2013; AFBA 2012) amidst the growing volume of food trade. In this regard, the AMS have expressed their intention to use global food standards as a basis for harmonization efforts at the regional level (AFBA 2012). There has however not been much progress in this regard (Lwin et al. 2017; Severino and Thuzar 2016; *The Star* 1 June 2015; USAID 2013).

Though much has been said about the restrictive nature of nutrition labelling, there has been no study, to the best of our knowledge that documents the economic implications of this regulation in the ASEAN context. ASEAN, to date, has largely focused on restricted use of certain substances in foods and feeds and their contact materials, while the issue of labelling has taken a back seat. The micro-evidence of this study therefore informs the debate on the importance of regional regulatory convergence[2] in nutrition labelling.

The chapter is organized as follows. The next section analyses the regulatory incidence and regulatory distance of the general labelling requirement, and variances in the core elements of nutrition labelling, to set the background of the study. Section "Survey Findings" details the research design and presents the results of the regional market survey and interviews with food exporters, trade associations and government officials. Section "Way Forward" concludes with some policy input, namely, the importance of moving forward with the harmonization process at the regional level. It also forwards specific interventions for regulatory convergence based on appropriate benchmarking of nutritional labelling.

Labelling Measures for Pre-packaged Food

Regulatory Incidence and Regulatory Distance

The PPF sector (see Appendix Table 10.6) in the region is highly regulated with technical barriers to trade (TBTs). TBTs constitute 40.6% of total public (mandatory) non-tariff measures (NTMs)[3] in the PPF sector in ASEAN (Fig. 10.1). Within the region, Malaysia records the highest number of TBTs (204) in PPF, followed by Brunei (163), Singapore (142) and Thailand (118). For Malaysia, Singapore and Brunei, TBTs also dominate in terms of the NTM-type in the PPF sector. Since nutrition labelling is a TBT measure, it is important to consider the incidence of labelling for TBT reasons (B31)[4] in the PPF sector. Figure 10.1 also presents the importance of B31 within the TBT chapter[5] for the individual AMS. Approximately 26.7% of the TBTs in the PPF sector in ASEAN is from sub-chapter B31.[6] The share of B31

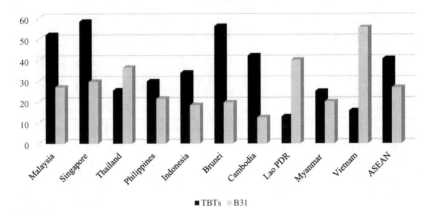

Fig. 10.1 ASEAN—TBTs and labelling requirements for TBT reasons in pre-packaged food (%). TBTs—share of total public (mandatory) NTMs in the PPF sector. B31—share of total TBTs in the PPF sector (*Source* Derived from ERIA-UNCTAD [2016])

in total TBT measures for PPF is highest for Vietnam, at 55.6%, which is also higher than the ASEAN average. The prominence of B31 in the regulatory framework of TBTs is also evident for Lao (40%).

Figure 10.2 further suggests that the regulatory distance (Cadot et al. 2015)[7] of labelling requirements for TBT reasons (B31) is not large ($D_{ij} < 0.5$) for all country-pairs. The regulatory distance is relatively large (albeit small at 0.25) for country-pairs such as Malaysia-Singapore, Singapore-Brunei and Singapore-Thailand, where the labelling regime in those country-pairs can be considered more dissimilar for PPF. Overall, the distance for the labelling framework for Malaysia-Thailand, Malaysia-Brunei and Thailand-Brunei is small relative to the other country-pairs in ASEAN.

The regulatory distance varies between the PPF subsectors as gleaned from Table 10.1. The regulatory distance is zero for HS16 (preparation of meat, fish or crustaceans, molluscs, etc.), suggesting that a similar requirement is imposed on all product items within this product group in the various bilateral country-pairs. Conversely, the regulatory distance, in relative terms, is high for HS17 (sugars and sugar confectionery), namely for Singapore's trade with all the other six ASEAN

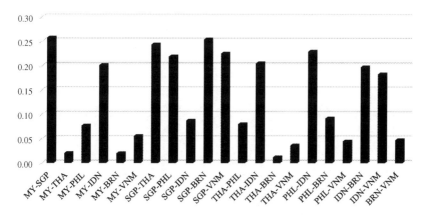

Fig. 10.2 ASEAN7*—regulatory distance of labelling requirements for TBT reasons in pre-packaged food. *ASEAN7 excludes Cambodia, Lao and Myanmar. MY—Malaysia; SGP—Singapore; THA—Thailand; PHL—Philippines; IDN—Indonesia; BRN—Brunei; CAM—Cambodia; MYA—Myanmar; LAO—Lao; VNM—Vietnam (*Source* Authors' own computations)

countries (Malaysia, Thailand, Philippines, Indonesia, Brunei and Vietnam). Likewise, regulatory distance is also somewhat high for HS09 (coffee, tea, mate and spices), specifically for Singapore's trade with Malaysia, Thailand and Brunei; and Indonesia's trade with Malaysia, Thailand, Philippines and Brunei.

Though closer regulatory distance for labelling requirements in the PPF may indeed make it easier to have a mutual recognition agreement (MRA) and/or harmonize the labelling requirement, there is still no empirical evidence to justify that a smaller regulatory distance will be associated with enhanced trade. More importantly, a similar labelling measure (B31) in two countries does not reflect nuanced differences in the labelling requirements within that particular measure. This is illustrated in the next subsection.

Variances in Nutrition Labelling

AFBA (2014) listed core variances in nutrition labelling as follow: variances in mandatory and voluntary labelling requirements; variances in nutrition information panel (NIP) formats and nutrition reference

Table 10.1 ASEAN7*—regulatory distance of labelling requirements for TBT reasons for pre-packaged food, by subsectors

Country-pair	HS04	HS09	HS16	HS17	HS18	HS19	HS20	HS21	HS22	PPF
MY-SGP	0.1212	1	0	0.8824	0	0.1053	0.0192	0	0.1364	0.2581
MY-THA	0.0909	0	0	0	0	0.0526	0.0192	0	0	0.0206
MY-PHL	0.1212	0.0513	0	0.3529	0	0.1053	0.0385	0	0.1364	0.0776
MY-IDN	0.1212	0.9231	0	0.0588	0.3333	0.0526	0.0192	0.0625	0.1364	0.2016
MY-BRN	0.0909	0	0	0	0	0.0526	0.0192	0	0	0.0203
MY-VNM	0.1212	0.0513	0	0	0.1818	0.0526	0.0385	0	0.1364	0.056
SGP-THA	0.0303	1	0	0.8824	0	0.0526	0.0192	0	0.1364	0.2439
SGP-PHL	0	0.1795	0	0.8182	0.5455	0	0	0	0	0.2194
SGP-IDN	0	0.0513	0	0.8462	0	0.0526	0.0192	0.0625	0.0909	0.0878
SGP-BRN	0.1212	1	0	0.8824	0	0.0526	0.0192	0	0.1364	0.254
SGP-VNM	0	0.1795	0	0.8824	0.1818	0.0526	0	0	0	0.2254
THA-PHL	0.0303	0.0513	0	0.3529	0.5455	0.0526	0.0192	0	0.1364	0.0806
THA-IDN	0.0303	0.9487	0	0.2353	0	0	0	0.1667	0.3	0.2054
THA-BRN	0.0909	0	0	0	0	0	0	0	0	0.0122
THA-VNM	0.0303	0.0513	0	0	0.1818	0	0.0192	0	0.1364	0.0366
PHL-IDN	0	0.8974	0	0.5882	0.5455	0.0526	0.0192	0.0625	0.0909	0.2295
PHL-BRN	0.1212	0.0513	0	0.3529	0.5455	0.0526	0.0192	0	0.1364	0.092
PHL-VNM	0	0	0	0.3529	0.3636	0.0526	0	0	0	0.0451
IDN-BRN	0.1212	0.9487	0	0.2353	0	0	0	0.0625	0.1364	0.1976
IDN-VNM	0	0.8974	0	0.2353	0.1818	0	0.0192	0.0625	0.0909	0.1829
BRN-VNM	0.1212	0.0513	0	0	0.1818	0	0.0192	0	0.1364	0.048

*ASEAN7 excludes Cambodia, Lao and Myanmar. MY—Malaysia; SGP—Singapore; THA—Thailand; PHL—Philippines; IDN—Indonesia; BRN—Brunei; CAM—Cambodia; MYA—Myanmar; LAO—Lao; VNM—Vietnam
Source Authors' own computation

values (NRVs); and different minimum and maximum limits for vitamins and minerals; and variances in tolerance levels (see also Tee et al. 2002, 80–86; Rimpeekool et al. 2015, 59–66). It is therefore important to examine the different requirements in the individual AMS for the seven core elements of nutrition labelling as depicted in Appendix Table 10.7.

There is a great deal of variation in the core nutrients that shall be declared on the NIP. The requirements range from four core nutrients (energy plus the three basic nutrients of protein, carbohydrate and fat), such as in Malaysia, to ten, such as in the Philippines. In addition to the basic nutrients, the most commonly required nutrients are saturated fat, sodium/salt, sugar, trans fat, cholesterol and dietary fibre. Some countries, such as the Philippines and Thailand, require the declaration of vitamins (A, B1 and B2) and minerals (iodine, iron and calcium). These different regulations require different mixes of nutrients.[8]

The NIP also lists the nutrients required with the quantity of the nutrient, usually in grams or millilitres, alongside. An additional requirement included in all regulations is the use of a reference unit, which is the quantity of each nutrient relative to a specific reference unit printed adjacent to the nutrient list. Three reference units are used: per 100 g/per 100 ml, per serving, and as a percentage of NRV/recommended daily intake/amount (RDI/RDA)/recommended energy and nutrient intake (RENI). Apart from the wide variation in the reference unit adopted by different countries, from some countries require more than one unit, such as Malaysia and Thailand. The different NRVs are most likely to pose challenges to the industry, especially if the percentage NRV is required to be declared on the NIP.

Survey Findings

Research Design

A survey method was adopted for the study and structured questionnaires were distributed by the FIA to PPF exporters and trade associations (namely AFBA members) in ASEAN. The questionnaire, comprising four sections, was designed to gather information on exporters' perspective on the complexity of the elements of nutrition labelling, business compliance issues and costs incurred from nutrition labelling, and opinions on the harmonization of nutrition labelling. Given a combination of concerns expressed (particularly for, and by, SMEs) and the need to ensure that the business costs of implementing any scheme are fully considered, the study adopted a comprehensive approach to most aspects of compliance costs (initial/recurring), which included administrative costs; testing costs; re-labelling costs; networking costs; transportation costs and inventory costs.

Prior to administering the survey, the questionnaire was subject to several rounds of expert review with the FIA and members of AFBA to ensure content and face validity of the instrument. The feedback and discussions helped improve the appropriateness of the questionnaire. The survey was then complemented with interviews with two selected firms and government officials from two Ministries/Government Agencies. The interviews were conducted to verify some of the results obtained from the survey.

The total sample of PPF exporters for the study is 26 (nine plants located in Malaysia, three each in Thailand and Indonesia, and 11 in the Philippines); 24 were respondents of the market survey and the remaining two firms were sourced for interviews. All firms are categorized as large firms, as many of the SMEs[9] are domestic-oriented and do not have the adequate export experience to provide reliable information on issues related to nutrition labelling. The key findings of the study are summarized in the following subsections.

Complexity of Regulations

Most of the ASEAN countries, with the exception of Thailand and the Philippines that have drafted their nutrition labelling regulations very similar to those of the Nutrition Labelling and Education Act of the United States (Tee et al. 2002), follow the Codex guidelines on nutrition labelling. Even then, the countries that follow Codex are at different levels of adopting/aligning to Codex. With the exception for

10 Regulatory Incoherence in Nutrition Labelling ... 211

the core nutrient list, declaration of carbohydrates and declaration of minerals and vitamins, most exporters find the four remaining elements of nutrition labelling to be more complex than the Codex guidelines (Table 10.2). Nutrition claims (including function claims), followed by NRVs, appear to pose major problems to exporters in the region given the highest responses for the categories of "more complex (ratings of 4 and 5) than the Codex guidelines" come from these two elements.

The reasons cited by the exporters for the complexity in nutrition labelling regulations across the region are reported in Table 10.3. The main reasons for the complexity in regulations related to the inconsistency in regulations that are largely not aligned to Codex. Importantly, the incoherency in regulations is noted even for the established markets in ASEAN, such as Malaysia, Thailand, the Philippines and Indonesia. They largely reflect the lack of alignment in the NRVs with the Codex guidelines. Conversely, the issue of a lack of transparency[10] in overall regulations per se apply to the newer member economies, the CLMV

Table 10.2 Distribution of responses based on level of complexity of nutrition labelling

Elements of nutrition labelling	Level of complexity				
	← Less complex		Codex	→ More complex	
	1	2	3	4	5
Core nutrient list		6	10	6	1
Nutrition information panel (NIP) format		5	6	8	4
Nutrient reference values (NRVs)		4	4	8	7
Declaration of carbohydrates	1	3	13	5	1
Declaration of minerals and vitamins	1	3	8	7	4
Tolerance level and compliance		5	5	9	3
Nutrition claims, nutrient function claims and other function claims	1	2	3	9	8

Notes Based on the 23 responses from the market survey. One respondent did not provide any feedback on the above table. Another respondent did not rate the tolerance level and compliance element

212 E. S. Devadason and V. C. Govindaraju

Table 10.3 Reasons for complexity in nutrition labelling

Main reasons	Yes	Explanations
Not aligned to international standards	20	• Incoherency in regulations across AMS • Particularly for THA, PHL and IDN • "Covered milk code products (milk for 3-years below)" has a different labelling requirement • Different number of core nutrients, MY (4 parameters), PHL (10 parameters), THA (6 parameters) • MY mandates both per serving and per 100 g OR 100 ml (if more than single serving size), while a majority of the other countries only require per serving • Not following Codex NRV, countries use their own RDI/RDA, while some have not developed their RDI • THA has own customized guideline daily amount (GDA) format and requirement and does not accept GDA of other countries • Different/missing NRV/RDA MYS, SGP, BRN • No harmonized NRV for THA PHL IDN Difficulty in meeting requirement to declare % NRV on nutrition facts • Different NIP format across AMS • IDN and THA have rigid NIP mandatory format • Calorie values in many ASEAN countries using 2000 kcal • MY requires carbohydrate to be available carbohydrate, while other countries require total carbohydrate • Stricter tolerance of declared values for VNM; minimum tolerance of sodium for THA • THA regulation requires 100% label declaration at the end of shelf life, PHL regulation only requires 80% label declaration at the end of shelf life
Requirements are not transparent	10	• Food regulation law for VNM (in English version) is hard to be found • No specific regulation for labelling in MYA • Not transparent for newer AMS (CAM, LAO, MYA, VNM) • Not transparent for THA, IDN and PHL • Percentage tolerance level has never been announced in writing for reference in THA, while it changes from time to time and varies upon each consultation with the officials in the case of VNM • Although nutrition facts are not required if there are no nutrient content/function claims made on the label for IDN, but if the label contains nutrition facts for other ASEAN countries, IDN requires it to be complied with IDN regulations. This requirement is not stated in writing and came to be known only when the product was being registered • Inconsistent requirements received during product registration from the FDA in IDN, VNM and BRN (different from the official document/not stated in official document/different from officer to officer)

(continued)

10 Regulatory Incoherence in Nutrition Labelling ... 213

Table 10.3 (continued)

Main reasons	Yes	Explanations
Frequent changes in labelling requirements	4	• Especially in IDN, THA and PHL • THA had few revisions in format and GDA values in span of 2–3 years • Although the AMS do not change labelling regulations regularly, frequent changes occur when the product shares a label with multiple ASEAN countries. For example, PHL revised its labelling regulation (general and nutrition labelling) in 2014 (AO 2014-0030); THA issued a new labelling regulation (Reg. 367) in 2014 (general labelling); IDN issued a new ALG which affects % AKG column in nutrition facts in 2016 • Even with a change in requirement every 2 years, some materials minimum order requirement (MOQ) is big and each order may last more than 2 years
Short grace period	3	• Particularly for IDN, THA and VNM • When pre-market approval including is needed, particularly in IDN, VNM • No grace period for new packaging implementation for VNM and MYA • Most countries allow for at least 1-year grace period for new regulations that entail changes in the label • Usually two years are given, however some changes may impact formulation and two years are definitely a challenge for reformulation and actual change
Others: local language; requirement for nutrition facts on individual packs, Healthier Choice Logo	2	• Local language is mandatory: issue for countries with small business volume • Especially for THA, IDN and VNM • PHL and IDN require nutrition facts on each individual pack (sachet, stick), even though they are in the wrapper bag, which is the selling unit, and nutrition facts are already provided on the wrapper bag. Individual packs are small, making it difficult to put nutrition facts on them • Tendency for countries to develop their own healthier choice scheme, and they are not ready to recognize each other country's logo (e.g.: THA, SGP, MY and BRN) • SGP "healthier choice symbol (HCS)" logo not recognized in MYS, leading to dual label for export and local sales

Notes The second column is based on the 22 responses from the market survey. Two respondents did not provide any feedback on the above table

AMS—ASEAN member states; MY—Malaysia; SGP—Singapore; THA—Thailand; PHL—Philippines; IDN—Indonesia; BRN—Brunei; CAM—Cambodia; MYA—Myanmar; LAO—Lao; VNM—Vietnam

countries, apart from Thailand, Philippines and Indonesia. In terms of the specifics of transparency in regulations, the lack of clarity and inconsistent requirements with the formal documents were observed by exporters when it comes to the guidelines on NIP and tolerance levels in the aforementioned countries.

The following are specific peculiarities expressed by the food exporters regarding the regulations per se:

* The format of the *Nutrition Information Panel (NIP)*[11] in Thailand is similar (but not identical) to that for the United States.
* In terms of the nutrient list and *declaration of minerals and vitamins*, Thailand is considered unique[12] in that vitamins A, B1 and B2, and calcium and iron need to be declared.
* Front-of-pack (FOP) signposting is also cited as an additional issue for one manufacturer in terms of exporting beverages to Brunei. This refers to the graphical format in the form of a heart-shaped logo as an interpretation of a cholesterol-free claim.

Compliance Costs

The common reasons for a change in nutrition labelling include the change in regulation in the export market, and product reformulation. The costs incurred and problems encountered from complying with nutrition labelling regulations are summarized in Table 10.4.

From Table 10.4, it is obvious that multiple costs are involved in the complying with an introduction or change in the legislative requirement in the ASEAN export market. The responses are at best mixed in terms of whether the compliance costs across the seven segments, as incurred by the firm, are on a one-off basis, or recurrent. Compliance costs are found to largely depend on the timeframe given to the manufacturer to adjust. Normally, the regulations provide a grace period (more than 1 year) for manufacturers to change product labels. During that period, the balance packaging materials and/or sticker labels will be cleared off; unless the customer requires the immediate use of new labels to comply with new rules.

Table 10.4 Compliance costs and problems related to nutrition labelling

Cost segments	Specific problems
1. Administrative costs	• Initial costs become recurring with constant changes • Extra resources needed to handle labelling matters • Hiring of additional staff with technical knowledge and skills; involves higher hiring costs/difficulty in getting talent/time needed to train new employees • Label development is very much dependent on regulatory personnel • For each revision of the label artwork, the support of the advertising agency is needed. The agency charges the service fee per time per one artwork. Some products have more than one pack size, so the numbers of artwork vary • Due to the local language requirement, there is a need for personnel with language proficiency to check and ensure the compliance with NIP and the claims
2. Testing costs	• Analytical tests need to be performed on a regular (yearly) basis • Systematic analytical checks are needed to validate the declared nutritional value complies with regulations • Certificate of authenticity (COA) is needed as supporting document for the Nutrition Information Table • Cannot proceed with label development without getting done the nutrient analysis report • No access to a validated database on nutrients • The database from GREAT (CAT) is useful, except for source countries who are not disciplined to do the necessary monitoring • Retesting to get missing data and reproduce consistent results. IDN officers are technically incompetent • IDN product registration requirement makes market testing almost impossible
3. Re-labelling costs	• Write-off costs for old packaging • Reprinting the label artwork incurs costs on new moulding, printing and services of the advertising agency and packaging material manufacturer • Labour costs for "stickering" • If unable to incorporate the information on the label, "stickering" is the only way to comply with local regulation • Additional resources needed to replace labels to conform to the new requirements

(continued)

Table 10.4 (continued)

Cost segments	Specific problems
4. Networking costs	• Identifying a common lab recognized by all ASEAN countries • IDN requests for accreditation certificate from a recognized lab, and information on the relationship between all parties on the lab report • With increasing tests to be performed, there is a continuous need to identify vendors
5. Transportation costs	• For MYA, need to submit the samples of the product in ready-to-launch appearance in every registration with the Food and Drug Administration (FDA) • IDN does not allow for more than five samples to be shipped, thereby increasing the burden for transporting of samples
6. Inventory costs	• Incurred only during the transition period, and the costs vary • Incurred if the grace period is shorter than 1 year. In some cases, even 1 year is too short, especially for products with less frequent production schedules or low sales volume. Packaging materials must be ordered at the minimum ordering quantity (MOQ), so the stock of printed packaging material may be high in inventory and cannot be used up faster than the 1-year grace period • Even with the grace period, there is a need to ensure no shortage of on-shelf products. Any shortage of on-shelf products will hurt the business directly as the consumers cannot find the products on shelf resulting in the loss of sales. It would also mean that the obligation under the sales contract made with the trade customers to ensure a continuous supply of products cannot be met, resulting in a compensation fee pay-out to the trader. For every change of label, there will always be more or less leftover stocks of the products with the old label that needs to be written off • Unnecessary waste in discarding outdated label, which is not due to lack of product quality or for safety reasons • Additional costs for handling and storage • More warehouse space needed to store multiple labels adds complexity to the operations side. It increases the risks of operation error due to two labels of the same product that looks similar
7. Other costs	• Change of labels requires existing registered product to be "re-registered"/updating of registration. Additional man hour/service cost from agency required to manage the change to get clearance from the Food and Drug Administration (FDA). Delay of clearance may result in out of stock in market and loss of market share/business opportunity (VNM, IDN, PHL)

Notes Based on the 23 responses from the market survey. MY—Malaysia; SGP—Singapore; THA—Thailand; PHL—Philippines; IDN—Indonesia; BRN—Brunei; CAM—Cambodia; MYA—Myanmar; LAO—Lao; VNM—Vietnam

Regulatory Consistency

All firms surveyed and interviewed look forward to some form of consistency in the seven elements of mandatory nutrition labelling, summarized hereafter from Table 10.5: (1) align core nutrient list with Codex; (2) consistent NIP format/design for ASEAN vs. flexible format (mixed views); (3) align country-specific NRVs with Codex or accept country

Table 10.5 Suggested changes for consistency in nutrition labelling

Core elements	Suggested changes/opinions
Core nutrient list	• Change requirement of total calorie to be stated in PHL • All types of fat, total sugars and sodium should be listed for relevant products • Align with Codex
Nutrition information panel (NIP) format	• Align country-specific format in THA, IDN and PHL with Codex • Format should be flexible in all markets • To declare only per serving • Specific design/format is needed for ASEAN (e.g. font style and size, table and etc.)
Nutrient reference values (NRVs)	• Give priority to total energy and macronutrients • Accept NRV of country of origin • Align country-specific NRVs in THA, IDN and PHL with Codex • If possible, the NRVs to be same for ASEAN • Nutrients should be computed based on a single dietary reference value instead of localized recommended energy and nutrient intake (RENI)
Declaration of carbohydrates	• Allow carbohydrate to be total carbohydrate in MY like other ASEAN countries, instead of requiring carbohydrate to be available carbohydrate
Declaration of minerals and vitamins	• Provide flexibility for the nutrients to be in either international unit (IU) or metric units in MY and PHL. MY requires all vitamins and minerals to be in metric units, while PHL requires vitamin A, D and E to be in IU • Align declaration of vitamins and/or minerals with Codex • Mandatory to declare only when a claim is made • Not relevant as bioavailability and presence is not consistent with label • Challenging as nutrition status differs across countries

(continued)

218 E. S. Devadason and V. C. Govindaraju

Table 10.5 (continued)

Core elements	Suggested changes/opinions
Tolerance level and compliance	• Suggest: same level in VNM as ASEAN countries, which is ±20%; change current allowance of ±10% of claim • Adopt consensus tolerance level that every ASEAN country accepts. Tolerance limit should be set based on necessity only. For example, vitamins and minerals without known toxicity should be allowed with open-ended upper tolerance (as long as they do not exceed the maximum daily nutrient limit, if any) • Example of common tolerance levels: tested value shall not be less than 20% from the declared positive nutrients (protein, vitamins and minerals); Tested value shall not be more than 20% from the declared negative nutrients (fats, trans fat, sugar) • Adopt consensus rounding rules and decimal point condition that every ASEAN country accepts. Different rounding rules and decimal point condition affect the declared values of nutrients on nutrition facts. There are cases when complying with one country's rounding rules or decimal point condition, causes non-compliance with another country
Nutrition claims, nutrient function claims and other function claims	• Align claim requirements with Codex • Adopt a consensus criteria for nutrient content and comparative claims that every ASEAN country accepts • Adopt a common list of nutrient function claim within ASEAN and capacity sharing, and a Mutual Recognition Agreement (MRA) on assessment of scientific substantiation for health claims • These claims should be optional

Notes Based on the 21 responses from the market survey. One respondent did not provide feedback on the above table. MY—Malaysia; THA—Thailand; PHL—Philippines; IDN—Indonesia; VNM—Vietnam

of origin NRVs; (4) only declare total carbohydrates (not available carbohydrates); (5) align declaration of minerals and vitamins with Codex vs. flexibility in declaring either in international units or in metric units (mixed views); (6) adopt a common tolerance (based on necessity) level for ASEAN, and adopt consensus rounding rules and decimal point condition that every ASEAN country accepts; and (7) adopt a common list of claims for the region and a consensus criteria for the assessment of scientific substantiation for health claims through a MRA.

Way Forward

The findings of the market survey of regional exporters in ASEAN suggest that nutrition labelling is complex due to the incoherence and lack of transparency of the regulations in the region. This impacts on business compliance costs. This suggests that although nutrition labelling is an NTM (TBT more specifically), it can turn out to be an NTB if the complexity of this regulation increases to point of limiting trade.

Though not all exporters desire nutrition labelling be made mandatory, there is a clear consensus when it comes to streamlining measures for the various elements of nutrition labelling to facilitate regional trade. The majority of firms support nutrition labelling be made mandatory on grounds that it provides a standardized way for food manufacturers to communicate with their customers. The firms that are not in favour of mandatory nutrition labelling are mainly from Thailand and Indonesia. Their reasons, apart from the high cost-per-unit of complying with regulations, are, that, some categories of PPF have limited nutritional importance, some food products have no/limited negative attributes to health, some food products do not have nutrition claims and some categories of packaging have limited space for posting nutrition information. For those that support mandatory requirements, they consider the Codex guidelines as a suitable benchmark given that a majority of the ASEAN countries have already adopted this international standard.

The debate should move beyond the option of voluntary versus mandatory, as even where nutrition labels are only required where a claim is made on foods with special dietary uses, the regulations usually also set out standards for the label format when they are applied on a voluntary basis. Accordingly even if the label is applied voluntarily, it still must follow mandatory standards on its format (Hawkes 2010). Further, nutrition labelling is already mandatory for some foods in Thailand and most foods in Malaysia, the core players of PPF trade in the region. Globally, nutrition labelling has also become an inescapable part of the industry and is becoming increasingly mandatory. It would therefore be in the best interest of the region to solidify its global market position by streamlining the regulations across the AMS.

Despite the mixed responses on making nutrition labelling mandatory, all exporters value harmonization. The industry and government pointed out some important factors for consideration in harmonizing the guidelines. This includes the following:

a. The nutritional contexts—different countries may be lacking or excessive in national diets, and national recommended daily intakes (RDI) may vary between countries;
b. The health burden—concerns and risks of unhealthy diets, obesity and other chronic disease are much higher in some countries than the others, and thus, would be more of a priority in some countries than others. For example, Kamis et al. (2015) argue the case for mandatory nutrition labelling with a more comprehensive labelling policy inclusive of the declaration on salt in processed foods in the case of Brunei. They forward this argument based on the problem of rising hypertension in Brunei and the fact that many manufacturers (mainly those in Brunei and Malaysia) did not display sodium or salt content on the packages based on the Healthier Choice Symbol (HCS) Nutrient Guidelines of Singapore.[13]
c. The level of consumer awareness/understanding and the importance of PPF in national diets—dictates the preference for mandatory guidelines and the extent of information needed on the label. In the case of Malaysia, nutrition labelling was made mandatory for a selected group of foods on the basis of those that were frequently consumed and in significant amounts and was important to the community. In Singapore, where consumer awareness is higher relative to most ASEAN countries, it has gone ahead with the HCS for the development of "healthier" products.
d. The consensus of ASEAN to harmonize nutrition labelling—consensus-building from regulators in ASEAN is important to move forward the harmonization process.

It is also important to bear in mind that complete harmonization through a single nutrition label may not be practical or politically feasible for the region (see also Tee et al. 2002). In this respect, priority should be given by the AMS to move ahead with the harmonization of

10 Regulatory Incoherence in Nutrition Labelling ...

guidelines in a selective manner that will produce the desired results. For this purpose, the following three-stage approach is considered appropriate:

i. Adopt a standard format, aligned to Codex, and identify the minimum (necessary and sufficient) requirements within the basic[14] nutrient list of Codex that should be declared at all times and made mandatory. The idea is to start with streamlining the selected nutrients (positive and less desirable nutrients) across the ASEAN members[15] in efforts to promote nutrition labelling as an information tool (narrow view to ensure honest commerce), rather than as a health promotion or marketing tool (expanded view of health as a stronger selling point of PPF).
ii. Give priority to streamline NRVs, as this is cited frequently by firms to be complex relative to the six other core elements of nutrition labelling. Inconsistencies in NRVs also prevail across countries.
iii. For the other remaining six elements of nutrition labelling, adopt a consensus on the following at the regional level:

*   standardize the NIP format (design/format) to prevent the use of a multitude of different formats by food companies;
*   a common declaration list of carbohydrates, and list of minerals and vitamins;
*   a common tolerance limit (based on necessity), with rounding rules and decimal point;
*   a common list of claims and criteria for nutrition (functional) claims.

The above recommendations suggest that: (a) not all elements of nutrition labelling can be made mandatory and harmonized; (b) even within those elements that should be mandatory, they need to be done sequentially, that is to align with the Codex guidelines before the identification of the mandatory requirements; and (c) a common consensus, list or criteria for the remaining voluntary guidelines be followed by MRAs.[16] The list or criteria adopted for the region should however be shown to be effective as the set of internationally approved requirements. It is also recommended, at least at this stage, that regulators do not focus on voluntary guidelines such as graphical formats that move beyond "healthy" to "healthier" food products given the development divide of the countries in the region. These voluntary regulations would only serve to deflect the goal in harmonizing mandatory standards.

Finally, ASEAN should also nurture bottom-up rapprochement especially in dealing with the harmonization or streamlining of technical requirements. At the regional level such as the ASEAN Consultative Committee on Standards and Quality (ACCSQ) platform, input from the food industry is important to harness the concerns of the industry players and undertakes regulatory changes that benefit the industry. Representation from the food industry in the working group is essential to inform the discussion on the complexity of the regulations, the extent of incoherence in the regulations, and more importantly on the minimum similarities in the requirements that would benefit the industry and facilitate regional trade.

Acknowledgements This study was funded by the Food Industry Asia (Singapore) and the ASEAN Food and Beverage Alliance (AFBA). A comprehensive version of this study entitled "Nutrition Labelling on Prepackaged Food: Impact on Trade in ASEAN" has been published as a Technical Report by AFBA on 28 February 2018 (see http://afba. co/wp-content/uploads/2018/02/Nutrition-Labelling-on-Prepackaged-Food-Impact-on-Trade-in-ASEAN.pdf).

Notes

1. The Codex Alimentarius is significantly relevant for international food trade, as the food standard (both product and process) issues cover specific raw and processed materials characteristics, food hygiene, pesticides, residues, contaminants and labelling and sampling methods.
2. The regulatory rapprochement includes coordination, mutual recognition or harmonization. Coordination refers to actions to narrow any significant differences between national-level food safety regulations. Mutual recognition involves the acceptance of different forms of food

10 Regulatory Incoherence in Nutrition Labelling ... 223

safety regulation among countries as "equivalent". Harmonization involves the standardization of all food safety regulations (Henson and Caswell 1999: Hooker 1999).

3. The NTMs aim to ensure food safety and animal and plant health; they also extend to other quality and technical aspects of food products.
4. The ERIA-UNCTAD (2016) database is based on the UNCTAD (2013) classification and does not distinguish finer levels of NTMs such as nutrition labelling within B31. In this respect, B31 is taken as indicative of nutrition labelling.
5. The TBT chapter has 9 sub-chapters (B1–B9) (UNCTAD 2013). Within those sub-chapters, the measures are further distinguished into 18 subgroups up to two levels.
6. The vast majority of labelling notifications to the WTO also relate to processed food (OECD 2003).
7. Determines the difference between the labelling requirement regimes of bilateral country-pairs. Simply put, it examines whether two countries impose the same B31 measure on the same commodities. In this analysis, if two countries apply B31 on product item s at the HS6-digit, then the regulatory difference is RDls$=0$; and RDls$=1$, otherwise. Regulatory distance (D_{ij}) between the two countries is then calculated as: $D_{ij} = \frac{sum\,of\,\text{RDls}}{count\,of\,\text{RDls}}$.
8. NRVs may be used for purposes beyond claims, and claims substantiation will require more than NRVs.
9. Worth mentioning here is that there is no standard definition of SMEs for ASEAN.
10. The regulations in Malaysia and Singapore are considerably more accessible, and thereby transparent, as the regulations are updated and the documents are readily available online.
11. Sometimes called "Nutrition Facts Panel".
12. Thailand is also unique in having three sets of conditions triggering the requirement for a nutrition label: foods with nutrition claims, foods which utilize food value in sale promotion and which define consumer groups in sale promotion (i.e. the usefulness or function, ingredients or nutrients of product to health for use in sale promotion and sales promotions that are aimed for specific consumer groups such as: students, executives, elderly groups); plus, as of 2007, a series of snack foods (fried or baked crispy potatoes, fried or baked popcorn, rice crackers

or extruded snacks, toasted bread, crackers, or biscuits and wafers) (Hawkes 2010).

13. The HCS guidelines consist of a set of nutritional (voluntary) criteria that food manufacturers need to adhere to in order to be eligible to carry a Healthier Choice Logo on their products. The guidelines include recommended level of fat, saturated fat, sugar, sodium and dietary fibre on a range of food products such as dairy products, cereals, seafood, meat and poultry, beverages, sauces, soups and convenient foods.

14. For example, the basic requirement for the core nutrient list as per the Codex recommendation is for the listing on the label energy plus three nutrients, proteins, available carbohydrates (dietary fibre, sugar, starch) and total fats.

15. The number of nutrients required on labels should be the lowest common nutrients required in the AMS.

16. Harmonization is time-consuming and involves consensus-building demands. Harmonization outcomes are politically and conceptually difficult to accomplish. Hence, it must be used sparingly.

Appendix

See Tables 10.6 and 10.7.

Table 10.6 Product description for subcategories of pre-packaged food

HS code	Product description
4	Dairy products; birds' eggs; natural honey; edible products not elsewhere specified
9	Coffee, tea, mate and spices
16	Preparation of meat, fish or crustaceans, molluscs, etc.
17	Sugars and sugar confectionery
18	Cocoa and cocoa preparations
19	Preparation of cereal, flour, starch/milk; pastry cooks' products
20	Preparation of vegetable, fruit, nuts or other parts of plants
21	Miscellaneous edible preparations
22	Beverages, spirits and vinegar

Source Based on the UNCOMTRADE commodity code description, https://comtrade.un.org/db/mr/rfCommoditiesList.aspx

10 Regulatory Incoherence in Nutrition Labelling ... 225

Table 10.7 Core elements of nutrition labelling

Elements of nutrition labelling	Description	Codex guidelines
Core nutrient list	"Core" nutrients are nutrients that require mandatory declaration wherever nutrient declaration is applied	Energy, protein, carbohydrate, fat, saturated fat, sodium/salt and total sugars
Nutrition information panel (NIP) format	The expression of nutrient content in the food product as amount per 100 ml/100 g, per serving size, etc.	Either per 100 g/per 100 ml OR per serving
Nutrient reference values (NRVs)	NRVs are a set of numerical values for the purpose of nutrition labelling and relevant claims. They are used as references when declaring the percentage of a particular nutrient against the recommended intake of that nutrient	For example, the NRVs prescribed for the following nutrients are: Vitamin A: 800 μg Calcium: 1000 mg Protein: 50 g
Declaration of carbohydrates	This refers to the expression of carbohydrates, and if dietary fibres and sugars are required to be declared as a subset of carbohydrates	Codex guidelines recommend that in instances where the type of carbohydrate is declared, this declaration should follow immediately after the declaration of the total carbohydrate content, e.g. "Carbohydrate ... g, of which sugars ... g, 'x' ... g" where "x" represents the specific name of any other carbohydrate constituent
Declaration of minerals and vitamins	The requirement(s) for declaring the presence of vitamins and/or minerals, e.g. if the content of that particular vitamin and/or mineral exceeds a certain amount	Vitamins to be declared if claims have been made and if they are present in amounts not less than 5% NRV per 100 g/100 ml/serving. Only vitamins and minerals for which recommended intakes have been established and/or which are of nutritional importance should be declared

(continued)

Table 10.7 (continued)

Elements of nutrition labelling	Description	Codex guidelines
Tolerance level and compliance	Tolerance limits refer to analytical values of the nutrient content as compared to the value claimed, e.g. for certain nutrients, the analytical value of the nutrient content shall be between 80 and 120% of the content claimed (i.e. tolerance of ±20%)	Not specified in Codex
Nutrition claims, nutrient function claims and other function claims	Nutrition claim: any representation which states, suggests or implies that a food has particular nutritional properties Nutrient function claim: a nutrition claim that describes the physiological role of the nutrient in growth, development and normal functions of the body Other function claim: refers to specific beneficial effects of the consumption of foods in the context of the total diet on normal functions or biological activities of the body	Under Codex, the only nutrition claims permitted are those relating to energy, protein, carbohydrate, and fat and components thereof, fibre, sodium and vitamins and minerals for which NRVs have been established

Source Compiled by authors through discussions with Food Industry Asia (FIA), Singapore

References

AFBA. 2014. *ASEAN Harmonization in the Food Sector*. ASEAN Food & Beverage Alliance (AFBA).

Alemanno, Alberto. 2015. "The Multilateral Governance Framework for Food Safety: A Critical Normative Overview." In *Food Safety, Market Organizatiom, Trade and Development*, edited by Abdelhakim Hammoudi, Cristina Grazia, Yves Surry, and Jean-Baptiste Traversae, 9–43. Switzerland: Springer.

10 Regulatory Incoherence in Nutrition Labelling ... 227

ASEAN Food & Beverage Alliance (AFBA). 2012. "Harmonization of Food Standards in ASEAN: A Shared Vision for Regulatory Convergence." https://foodindustry.asia/documentdownload.axd?documentresourceid=473.

Bode, John. 2017. "Adult Supervision Needed in Food-Labeling Regulatory Policy." *Forbes*. February 16. https://www.forbes.com/sites/realspin/2017/02/16/adult-supervision-needed-in-food-labeling-regulatory-policy/#791bc0264cc3.

Cadot, Olivier, Ernawati Munadi, and Lili Yan Ing. 2015. "Streamlining Non-tariff Measures in ASEAN: The Way Forward." *Asian Economic Papers* 14 (1): 35–70.

Corazon, V. C. B., and Ma Isabel Z. Cabrera. 2008. "Recommended Dietary Allowances Harmonization in Southeast Asia." *Asia Pacific Journal of Clinical Nutrition* 17 (S2): 405–408.

Devadason, Evelyn S. 2016. "More Harmony Needed in ASEAN Food Standards, East Asia Forum." September 20. http://www.eastasiaforum.org/2016/09/10/more-harmony-needed-in-asean-food-standards/.

Gautier, Clemence. 2010. "Labelling Food Products in ASEAN: A Juggling Act." *American Chamber of Commerce in Thailand, Bangkok*, 14.

Hawkes, Corinna. 2010. "Government and Voluntary Policies on Nutrition Labelling: A Global Overview." In *Innovations in Food Labelling*, edited by Janice Albert, 37–58. Cambridge: Woodhead Publishing Limited.

Henson, Spencer, and Julie Caswell. 1999. "Food Safety Regulation: An Overview of Contemporary Issues." *Food Policy* 24 (6): 589–603.

Hooker, Neal H. 1999. "Food Safety Regulation and Trade in Food Products." *Food Policy* 24 (6): 653–668.

International Life Sciences Institute (ILSI) Southeast Asia Region. 2014. "Nutrition Labels and Claims—Updates and Future Directions in ASEAN and Other Regions." *ScienceInSight Newsletter*, 3–7. ILSI: Singapore.

Kamis, Zakaria, Roseyati Yaakub, Sok King Ong, and Norhayati Kassim. 2015. "Sodium Content of Processed Foods in Brunei Darussalam." *Journal of Health Research* 29 (3): 153–164.

Kasapila, William, and Sharifudin M. D. Shaarani. 2011. "Harmonisation of Food Labelling Regulations in Southeast Asia: Benefits, Challenges and Implications." *Asia Pacific Journal of Clinical Nutrition* 20 (1): 1–8.

Lwin, May O., Jerrald Lau, Andrew Z. H. Yee, and Cyndy Au. 2017. "Nutrition Labelling in Health and Risk Messaging in Asia, Health and Risk Communication." In *Oxford Research Encyclopedia of Communication*, edited by Roxanne Parrott. Oxford: Oxford University Press. https://doi.org/10.1093/acrefore/9780190228613.013.307.

Miller, Lisa M. Soederberg, and Diana L. Cassady. 2015. "The Effects of Nutrition Knowledge on Food Label Use: A Review of the Literature." *Appetite* 92: 207–216.

OCED. 2003. *Analysis of Non-tariff Measures: The Case of Labelling—Overview and Analysis of WTO Data.* Paris: Organisation of Economic Cooperation and Development.

Othman, Noraini Mohd. 2014. "Food Safety in Southeast Asia: Challenges Facing the Region." *Asian Journal of Agriculture and Development* 4 (2): 83–92.

Pettman, Simon. 2013. *Standards Harmonisation in ASEAN: Progress, Challenges and Moving Beyond 2015.* ERIA Discussion Paper 2013–30. Jakarta: Economic Research Institute for ASEAN and East Asia (ERIA).

Rimpeekool, Wimalin, Sam-ang Seubsman, Cathy Banwell, Martyn Kirk, Vasoontara Yiengprugsawan, and Adrian Sleigh. 2015. "Food and Nutrition Labelling in Thailand: A Long March from Subsistence Producers to International Traders." *Food Policy* 56: 59–66.

RSIS. 2013. *Expert Group Meeting on the ASEAN Economic Community 2015: Opportunities and Challenges for Food Security.* Singapore: Rajaratnam School for International Studies (RSIS).

Severino, Rodolfo C., and Moe Thuzar, 2016. "ASEAN Economic Cooperation and its Political Realities." In *Moving the AEC Beyond 2015: Managing Domestic Consensus for Community-Building,* edited by Tham, Siew Yean, and Sanchita Basu Das, 24–43. Singapore: Institute of Southeast Asian Studies (ISEAS).

Tee, E-Siong, Suryani Tamin, Rosmulyati Ilyas, Adelisa Ramos, Wei-Ling Tan, Darwin Kah-Soon Lai, and Hataya Kongchuntuk. 2002. Current Status of Nutrition Labelling and Claims in the South-East Asian Region: Are We in Harmony? *Asia Pacific Journal of Clinical Nutrition* 11 (2): S80–S86.

The Star. 2015. "Standardise ASEAN Business Environment." June 1. http://www.thestar.com.my/metro/smebiz/news/2015/06/01/standardise-asean-business-environment/.

UNCTAD. 2013. *Non-tariff Measures to Trade: Economic and Policy Issues for Developing Countries.* Geneva: United Nations Conference on Trade and Development.

United States Agency for International Development (USAID). 2013. "Nontariff Barriers to Trade: Regional Agricultural Trade Environment (RATE) Summary." https://www.usaid.gov/sites/default/files/documents/1861/Nontariff_barriers.pdf.

Online Databases

ERIA-UNCTAD. 2016. TRAINS: Non-tariff Measures (NTMs) Based on Official Regulations, available at http://asean.i-tip.org/?platform=hootsuite.

UNCOMTRADE. 2016. Available at: https://comtrade.un.org/db/dqQuickQuery.aspx.

11

Real-Life Moral Dilemma Discussion (Re-LiMDD) Among Young Adolescents: A Comparison Between Malaysia and Indonesia

Vishalache Balakrishnan

Introduction

Sociocultural issues are becoming more complex and borderless in the current digital era. Society overall finds adolescents more carefree and hedonistic in nature. However, this phenomenon is no difference even during the times of early philosophers such as Socrates who commented that adolescents at that time were also impolite, disrespectful and did not honour the elders. Social issues among adolescents have become more complex with the development of technology. Morality and moral are transforming in the current digital era. Moral is defined in so many perspectives and meaning that it is seen with positive and negative implementations. For this chapter purpose, moral is understood from the original language of Latin "mores" which means way. Bull (1969) considered moral as a code of action that is practised and accepted in one society and the sub-society within that bigger society.

V. Balakrishnan (✉)
Faculty of Education, University of Malaya,
Kuala Lumpur, Malaysia
e-mail: visha@um.edu.my

© The Author(s) 2019
A. Idris and N. Kamaruddin (eds.), *ASEAN Post-50*,
https://doi.org/10.1007/978-981-13-8043-3_11

231

When these codes are abandoned or questioned, the individuals within the society are considered immoral and issues of morality will start building up. However, the issues of morality which are considered serious in one society might be seen as a norm in another society. Thus, morality can be very subjective and different between one society and another.

Moral issues or moral problems exist when there are conflicts in opinions, belief systems, values, culture and rule of law, from the micro- to the macro-perspective (Balakrishnan 2009). With current fast development in technology and adaptation of different ways of lives, even with a society or sub-society, moral issues exist. What more between nations or continents; it has become an ongoing struggle for humanities to face daily life and actions dealing with internal and external aspects of moralities.

Many times, an individual is seen as a perfect model for his or her society but once it is known that the individual is a gay or lesbian within the society which sees LGBTQ as not accepted, then the individual becomes a mismatch. Such situations become more and more popular in current times and need lots of discussions and open dialogues. Many times, adolescents are silenced due to their cultural set-up, relational communications and strong conventional belief systems, which have been followed for generations; there is never an opportunity for adolescents to speak openly and honestly.

Issues of physical and mental phenomena such as stress, depression, obesity and suicide are also on the rise among adolescents and adults, even among influential individuals in the current era. The possibility of not able to be what they want to be and always putting on a mask to please their society has become a possibility in many instances. Non-risk takers in life who are unable to speak up become individuals who others see as troubled but tend to do things that harm themselves and at times harm others.

Being able to be honest, voicing of what is undergoing and be sincere in all thoughts, feelings and actions is a simple common sense philosophy in life. To be able to do such things, one needs to be able to look their lives with whatever that one is in communication with; let it be themselves, their family, their society, their workplace, their creator and anything and everything which is under the sun. Such a way of life can be adapted and taught to adolescents if certain strategies are being applied from young. These are lifelong strategies which need to be taught, nurtured and adapted as individuals grow to become more matured and wise. It is using real-life moral dilemma discussion (Re-LiMDD) in daily life.

In theories of moral development, life is always linked to early development which means when an individual is young, what is instilled in that individual goes a long way in his life, let it be habits, values and inter- as well as intra-motivation to do something. All these become that individual's asset and liabilities as he faces daily life. One of the strategies to overcome challenges in such a scenario is using real-life moral dilemma discussion.

Real-Life Moral Dilemma Discussion (Re-LiMDD)

Many times, when things are right 'according to one's owe principles or one's environment where society accepts or rejects one's action, there is a clear need to know how to reach such an equilibrium' (Balakrishnan 2009). It always starts from self, reaching out to society and the decision of society let it be workplace or family will finally make one decide whether the action taken is acceptable or vice versa. However, before such action is being taken based on the decision, there is lots of mental turbulence taking place in one's head, and one's heart. Educating that two components are where Re-LiMDD comes into play.

In my thirty years of educating adolescents, I realize that they are always in a state of uncertainty. Their parents do not favour sometimes what they need or want or society and they tend to feel sad and depressed. That stage of mind and body is increasing in today's world where suicide and mental health issues are on the rise. The adolescents feel that they have no voice and even if they are given the space to voice out their feelings and needs, the elders in their environment tend to already make the final decisions for them; which school to study, what course to take, who they should friend, who they should marry, where they should stay, what car they should buy and the list goes on. Thus, Re-LiMDD is a simple but effective way to educate both the adolescents and their connections to see the wider picture, make decisions wisely and take actions effectively when facing a moral dilemma.

What are moral dilemmas? Moral dilemmas are situations in which an individual, a family or a society face conflicting situations in which there are a few alternatives to choose from to make a moral decision. Moral dilemmas exist due to clashes in values between one or more persons (Balakrishnan 2009). At times, the moral dilemmas are within the individual. At other times, the moral dilemmas involve individuals, groups, society, nation and the entire world.

Usually, a moral dilemma consists of one or several issues, involving one or more characters, which an individual must face and make a decision. The decision made and action that follow-up is based on several factors such as rational reasoning, types of moral orientation that one is brought up in: justice or care and many other cultural and environmental factors. Societal needs to think and work together on moral issues has increased tremendously (Austin 2000), shifting the emphasis from individual efforts to group work and from independence to the community (Leonard and Leonard 2001). As one cannot separate water into its distinct parts (hydrogen and oxygen) and still maintain the integrity of water, so, too, one cannot separate the individual from the context and still have a complete understanding (Vygotsky 1977, 1986). The unification of a person within that social, cultural, historical and political context informs our understanding of this dialectical relationship. This Vygotskian metaphor of water can be applied to the process of decision-making in life. As Vygotsky clearly states that education is meaningless outside the real world if one is within an individual is not applied when facing challenges, conflicts or difficulties in the real world.

In this comparative research, 15 Malaysian adolescents and 15 Indonesian adolescents were the participants involved. They underwent the process below to identify their own real-life moral dilemmas and partake in the Re-LiMDD (Fig. 11.1).

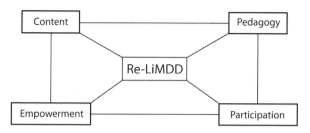

Fig. 11.1 Four components of Re-LiMDD

Content

The content which is the real-life moral dilemmas were provided by the participants from Malaysia to Indonesia. They wrote their moral dilemma or one that they are facing currently during the research duration. They also were allowed to use any other dilemmas, which were presented to them, for example, their friend or family members' moral dilemmas. To safeguard their privacy and confidentiality, no real names were required. They were encouraged to provide a pseudonym.

Pedagogy

The pedagogy for Re-LiMDD is dialoguing, discussion and engaging in critical thinking processes. The pedagogy is transformative in nature and develops in students the knowledge, skills and values needed to make good moral choices and resolve moral conflicts amicably. Decisions, which were made after the Re-LiMDD, had to be reflected upon. In other words, the pedagogy for Re-LiMDD must allow reflective decision-making with collaborative and personal moral action.

Empowerment

Power-sharing is essential in implementing Re-LiMDD. It must be between students and students, and teacher and students. Each party should feel comfortable and confident that they have equal power and

236 V. Balakrishnan

privilege to voice their opinions, suggestions and arguments. The final decision to take the appropriate action is up to the individual with the moral dilemma but the Re-LiMDD has made his or her thought more elaborate and wiser.

Participation

The participants take an active participation role. There are times when they become a capable peer who leads the group discussion. It all depends on their experience and their funds of knowledge. The role of the capable peer is taken up in various forms and different individuals too can take this role if the dilemma individual lacks the expertise. However, the notion of power-sharing is important and participants tend to listen and dialogue better when there are fewer constraints from the others exercising an authoritative role. Finally, as the four components above are interrelated, they all share equal weight in Re-LiMDD.

What Young Adolescents Describe as Moral Dilemmas?

In this chapter, a comparative analysis is reviewed and narrated between adolescents in the University of Malaya, Malaysia and adolescents studying in Universitas Pendidikan Bandung (UPI) Bandung, Indonesia. The research was conducted using the action research approach focusing on "participatory action research" (PAR). Using focus group discussions as the main tool, both groups experienced the use of their own moral dilemmas to apply Re-LiMDD in their daily lives.

Data collected were analysed using the thematic approach where each moral dilemma presented by the participants underwent the Re-LiMDD process. Both the Malaysian and the Indonesian adolescents find relational moral dilemmas very difficult to resolve. Table 11.1 shows a comparison of what they describe as moral dilemmas in their current stage of life.

Table 11.1 Comparison of moral dilemmas

Participants	Malaysia	Indonesia
Total	15	15
Age group	20–21	20–21
Gender	7 male students, 8 female students	7 male students, 8 female students
Moral dilemmas	Involving family members Involving friends Sexual relationships Career and life Self-motivation	Sexual relationship Sibling rivalry Injustice within society Career and decision-making Friendship and cultural taboos
Re-LiMDD progress	Actively involved	Actively involved
Moral Orientation	More than 50% participants used justice orientation	More than 50% participants used care orientation
Recommendations	More voice provided	More voice provided

Source Compiled by author

Conclusion

There is not a single or best pedagogical answer that would suit all contexts and any initiative is still just one of the many possibilities with their own strength and limitations (Chen 2008). To a certain extent, I agree with Chen, but being a social science researcher I feel compelled to research, analyse and construct integrative and alternative approaches to providing adolescents with strategies that help them cope with daily moral dilemmas. It is important that the weaknesses of a certain approach are seen with a proactive perspective and distinct alternative approaches are articulated. Based on my research, Re-LiMDD made some participants see the potential for a future impact for the nation as a whole.

Coming from policies across the ASEAN border, policymakers in different ASEAN countries need to have intelligent quotient (IQ), emotional quotient (EQ) and lately cultural quotient (CQ) in dealing with delicate issues such as self-development and societal movement. They need collaboration between the different nations to ensure that future adolescents can develop and live within a world that is borderless yet provides a comfortable environment that they are aspiring for.

References

Austin, Wendy. 2000. "Ethics and the Stigma of Mental Illness." *In Touch: The Provincial Health Ethics Network* 2 (12): 1–2.

Balakrishnan, Vishalache. 2009. *Moral Education for University and College.* Subang Jaya: Arah Pendidikan.

Bull, Norman J. 1969. *Moral Education.* London: Routledge & Kegan Paul.

Chen, Laiz. 2008. "Education for Community Cohesion: Lowest Common Denominator or Daring to Be Different?" *Journal of Critical Literacy: Theories and Practices* 2 (1): 76–86.

Leonard, P., and L. Leonard. 2001. "Assessing Aspects of Professional Collaboration in Schools: Beliefs Versus Practices." *Alberta Journal of Educational Research* 47 (1): 4–23.

Vygotsky, Lev Semionovich. 1977. "Play and Its Role in the Mental Development of the Child." In *Soviet Developmental Psychology,* edited by Michael Cole, 76–99. New York: M.E. Sharpe.

Vygotsky, Lev Semionovich. 1986. *Thought and language.* Cambridge, MA: MIT Press.

12

Challenges and Opportunities; Lessons for ASEAN Post 50

Nurliana Kamaruddin and Aida Idris

Navigating a Changing World

Ten years after the 1997 Asian Financial Crisis, the signing of the ASEAN Charter in 2007 and the launching of the ASEAN Community in 2015 showcased the region's capacity to evolve and progress. Although there have been many positive changes in the Southeast Asian region, ASEAN as an organization continues to face many challenges. As explored in the first chapter of the book, the economic, political and social disparity among the ten countries in the region complicates the effort to establish a cohesive ASEAN community. The chapters in this book have merely touched upon some of the contemporary issues for

---

N. Kamaruddin (✉)
Asia-Europe Institute, University of Malaya, Kuala Lumpur, Malaysia
e-mail: nurliana.k@um.edu.my

A. Idris
Faculty of Business and Accountancy, University of Malaya,
Kuala Lumpur, Malaysia
e-mail: aida_idris@um.edu.my

© The Author(s) 2019
A. Idris and N. Kamaruddin (eds.), *ASEAN Post-50*,
https://doi.org/10.1007/978-981-13-8043-3_12

ASEAN member countries. For ASEAN to effectively move forward as a regional organization, it would be important for members to recognize the challenges, both internal and external, that might prove to be obstacles to progress.

These would include recent events that have contributed to a regression on ASEAN's effort to achieve unity. As mentioned earlier, Myanmar's treatment of the Rohingya minorities in its state of Rakhine has drawn severe criticism from the international community not only towards Myanmar but also to ASEAN's inaction on the matter. The issue has also contributed to disagreements among ASEAN members as well with Malaysia criticizing and disassociating itself from ASEAN's joint statement on the issue (CNA 2017). ASEAN also remains divided concerning the best action needed to deal with China's presence in the South China Sea and the multiple existing claims on the Spratly Islands. Vietnam and the Philippines are pushing for ASEAN to take a tougher stance against China even as China increases its military presence in the area (Chan and Li 2015).

Southeast Asia's central position in the geography of Asia and the major trade routes passing through the sea lanes located in the region means that ASEAN's importance to larger more powerful nations should not be underestimated. ASEAN's relationship with the larger economic powers of East Asia in general and China, in particular, will continue to be a major part of ASEAN's foreign relations. In the coming decades, ASEAN will continue to play an important role not only in managing its external relationships with the big powers but also in becoming the catalyst to spearhead more comprehensive and dynamic relationships among the ASEAN member countries. ASEAN's ability to successfully realize its goal to establish an ASEAN community depends not only on the political will of member countries' leaders but also meaningful grass-roots cooperation. More effort is needed into making the three ASEAN pillars of political-security, economy and socioculture communities into reality. The next section identifies some areas for the consideration of policymakers not only at the ASEAN level but in national governments of member states as well.

Moving Forward

Despite the challenging international and regional environment, there is vast potential and opportunities for ASEAN to harness as it moves forward. The question remains whether ASEAN member countries will be able to make good on the agreements and policies it has enacted in the last decade or so. ASEAN not only needs to ensure that it remains relevant in the twenty-first century but that it can also be a catalyst for continued improvement among member countries. Considering the establishment of the ASEAN Community, the three pillars of the ASEAN community reflect ASEAN's desire to create a "community of opportunity" for citizens of the ASEAN region (ASEAN 2015). However, ASEAN has been more successful in some areas such as economic cooperation and community activities but less so in political-security effort.

The ASEAN Economic Community have led to deepening regional cooperatives and the under the current stewardship of Singapore, five "key thrust" is established. These are promoting innovation and e-commerce, improving trade facilitation, deepening services and investment integration, cultivating a conducive regulatory environment and progressing ASEAN's external relations (ASEAN 2018). ASEAN member countries continue to work on free trade agreements with external partners like China and India, as well as the Regional Comprehensive Economic Partnership (RCEP).

Activities under the ASEAN SocioCultural Communities have led to initiatives in various sectors meant to improve the living standards of ASEAN citizens and enhance protection of environment, culture and heritage. For example, efforts focusing on education have led to mechanisms like the ASEAN University Network (ASEAN 2017). Efforts to improve rural poverty led to the establishment of the ASEAN Multi-dimensional Poverty Index (MPI) (ASEAN 2017). On the other hand, ASEAN's effort to enhance human rights, combat corruption and promote good governance under the ASEAN Political-Security Community remains less than successful.

In line with these challenges, this chapter identifies three areas for the consideration of policymakers both at the national and regional level. These are (1) exploring new roles for cooperation in the existing architecture (2) enhancing effort to standardize institutional regulations (including economic and educational institutions) and (3) empowering the people-to-people and civil society network.

New Roles for Cooperation

With the establishment of the ASEAN Charter, ASEAN has begun the important move towards becoming a rules-based organization. Although it remains limited by its policy of "non-interference", this does not mean that ASEAN member countries are not able to continue forging more comprehensive partnerships. More importantly, ASEAN's existing mechanism can, and should be, utilized to explore new capacities for cooperation. The changing social structure in the next 50 years would also mean many new cooperation opportunities for ASEAN to explore in order to deepen ties for its member states. Shifting its focus from traditional cold war security concerns, ASEAN has made impressive strides in several sectors.

Political and social cooperation have also resulted in many initiatives with varying degree of success. For example, the ASEAN Agreement on Disaster Management and Emergency Response (AADMER), which came into force 2009 led to the establishment of the Coordinating Centre for Humanitarian Assistance on Disaster Management (AHA Centre) in 2011 (AHA Centre 2018). On the other hand, ASEAN's Agreement on Transboundary Haze Pollution (AATHP) signed in 2002 is generally regarded as a failure due to lack of enforcement, and ASEAN is not likely to achieve its goal to be haze-free by 2020 (Biswas and Tortajada 2018, 13).

Externally, ASEAN should also continue to pursue improvements in its relations with major powers like the United States and EU, but the focus on East Asia as a region would remain one of the foremost importance for ASEAN. Therefore, it would also be important for ASEAN to leverage and reinvigorate existing regional mechanisms in order to ensure

12 Challenges and Opportunities; Lessons for ASEAN Post 50   243

it remains a relevant player in the larger East Asian region. Its effort to maintain ASEAN centrality in any East Asian regional architecture will continue to be shadowed by the much larger, more developed China, Japan and South Korea. Consequently, relations with the aforementioned countries can and should be leveraged to ASEAN's advantage.

China's continued growth is especially significant in the economic sector as China represents the largest share in ASEAN's international trade partner (ASEAN Secretariat 2018, 34). Therefore, as explored in Chapter 4, the increase in Chinese FDI to ASEAN since the signing of the 2009 ASEAN–China free trade agreement would inevitably mean a bigger presence of the country in the region. It is important to note that aside from the market size and strategic assets of a country, political stability plays an important factor in attracting Chinese FDI. Chapter 2 has provided an in-depth exploration as to why China's political and economic approach and its treatment of ASEAN as a regional organization is also likely to remain divisive. Consequently, ASEAN's effort to spearhead East Asian regionalism will also need to take into consideration how to balance China's presence in the region with long-time partner Japan as well as the possibility of increasing influence from South Korea due to its New Southern Policy as explored in Chapter 3.

Standardization and Harmonization

One of the most important aspects of ASEAN member countries is economic growth. Economically, ASEAN has seen an increase in trade and cooperation. By 2016, intra-ASEAN trade was the largest share of trade among ASEAN members. Member countries through the ASEAN Consultative Committee on Standards and Quality (ACCSQ) have also continued work towards harmonizing trade standards. However, this remains difficult as the example concerning the nutrition labelling for pre-packaged food explored in Chapter 10. Priority should be given to streamlining regulations and policies in order to effectively increase trade. Engaging all stakeholders especially businesses and industry players will continue to be important for governments to continue making progress among ASEAN members.

Poverty reduction and economic development have been a major agenda for ASEAN and its member countries. However, inequality among and within ASEAN member countries still need to be addressed. According to the 2017 UNESCAP SDG Progress Report, Southeast Asia is the only region in the Asia Pacific to experience widening inequality (UNESCAP 2017, ix). For example, Thailand's top 1% controls 58% of the country's wealth while the combined wealth of the four richest in Indonesia is more than that of the poorest 100 million people (Maizura 2018). Inequality exists not only between within countries but between member countries as well.

Among the CLMV countries, Cambodia and Vietnam have made some progress to achieve comparable income level with a few of the older ASEAN countries, but Laos and Myanmar have been much less successful (Furuoka 2018, 4). Consequently, Cambodia, Laos, Myanmar and Vietnam's (CLMV) effort to catch up with the other ASEAN members can be accelerated through more efficient standardization of the ASEAN market as a whole. The economic and education structure needs to be adaptable to the rapid changes brought about by the industry 4.0 revolution.

Improvement of the education sector is crucial, not only to ensure that noted improvements can be made in the human resource of all countries, especially for the CLMV as this is the best way for countries to upgrade their economies in this new age. Coordination and standardization among ASEAN countries in the education sector such as the Asian Qualifications Reference framework discussed in Chapter 6 are one such step that needs to be properly carried out with problems like the lack of coordination and transparency be given priority. This in return would greatly contribute to ASEAN's ability to improve mobility among its higher education institutions which is key to building better regionalization.

Harmonization and enforcement of environmental agreements and laws are also another concern that ASEAN member countries need to pay attention to. As ASEAN continues to urbanize, environmental challenges as presented in Chapter 9 would be further exacerbated if no meaningful effort is put in place to tackle the issues. Furthermore, the lack of any standard legal measures such as those discussed in Chapter 8 limits the ability for any regional effort to mitigate and enforce environmental objectives.

12 Challenges and Opportunities; Lessons for ASEAN Post 50   245

Empowering the Grass Roots

ASEAN member countries would also reap long-term benefit by investing in local community development. State investment should also be directed not only for market-based formal education but also towards non-traditional education and enhancing lifelong learning. As explored in Chapter 5, development programmes with strong education components are more like to empower a community and create long-lasting change. This also allows for governments to implement social safety nets for those who might not have a chance to fully benefit from the formal education system and provide marginalized communities with a means to upgrade or diversify their economic revenues. Other forms of non-formal education can also be utilized to provide new possibilities that could generate a holistic approach to education. Chapter 11 discussion of Real-Life Moral Dilemma Discussion (Re-LiMDD) provides one such example of an alternative approach to empowering the younger generation.

Such investments can and should be broadened beyond local communities and another important evolution that ASEAN should focus on is building relationships among ASEAN member countries that are able to transcend government-to-government relations to a more comprehensive grass-roots connection. More importantly, for ASEAN Community to be realized, bottom-up measures need to be strengthened through fostering better people-to-people and civil society networks. Civil society networks provide a crucial means of social inclusion as well as support for minorities and the most vulnerable. One such support is in the issue of migration.

As pointed out in Chapter 7, intra-ASEAN migration will only continue to increase. As the world continues to globalize, efforts to cultivate the ASEAN community should also extend to facilitating the mobility of ASEAN's citizens. The gaps in regional- and state-level effort to overcome difficulties faced by migrants can also be filled through community and non-governmental effort. This includes cultivating better awareness of migrant conditions and the complexity of issues such as forced migration and refugees. Accordingly extending community-level effort would provide important support for governments in events where governments are short on, or unable to provide, resources and services to the people.

Conclusion

When ASEAN celebrated its 50th anniversary, the late Dr. Surin Pitsuwan, former Secretary General of ASEAN stated that ASEAN had evolved "into a community", and that ASEAN could "face and successfully manage a lot of contending pressures, conflicting interests around us and within us, and also a lot of changes in the environment of Southeast Asia, of East Asia, (and) of the global community" (Pitsuwan 2017). This reflects the optimism that ASEAN would continue to facilitate growth and security in the region. However, questions remain as to whether ASEAN would be able to make meaningful progress on the goals of achieving a comprehensive ASEAN Community even though it has been more than ten years since the signing of the ASEAN Charter in 2007.

ASEAN will continue to face many more challenges, but the most important challenge would be generating and maintaining the political will to commit to the various initiatives established under the ASEAN aegis. The complexity of this new era, as well as the ever-increasing demands of fast-paced globalization, means that ASEAN now more than ever need to play a proactive role to facilitate development in the region. Post 50 ASEAN will need to chart a new course that would empower and include not only the governments of member countries but also other stakeholders such as businesses, civil society and local communities.

References

AHA Centre. 2018. *Operationalising One ASEAN One Response.* Jakarta: The AHA Centre.

ASEAN. 2015. *Fact Sheet—ASEAN Community.* Jakarta: ASEAN Secretariat.

ASEAN. 2017. *Fact Sheet of ASEAN Socio-Cultural Community (ASCC).* Jakarta: ASEAN Secretariat.

ASEAN 2018. *ASEAN Economic Integration Brief,* No. 3. Jakarta: ASEAN Secretariat.

ASEAN Secretariat. 2018. *ASEAN Key Figures 2018.* Jakarta: ASEAN Secretariat.

12 Challenges and Opportunities; Lessons for ASEAN Post 50   247

Biswas, Asit K., and Cecilia Tortajada. 2018. "Managing Indonesian Haze: Complexities and Challenges." In *Pollution Across Borders: Transboundary Fire, Smoke and Haze in Southeast Asia*, edited by Euston Quah and Tsiat Siong Tan, 1–18. Singapore: World Scientific Publishing.

Chan, Irene, and Mingjiang Li. 2015. "New Chinese Leadership, New Policy in the South China Sea Dispute?" *Journal of Chinese Political Science* 20: 25–50.

Channel News Asia (CNA). 2017. "Malaysia Disassociates Itself from ASEAN Statement on Myanmar's Rakhine State." *Channel News Asia*, September 24. Accessed December 31, 2018. https://www.channelnewsasia.com/news/asia/malaysia-disassociates-itself-from-asean-statement-on-myanmar-s-9246494.

Furuoka, Fumitaka. 2018. "Do CLMV Countries Catch Up with the Older ASEAN Members in Terms of Income Level?" *Applied Economics Letters*. https://doi.org/10.1080/13504851.2018.1489494.

Maizura, Ismail. 2018. "Southeast Asia's Widening Inequalities." *The ASEAN Post*, July 17. Accessed January 8, 2019. https://theaseanpost.com/article/southeast-asias-widening-inequalities.

Pitsuwan, Surin. 2017. "Challenges for ASEAN in the Changing Regional and Global Landscape." Speech presented at the Symposium on the 50th Anniversary of ASEAN with H.E. Dr. Surin Pitsuwan, Former Secretary-General of ASEAN, ASEAN-Japan Centre, Tokyo, Japan. Accessed January 2, 2019. https://www.asean.or.jp/ja/wp-content/uploads/sites/2/2017/06/For-WEB-Symposium-on-the-50th-Anniversary-of-ASEAN-Verbatim-of-Keynote-Speech-by-Dr.Surin_.pdf.

UNESCAP. 2017. *Asia and the Pacific: SDG Progress Report*. New York: United Nations.

Index

A

adolescents 231–234, 236, 237
air pollution 156, 158, 166, 169, 181, 183–188, 196
ASEAN Declaration Against Trafficking in Persons Particularly Women and Children 140
ASEAN Declaration on Transnational Crime 140
ASEAN Environmental Cooperation 157
ASEAN Free Trade Area (AFTA) 19, 20, 36
ASEAN Higher Education Harmonisation 128
ASEAN-Korea 38, 40, 41, 46
ASEAN Ministerial Meeting on the Environment (AMME) 159
ASEAN Qualification Reference Framework 109, 126
ASEAN-ROK Free Trade Area (AKFTA) 39, 40, 47, 48
Asian Financial Crisis 36, 239
Association of Southeast Asian Nations (ASEAN) 1–10, 13–31, 35–49, 54–57, 62–66, 71–75, 82, 84–88, 90, 93, 95, 96, 101–111, 113–115, 118–120, 122, 123, 125–129, 135–151, 155–173, 177–184, 186–197, 204–206, 209–214, 216–223, 237, 239–246
ASEAN6 3, 4, 10, 36
ASEAN7 207, 208

© The Editor(s) (if applicable) and The Author(s), under exclusive license to Springer Nature Singapore Pte Ltd. 2019
A. Idris and N. Kamaruddin (eds.), *ASEAN Post-50*,
https://doi.org/10.1007/978-981-13-8043-3

250   Index

B

Bangkok Declaration on Irregular
Migration 140, 142
Belt and Road initiative (B&R initiative) 7, 22, 25, 27, 29,
55

C

China 6–8, 10, 13–30, 38, 39, 45,
46, 49, 53–57, 60–64, 66,
71–75, 135, 138, 168, 240,
241, 243
China FDI 21, 22, 243
China trade 37
Climate change 3, 10, 156–159,
165–170, 173, 174, 181, 183,
187–192, 194, 196
Cold War 1, 14, 17, 101, 242
Consensus on the Protection and
Promotion of the Rights of
Migrant Workers 140, 143

D

Declaration on the Protection and
Promotion of the Rights of
Migrant Workers 140
discourse analysis 140
Dunning's OLI (ownership-location-internalization paradigm)
framework 57, 58

E

Economic Development
Cooperation Fund (EDCF)
43, 44

H

Hallyu 40
Hanoi Plan of Action (HPA) 36,
140, 160
human capital development 82, 83,
86, 87, 103

K

KA programme 93–96

L

linguistics 140

M

Maritime Silk Road (MSR) 21, 27,
29, 55
migration 7, 136–143, 146–151,
158, 166, 169, 245
moral decisions 234

N

national qualification framework
(NQF) and quality assurance 103
non-tariff measures (NTM) 19, 205,
206, 219, 223
nutrition labelling 203–205, 207,
209–212, 214, 215, 217,
219–221, 225, 243

O

Overseas Foreign Direct Investment
(OFDI) 55, 57, 60–63, 65, 66,
69–72, 74, 75

Index   251

P

pre-packaged food 208, 224

R

Real-Life Moral Dilemma Discussion
(Re-LiMDD) 233–237, 245
Regional Comprehensive Economic
Partnership (RCEP) 7, 15, 21,
23–25, 27, 29, 241
Republic of Korea (ROK) 36, 39, 40

S

Silk Route Fund 21
sustainable development 7, 9, 89–92,
95, 96, 107, 120, 143, 156,
158, 171, 179, 194

T

technical barriers to trade (TBT)
205, 206, 208, 219, 223
territorial claims 18, 28

Trans-Pacific Partnership (TPP) 7,
21, 23, 24
Trans-Pacific Partnership Agreement
(TPPA) 15

U

Urban population 177, 178, 189,
192, 196, 197

V

Vientiane Action Programme (VAP)
140, 143

W

water pollution 181, 192–196